# Chaucer's
# Chain of Love

# Chaucer's Chain of Love

## Paul Beekman Taylor

Madison ● Teaneck
Fairleigh Dickinson University Press
London: Associated University Presses

Associated University Presses
440 Forsgate Drive
Cranbury, NJ 08512

Associated University Presses
16 Barter Street
London WC1A 2AH, England

Associated University Presses
P.O. Box 338, Port Credit
Mississauga, Ontario
Canada L5G 4L8


The paper used in this publication meets the requirements
of the American National Standard for Permanence of Paper
for Printed Library Materials Z39.48-1984.

**Library of Congress Cataloging-in-Publication Data**

Taylor, Paul Beekman, 1930–
    Chaucer's chain of love / Paul Beekman Taylor.
        p.   cm.
    Includes bibliographical references and index.
    ISBN 0-8386-3682-9 (alk. paper)
    1. Chaucer, Geoffrey, d. 1400—Criticism and interpretation.
2. Love in literature.   3. Christian poetry, English (Middle)—
History and criticism.   4. Christian pilgrims and pilgrimages in
literature.   5. Philosophy, Medieval, in literature.   I. Title.
PR1933.L6T38   1996
821'.1—dc20                                                   96-17171
                                                                   CIP

PRINTED IN THE UNITED STATES OF AMERICA

*This book is for Rose-Marie,*
*who inspired it and*
*whose love is its context.*

# Contents

# Acknowledgments

A VERSION OF CHAPTER 3 APPEARED EARLIER AS "CAVE AND WEB: VISION and Poetry in Chaucer's *Legend of Good Women*," *Poetics: Theory and Practice in Medieval English Literature,* ed. Piero Boitani and Anna Torti (Cambridge: Derek Brewer, 1991), 69–82. Portions of chapters 6 and 7 appeared in *Swiss Papers in English Language and Literature,* volumes 3 (1987) and 4 (1988), 124–35 and 133–46, respectively. A version of chapter 2 is forthcoming in *Exemplaria* under the title "Time in the *Canterbury Tales.*"

My colleague George Steiner read an earlier draft of this work and made valuable suggestions for revision, and my colleague Wlad Godzich read a subsequent draft. My debt to both is considerable, but where this book has failed their expectations, I must take the blame.

9

# Chaucer's
# Chain of Love

# Prologue: A Tale of Two Cities

*Amor mundum fecit*

> . . . al this ground on which we been ridyng,
> Til that we come to Caunterbury toun,
> He koude al clene turnen up-so-doun,
> And pave it al of silver and of gold.
>
> (*CT* 8, 623–26)

THIS BOOK IS ABOUT THE PHILOSOPHIC, LINGUISTIC, AND MORAL IMPLICA-tions of the juxtaposition between the actual road to a shrine and the potential pavement to the grace it figures. The putative power to transform the pilgrim's path from vernal mud to eternal gold figures the power of grace to transform Canterbury into heaven, and the pilgrims' hard pedestrian step into a soul's aery float.[1] That magical force figures the creative *logos* which reifies a divine idea into an organization of things and signs and the writer's transformation of his thought into word and into the structure of story. Most important for this study, it figures the love which makes new life out of old.

Chaucer is a love poet; that is, Chaucer conceives of love as the philosophic principle behind the ontological fact of creation. Man's art, like the road built across the hills of Kent, is a figure of the love that mediates man's will. Figures of love inform nature, poetry, and books. They link worlds of things with worlds of deeds and thoughts. At the beginning of the pilgrimage road is the worldly London whose Tabard Inn is a sign of worldly appetite; at its terminus is the spiritual Canterbury with its shrine of Thomas à Becket. The path that links the two is a way to leave and return, an escape path from the city of sin and a return route to the haven of God's presence.[2] It is Saint Cecile's "wey to blinde," a track of restoration of spirit to its pristine purity.

It is also a trail of words. In short, though the Canon's Yeoman is undoubtedly thinking of something else, his pilgrimage path figures the bond of love that holds man to God. That bond in the poetry of Geoffrey Chaucer is the topic of this book, and its subject is the tortuous quest to see, speak, and write that bond into being; that is, to translate apprehension

13

of things into comprehension of their meanings figured in language. Seeing is a coordinate activity of relating sight to insight, thing seen to idea conceived. Ideas, however, have a tendency to run loose from words' control. In the case of the Canon's Yeoman, Harry Bailly's trained hosteler's eye spies a cheat by his verbal and sartorial array. Why is the Canon so "sluttish . . . if that his dede accorde with thy speche?" (*CT* 8, 636–38) he challenges, and the Yeoman is incapable of translating the claim of his lord's science into an explanation of the Lord's art: "We mowen nat, although we hadden it sworn" ( 8, 681), he admits, and the accidental timing of his confession seems apt, for the pilgrimage goal is but five miles down the road.

Any *array* is a sign to be read, whether it is the shapes of nature or the dress ordained for someone by civil regulations as a emblem of social estate. A tabard is an array of the lower classes; the Tabard Inn is a place of refreshment; and, as the starting point for pilgrimage, it is a sign of the worldly array to be put aside for the cover of grace in Canterbury. *Cover* is pertinent here, for array covers an essential form: clothing for a body, the Tabard Inn for worldly appetites, the shrine of Becket for spiritual intercession, and the words of the pilgrims along the road for a spectrum spanning worldly and spiritual thought.

The Canon's Yeoman's words to cover his master's cheating arts hint at something of the power of true art to reveal the spiritual gold inherent in natural dross, just as the silver and gold path to Canterbury leads to the treasure of grace at its terminus. The Nero of the Monk's tale, whose rule in the City of Love reflects the rule of love in the Heavenly City, has his own particular strategy for spying beneath nature's array to discover hidden powers. The Monk describes him as a man so extravagant of habit that he throws away his clothes after a single wearing. Perhaps dissatisfied at the loss of his first array—the womb of his mother—he decides to test its perfection:

> His mooder made he in pitous array,
> For he hire wombe slitte to biholde
> Where he conceyved was—so weilaway
> That he so litel of his mooder tolde!
>
> (7, 2483–86)

Looking into the matrix of one's biological conception is an inquest into spiritual origins of things before the *idea* of life is arrayed in body, name, and fame. Agrippina's womb, like Harry's Tabard Inn, is a point of departure on the dual highway of body and spirit which pilgrimage constitutes. Nero's blindness to the essential *nexus* between the two is revealed in his terse and remorseless postmortem praise of his mother's dead figure: "A fair womman was she!" (7, 2488). The physical fairness which he so unnaturally despoils is remembered, but beyond Nero's ken is an invisible form of beauty which he cannot mar. Nero sees the one but not the other.[3] Alone later, with Fortune's array withdrawn from him, pursued by his people, he searches vainly for cover, and finally kills himself in a garden, which is itself an image of the womb from which he first emerged into life (7, 2530–50).[4] Man's enduring array is not of the body but of the soul.

Array is all those things intermediary between eye and object of its attention, like the path that stretches before the pilgrims as they pass eastward toward the shrine at Canterbury. Clothing, womb, road, and words are mediants between thought and act. They are the connecting material in the triadic structure of man's life between conception and termination, and in the world's life between Creation and Doomsday. The pilgrimage of Chaucer's *Tales* whose terminus—which we do not see anyone reach—is redemption, depicts man moving from sin toward grace.[5] Along the way, pilgrim and reader of pilgrimage are involved in speaking and hearing distinctions between oppositions such as experience and authority, earnest and game, learned and lewd, and private and public.[6] Extremes are more easily conceptualized and described than the plasticity of things between, but Chaucer's verse draws our eyes insistently towards those uncertain shapes of things between beginnings and ends, between things to perceive and ideas to conceive. Man lives in a middle ground, *nel mezzo del commin,* like the bright winter hall through which the sparrow-soul flies for an instant before disappearing again into the ageless dark from which it came.[7]

The spiritual chain of love is life's invisible and ungraspable guiding principle of being. It is not surpising, however, that assertions of its existence, such as the Canon's Yeoman's bragging of his lord's powers and Nero's search for the array of his conceiving, are usually denied; for Chaucer's poetry exposes the visible disorder of man's experience out of which he would find order. Although Harry treads a road toward a rehearsal of his initial and ultimate union with God, he does not read the spiritual implications of the Canon's silver and gold. Both he and Nero are incapable of seeing any deeper into being than a knife can cut.[8]

Chaucer's narrative style consistently questions the philosophical ideas of order which his characters have trouble coordinating with their experience. As the cases of Harry Bailly and Nero exemplify, the issues are semiotic and epistemological. They concern reading signs. Chaucer is a philosophical poet,[9] but his language engages in ideas without arguing for a single particular truth. He disdains making systems of thought out of his fictional ordering of experience, but he delights in the artifice that makes riot of philosophical certainties. One plays well with ideas one knows well. It may be that Chaucer's poetry is so alive with gusto for the things of this world because the author is confident in the existence of the next. Though both man and his art are imperfect, neither is lost. Poetry and pilgrimage, and particularly the poetry of pilgrimage, draw a man back toward a primal perfection. Neither foot, mouth, nor pen can get him there, but each can move him closer to the One who will.

In one respect, then, this is a study of the career in Chaucer's longer poems of a philosophical idea figured by images of a bond like the Canon's road between two extremes. Inevitably, in tracing that idea and its images, I dwell on Chaucer's language, for words bind ideas and things. Chaucer's poetry ties and unties those bonds simultaneously. The polysemy of his language pulls words toward opposing ideological poles. It is as if Chaucer sends words on their way, and then, like a god observing the process of the life he initiates, follows their errant traces without appearing to meddle with their semantic vectors, no matter the confusion they spell.

My philological observations are meant to collaborate with information about the text. They mean to conjoin semantic references with narrative ideas. I am convinced that Chaucer's free-flowing style is congruent with his reading of the vast and rich store of his authorities. He shapes the language and ideological content of philosophy in his making of story but does not order his story to serve philosophy. This book is not, then, a "history of ideas" or a chronology of influence, but rather an exposition of Chaucer's play with ideas, his juggling with interrelated images drawn from his social and intellectual environment, his manner of making a synchronicity out of the diachronic jumble of past and present.

A reading of Chaucer suggests its own theory. One component of this theory is Chaucer's stylistic and narrative *aporia,* the doubt of certainty of meaning in word, narrative, and structure. One is made aware by Chaucer's style of the insufficiency of linguistic and intellectual references to limit meaning, for Chaucer's poetry is ideologically open-ended. Its implicit questioning of structural and semantic closure fractures meaning several ways. Chaucer's poetry invites a plurality of readings and denies the exclusivity of any one. Similarly, Chaucer characteristically refuses to indicate an authorial preference.

So, I am not so much concerned with establishing new readings as much as I am in uncovering paths to new meanings. I have no stake in any particular critical stance. There are many rooms in the mansion of Chaucerian criticism. I appreciate a dramatic principle at work in the *Tales* as well as a drama of style, an inorganic structure, a counterplay of narrative voices, fideism, philosophical doubt, and much more than is in my immediate recall. No single way of reading dominates the pleasure of the text for me to the exclusion of another. I see both weasel and whale in the skies of Chaucer criticism.

The Notes and Bibliography fail to quit my debt to my peers. Many of my facts and observations have sources I have lost sight of. I realize that I tread a similar critical path as Robert M. Jordan, Jörg O. Fichte, Piero Boitani, V. A. Kolve, and D. W. Robertson, Jr., just to mention a few who have frolicked in Chaucer's ideological gardens. I would join them in showing how much Chaucer's poetry engages the things of this world while peering behind for a glimpse of a world that once was and may yet be.

# 1

Chaucer's Chain of Love in the European
Tradition

> ... hanging in a golden chain
> This Pendant World.
> —Milton, *Paradise Lost* 2, 1051–52

> Vast Chain of Being! which from God began,
> Natures ethereal, human, angel, man,
> Beast, bird, fish, insect, what no eye can see,
> No glass can reach! from Infinite to thee,
> From thee to nothing.
> —Pope, *An Essay on Man* 1, 8, 237–41

IN THE KNIGHT'S TALE, A STERN AND IMPERIOUS THESEUS REDRESSES
the disarray of Palamon's and Arcite's amatory pursuit of Emily by
turning it into a competition for marriage. When Palamon survives as
the sole claimant for her hand, the stately Duke of Athens calls the couple
together to explain that their proposed marriage would imitate and join
the cosmic bond of all things. He makes this point at length in a passage
too complex for cursory comment, perhaps far too rich for the context
in which the Duke of Athens spreads before this select audience of two
a blueprint for the mansion and furniture of their existence:

> "The Firste Moevere of the cause above,
> Whan he first made the faire cheyne of love,
> Greet was th'effect, and heigh was his entente.
> Wel wiste he why, and what thereof he mente,
> For with that faire cheyne of love he bond
> The fyr, the eyr, the water, and the lond
> In certeyn boundes, that they may nat flee.
> That same Prince and that Moevere," quod he,
> "Hath stablissed in this wrecched world adoun
> Certeyn dayes and duracioun

18

> To al that is engendred in this place,
> Over the which day they may nat pace,
> Al mowe they yet tho dayes wel abregge.
> Ther nedeth noght noon auctoritee t'allegge,
> For it is preeved by experience
> But that me list declaren my sentence.
> Thanne may men by this ordre wel discerne
> That ilke Moevere stable is and eterne.
> Wel may men knowe, but it be a fool,
> That every part dirryveth from the hool,
> For nature hath nat taken his bigynnyng
> Of no partie or cantel of a thyng,
> But of a thyng that parfit is and stable,
> Descendynge so til it be corrumpable.
> And therfore, of his wise purveiaunce,
> He hath so wel biset his ordinaunce
> That speces of thynges and progressiouns
> Shullen enduren by successiouns,
> And nat eterne, withouten any lye.
> This maystow understonde and seen at ye."

> (*CT* 1, 2987–3016)

Leaving aside for the moment the question of the pertinence of such an exposition to its fictional occasion, this passage, replete with the familiar jargon of scholastic humanism of Chaucer's day, is a careful Neoplatonic exposition of the creation of the world and of the forces that govern its process. The chain of love with which God holds the elements in place is at once a metaphor for the imperceptible and perceptible forms and motions that govern the visible world and a model for poetic structure. In short, the shape of Theseus's speech as well as the book which contains it imitates the shape of the world.

The source of the chain image and its long history before Chaucer's time are identified succinctly in the notes to any current classroom text of Chaucer's works. The extensive scan I offer in the following pages is intended to both identify the importance of the chain image in the authoritative scientific lore upon which Chaucer draws for his Neoplatonic model and to explicate Theseus's version of it. The background of Theseus's passage is Chaucer's encyclopedic reference book for his poetic enterprise.

Theseus, though he rules in Athens before the Trojan War, uses a metaphor of a chain found in Homer's eighth book of the *Iliad* where Zeus challenges the bickering gods to test his power by stretching a cord between himself and the earth and trying to pull him down by it.[1] This image of a nexus between heaven and earth was interpreted by philosophers as a cosmic bond. In Plato's *Theaetetus*, 153c–d, Socrates says that

Zeus and the chain represent the sun and its orbit, and, as long as Zeus controls the chain, all things remain stable and durable both in heaven and on earth, but if the sun is blocked in its course, all things decay. In the *Timaeus,* the best known of Plato's dialogues in Chaucer's intellectual world, thanks to Chalcidius's fourth-century translation and commentary, Timaeus explains to Socrates and Hermocrates that the cosmic chain is the essential cohesive structure in the universe. The crucial passage, 31b–c, appears as follows: *Ignem terramque corporis mundi fundamenta iecit deus, quoniamque nulle suo sine adiunctione tertii firme et dissolubiliter cohaerent. Nexu enim medio extrema nectente opus est. Nexus uero firmissimus ille certe est, qui et se ipsum et ea quae secum uinciunter facit unum* [Of fire and earth god made the base of the world body; yet, it is not possible for two things to be joined firmly and indissolubly without a third. An intermediary bond must connect the extremes. The firmest (Plato has *kallisto,* "fairest") of bonds is that which unites into one thing both itself and the things it binds together].[2] In *Timaeus* 32c, the bond is called *philia* [love], and this is Chaucer's ultimate source for the conceit.

Some fifty years after Chalcidius, Macrobius's *Commentary* on Cicero's *Somnium Scipionis* explains that "the close observer will find that from the Supreme God even to the bottommost dregs of the universe, there is one tie [*uinculis religans*], binding at every link and never broken. This is the golden chain of Homer which, he tells us, God ordered to hang from the sky to the earth" (1, 14, 15).[3] Macrobius had explained earlier (1, 6, 24) that two is the first whole number which is a binding mean between extremes, in imitation of the Creator's *insolubili uinculo* [unbreakable chain] which binds the four elements. The numbers between two and four, and all the numbers in any series that links first and last, constitute a *tertium quid* in what C. S. Lewis has more recently labeled "the principle of the triad."[4] The first number and last numbers in a series and the mediant number(s) between them are a conceptual triadic figuration of the cosmos in Chaucer's Platonic Christianity.[5]

The mediant bond between extremes, which is Plato's structural principle of the universe, becomes easily elaborated into both spiritual and natural structures. In *Boece* 1, m. 5, Boethius's prayer translates the Platonic chain into a typology that recalls Christ's assignment of Peter as bond between heaven and earth (Matthew 16, 19, and 18, 18): "Thow governour . . . fastne and ferme thise erthes stable with thilke boond by whiche thou governest the hevene that is so large." Lady Philosophy's subsequent explanation of God's governance establishes a common medieval reading of the cosmic *tertium quid* as a power of love:

Hanc rerum seriem ligat
Terras ac pelagus regens
Et caelo imperitans amor.

(*Cons.* 2, m. 8, 13–15)

[Al this accordaunce and ordenaunce of thynges is bounde with love, that governeth erthe and see, and hath also commandement to the hevene.] William of Conches' *Commentary* on these lines explains the bond as *divina et benigna concordia . . . divina amore* [divine and benign concord . . . divine love].[6] In *Inferno* 11, 56, Dante's Virgil speaks similarly of *lo vinco d'amor che fa natura* [the knot of love which nature made]. In his *Convivio* 3, 7, 2, that knot is *la divina bontade.*[7] At the close of the *Commedia,* Dante looks into the light of Infinite Good, where he sees the essential knot behind things: "legato con amore in un volume / ciò che per l'universo si squaderna" (*Par.* 33, 87–88). [bound by love into one volume that which is dispersed in leaves throughout the universe]. So Dante's bond of love shapes a book and the words it contains.

The knot of love is God himself. *Voi che'ntendo il terzo ciel movete* [You who by intellect move the third heaven (Venus)], Dante exclaims to God in *Convivio* 2, 3, 7. As the moment of his long-desired consummation of love draws near, Chaucer's Troilus cries out to Venus, "Benygne Love, thow holy bond of thynges" (*Tr.* 3, 1261). This bond is a principle of nature as well as love and reason. In the *Roman de la rose,* 16786, Nature boasts that she, as God's regent on earth, is the guardian of the *bele chaeine dorée;* and in his *Troy Book* 2, 2188, Lydgate speaks of "Kynde's large cheyne."[8] The bond of love, then, links God's being, art, and nature.

At the lower reaches of the chain in the realm of nature, the bond of love is only physical, unattended by spirit. Such love is a counterweight pulling man down toward physical pleasure and away from spiritual exaltation. The tenth-century lyric "Flane cum terram" scorns those who flee Zephirus's inspirational breath of love: ". . . tua grate sociari legi / colle nequibunt" [And your necks will not be able to be joined to the law of pleasure's rule].[9] To refuse physical love is to refuse the universe, but to embrace sexual love alone is to be bound, as the same lyric warns, in the hellish depths of *catena arte Vulcani* [Vulcan's constricting chain]. In the same spirit, in his "Lenvoy a Bukton," Chaucer calls marriage the "cheyne of Sathanas," and his "Lenvoy de Chaucer à Scogan" lists humorously the cosmic disasters consequent upon scorning the behavior implicit in bonds of love. Peter of Blois's lyric "Grates ago Veneri" praises sexual desire as a *firmo nexus.*[10] For the medieval exegetes, the two extreme links of the chain of love are *caritas* and *cupiditas.*

All of these ideas reside in Theseus's figure of the bond of love, and the implications of the bond color the remainder of his exposition to Palamon and Emily. Following his argument requires an understanding of the basic tenets of Chaucer's received theology. To begin with, since the chain of love connects nature with God, it is for the philosophers the bond between the universe's efficient and its final cause.[11] It descends from the invisible cosmic *dessus* of creation to the *dessous* of man's lowest natural qualities, which Theseus identifies as corruptibility. It reaches from God's idea to man's basest senses, and among the things between are reason and word. Boethius measures the distance between idea and sense with the female figure of Philosophy. From the *Pi* (*Pratica*) woven on the lower hem of her dress to the *Theta* (*Theoretica*) of the upper runs a ladder motif.[12] Similarly, the pure mind and body of a virgin is an image of the *vita angelica* that links earthly and heavenly perfection in love.[13] The virgin's love is an emanation of *Venus caelestus,* but those who prefer only kindly affections are held toward *Venus vulgaria.*[14] The Provençal love-poet Jaufre Rudel (fl. 1140–50) praises God as the source of both loves: "Dieus que fetz tot quant vi ne vai / E formet sest'amor de lonh" [God made all that comes and goes, and formed that love far away].[15] *De lonh* is both the distance between man and God and between the lover and his lady.

In the ontology of gender, the cosmic chain is a female force. For philosophers such as Alain de Lisle, grammatical gender has ideological import,[16] and *catena* is, appropriately, a feminine noun. Theseus character-izes the chain of love as a reification of God's "wise purveiaunce," which in Boethius's Latin is both a feminine noun (*providentia*) and a feminine force mediated by the Virgin Mary. Boethius explains it as the matrix of all order: *concurrere uero atque confluere causas facit ordo ille ineuitabili conexione procedens, qui de prouidentiae fonte descendens cuncta suis locis temporibusque disponit* (*Cons.* 5, pr. 1, 55–58) [Thilke ordre, proced-inge by an uneschuable byndinge togidre, whiche that descendeth fro the welle of purveaunce that ordeyneth alle thingis in hir places and in hir tymes, makith that the causes rennen and assemblen togidre]. The "uneschuable byndynge" is union of God with matter, and the "welle" is source of all life.[17] The statement that "purveaunce knytteth alle thingis in hir ordres" (Book 4, pr. 6, 66–67) is the direct source of Theseus's conception of the chain binding the elements.

In Boethius's summary of the first part of *Timaeus* in the ninth meter of Book 3, the masculine counterpart of female matter, which Theseus identifies as "Prince and Mover," is *principium, uector, dux, semita, terminus idem* (28), which Chaucer renders as "Begynnynge, berere, ledere, path and terme" (47–48). In Book 4, pr. 2, 12–14, Boethius explains that human power, or *potestas* (f.) collaborates with will, *voluntas* (f.) to effect action, *actus* (m.). I am reminded of Bernard Silvester's

*Commentary* on Martianus's *Marriage of Mercury and Philology,* where Jove figures the power of action and Juno that of divine will.[18]

Purveyance, the invisible matrix of all matter, produces the ordinance (*ordo,* m.) which arranges matter into substance and form. *Providentia* translates Plato's *noys,* and both are figured, like Alain's Natura and Boethius's Philosophia, in feminine form.[19] Bernard Silvester explains *noys* in *Cosmographia* 1, 2, 8–9, as *scientia et divinia voluntatis ad disponsitionem rerum* [knowledge and divine will for the ordering of things] and it is mediant between divine will and created things.[20] The birth of the universe, Bernard explains, takes place in the divine mind before it is reified in matter.

If feminine Providence is the invisible shaping principle of the universe, feminine Nature is its visible form, the *tertium quid* between the invisible world of idea and the visible world of matter. Nature is the agency of *noys* in the creative act, intermediary between God and man, and her realm stretches, as Aldhelm's *De Creatura* riddle pronounces, from higher than the sky to lower than the earth.[21] Stretching from God to man, and from idea to matter, Nature has both invisible and visible manifestations. At the end of his ascension toward God, Dante catches sight of the *forma universal di questo nodo* (*Par.* 33, 91), the universal form of this knot, or chain, of love. Bernard Silvester's nature is a *sacer nexus* (*Cosm.* 2, 10, 17–18).[22] For a creature to exist, Bernard adds, his soul must be joined to a body, and the Greek word *demas,* he expounds, means both "body" and "chain."[23]

Chaucer's Physician describes Nature as God's mediator for the shaping of earthly forms as well as the principle wherby those forms are capable of taking on new matter and shape:

> . . . He that is the formere principal
> Hath maked me his vicaire general,
> To formen and peynten erthely creaturis
> Ryght as me list. . . .
>
> (6, 19–22)

"Peynten" designates the attributing of senses and looks. "As me list" sounds like blasphemous willfulness, but it can be explained as a composite of Nature's will and God's providence. What is particular to Nature's power for the Physician, however, is her attention to the painting of woman's beauty.[24]

Like the sunbeam, the bond of love is a universal *connexio* that emanates from God and contains all perfect forms of nature. Taking a lead from Plato, Boethius has the sun's orbit bind the universe in *allyaunce perdurable* (*Boece* 2, m. 8, 1–6).[25] It is one of those appropriate sound-sense coincidences that *dies dominicus,* God's day, is English *Sunday,* the day of the Sun/Son, or love. Since fire is the lightest and highest natural element, light is the purest form in nature and a perceptible avenue to God's person. For the Neoplatonists, the World Soul is both luminous and pneumatic. For Robert Grosseteste, light is the most pervasive feature of the universe and the most perfect of all corporeal things, combining the natural and the supernatural in one.[26] Grosseteste pictures creation as a point of light radiating outward from a central *lux* to a sphere of *lumen.*[27] Similarly, Dante distinguishes between the *luce etterna* of God and the *alto lume* of his manifest presence (*Par.* 33, 84, 116, and 127). This design is repeated in Nicholas de Cusa's image of the moral universe as a descent of spirit in a "fine point evenly enlarging itself to form a cone whose base has diameters outrageously infinite."[28] Dante's light of pure vision of the Godhead descends from the *Mobile Primo* (*Par.* 30, 100–108) and is dispersed as a *trine luce* "threefold light" (*Par.* 31, 28).

It is nature that fills the space between God's unseen light and man's ocular light, and Chaucer's Parson alludes to the power over nature of the spiritual light of salvation in the process of penance that transforms "the body of man, that whilom was foul and derk . . . moore cleer than the sonne" (10, 1078). The alchemist who is dedicated to transforming dark metals to light mimics the Creator. Visible things are but a dark likeness of their invisible source. Boethius observes that God is the *verus sol* (*Cons.* 5, m. 2, 14), the "verrai sonne," since he sees in his thought all things.

That power that transforms God's thought into things and matter into substantial form is what Theseus calls "ordinaunce." It consists of the laws of order in which God's purveyance is conjoined with matter. Before it is touched by thought, matter is chaos, what Sapientia 11, 18, identifies as the *materia invisa* [formless matter] out of which God shaped the world. Touched by God's thought, matter becomes substance whose visible appearance is accident. Familiar to Chaucer is the conventional philosophical jargon of the schools used by Jean de Meun's Nature:

> Et muent par lor influances
> Les accidens et les sustances
> Des choses qui sont sous la lune.
>
> (*RR,* 16955–57)

[The things that reside beneath the moon alter under the influence of accident and substance.] *Accident* is the philosophical term for the worldly appearance of form, the perceived shape of something. Aristotle distinguishes between the accident of a thing, which is perceived by the senses,

and its primal and alterable form, *ousia,* or res.[29] Chaucer's Pardoner
utters a disparaging remark about the Host's occupation in these terms:

> Thise cookes, how they stampe, and streyne, and grynde,
> And turnen substaunce into accident
> To fulfille al thy likerous talent!
>
> (6, 538–40)

The accident of the cook is the pleasing appearance of food whose substantial quality and nourishment, suggests the Pardoner, are questionable.

In the biology of creation, accident is the outward show of a substance's
ideological code, without which nothing in nature can exist. Aristotle
teaches that a thing's design combines with its capacity for change,
*steresis,* and inchoate material, *hyle,* to make a bond between divine
thought and nature.[30] He explains substance as a triad of form, matter,
and combinations of them (*De Anima* 3, 2, 414a). Dante's comparable
triad in the *Commedia* is *sustanza e accidenti e lor costume* [substance
and accident and their relation] which he is privileged to glimpse through
God's transcendental light.[31] In his 1379 Oxford lectures published under
the title *De Eucharistia,* Wyclif argues against the dogma of transubstan-
tiation on the grounds that substance cannot be annihilated.

The purveying God whose nature conjoins matter with form is a *Deus
otiosus,* unmoved; but *otium* in created things is contrary to their nature.
In man it constitutes sloth, personified in feminine form in the *Roman
de la rose* as Oiseuse, Chaucer's Ydlenesse. As unmoved Mover, God is
like an architect whose plans are carried out by a craftsman. So Theseus,
who sits like a god on a throne (1, 2528–29), orders the construction of
a theater of the world in order to fulfill providence (1, 1842–44). Timaeus's
artificer-god uses shapeless *hyle* as his building material (*Timaeus* 28a);
and, commenting on this passage, William of Conches explains that God is
*faber, volens aliquid fabricare, prius illud in mente disponit* [the craftsman
who, wishing to make something, orders it first in his mind].[32] In *De
Planctu Naturae,* 3 [pr. 3], Alain's Natura announces: *ille me opifex
operis, ego opus opificis* [God is the creator of my work; I am the creator's
work].[33] Both Chalcidius and Bernard Silvester conceive of God as an
*opifex,* while Boethius calls him the *artifex* who joins "the purveaunce
[which] is an unmoevable and symple forme of thinges to doone and the
moevable bond and the temporel ordenaunce of thinges" (*Boece* 4, pr. 6,
102–5). Chalcidius calls him *genitor* as well, but the architectural figure
is predominant in the Platonic tradition. Cicero calls the creator *aedificator*
and Alain de Lisle calls him both *Opifex* and *Artifex.* Chaucer's Pandarus
assigns himself the role of *artifex* when, in playing *tertium quid* between

Troilus and Criseyde, he "caste his werk ful wisely or he wroughte" (*Tr.* 1, 1070).

Chaucer compares the poet to an artificer (*Tr.* 1, 1065–69)[34] and the Merchant compares his salacious Januarie with Solomon in his skill as architect of gardens and temples (*CT* 4, 2291–96). The young folk of Kayrrud in the Franklin's tale make "ordinaunce / Of vitaille and of oother purveyeiaunce" in collaboration with nature to make a "verray paradys" (5, 902–12). Ralph of Longchamps's commentary on Alain's *Anticlaudianus* lists God, Nature, Fortune, and Sin in a hierarchy of *artifices.*[35] God designs, Nature fashions things out of preexistent raw materials, Fortune produces the fortuitous events and effects of things, and Sin is responsible for vices.

A more common term in Chaucer's poetry for accident, the visible manifestation of an essential form, is *countenaunce.* Grisilde's countenance in the Clerk's tale, when Walter announces that her daughter is to be taken away and killed, hides her horror and sadness (4, 499). Pandarus makes much of Troilus's countenance in his account to Criseyde of the hero's complaint on his secret love in the garden (*Tr.* 2, 552). Since Pandarus seems to be inventing the story to whet his niece's love interest, the story is itself a countenance with hidden intent behind it. The deceit that the term often carries into a literary context is most obvious at the end of the Cook's fragmentary tale of a young wife who "heeld for contenaunce / A shoppe, and swyved for her sustenance" (1, 4421–22). Her shop is an appearance of bourgeois respectability to the public, but it conceals the prostitution that provides a private income.

Theseus attributes to the chain of love the binding of the four elements, "in certeyn boundes," and this organization of the created material of the universe is understood as the principle of plenitude, which holds that there is a place for everything, that everything has its proper place, and that no space is void.[36] W. H. Auden sums up the implications of this principle by explaining that once creation was completed, "every kind of thing which could possibly exist was already there without room for the admission of any extra novelty, and arranged in an orderly and rationally comprehensible hierarchy of being."[37] Plato's Timaeus explains the concept of a universe without a void by the fact that the All contains everything (*Timaeus* 58b–c). He is *pleroma,* fullness. "I am who / Fill Infinitude, not vacuous the space," thunders Milton's God (*Paradise Lost* 7, 168–69). Plotinus calls space a container of bodies (*Ennead* 4, 3, 20). Even darkness and emptiness are not *nothing,* explains Fredegius, neither voids nor absences but things in themselves.[38]

The proper place for anything is its blueprint location in God's design for creation, but its actual place is elsewhere. Before the chain of love ordered things within bounds, the *hyle* of the universe contained neither form nor order. Ovid's account of creation begins: "nec circumfuso pende-bat in aere tellus / ponderibus librata suis . . ." *Metam.* 1, 12–13)[39] [The earth did not yet hang in the air poised by her own weight]. Following Aristotle and Plato in ordering the elements and binding them together by love, Ovid identifies the bond as *concordi pace* (1. 25). Augustine calls it the "appointed order of things transitory" (*De Civ.* 12, 4–5).[40] Each thing in nature has its own hierarchal order of location, divisible into smaller orders down to the smallest measurable item. Chaucer parodies the view of God as one and indivisible, while creation is infinitely divisible, in his comedy of orders in the *Parliament of Fowls*.

Gower's *Prologus* to *Confessio Amantis* explains the necessity of such natural diversity:

> . . . If a man were
> Mad al togedre of a matier
> Withouten interrupcioun,
> Ther sholde no corrupcioun
> Engendre upon that unite;
> Bot for ther is diversite
> Withinne himself, he may nat laste,
> That he ne deieth ate laste.
>
> (983–90)[41]

So man must die in order to rejoin his source, and his matter must decay in order that he die. As old things die and transitory things like Malkyn's maidenhead disappear, form must seek out new matter in order to maintain the balance of plenitude. It is by this philosophical principle that Chaucer explains in *The Legend of Good Women* why Jason turns to Phaedra as his lust for Medea wanes; and the accident of cooks, remarks Chaucer's Pardoner, turns quickly to "dong and corrupcion" (6, 535).[42]

Timaeus goes on to explain that since all divisible things are unequal, each order has its own hierarchy as well as its proper place in a larger hierarchy (*Tim.* 58b). *Fauna* and *flora,* lions and worms, roses and weeds, wine and ale, kings and beggars each have their zeniths and nadirs. That which holds any two items together in any hierarchal relationship is their "natural piety," a name for the bond holding unequal things in harmonious accord.[43] As Milton's Raphael explains to Adam:

> The grosser feeds the purer, Earth the Seas,
> Earth and Sea feed Air, the Air those Fires
> Ethereal.
>
> (*PL* 5, 416–18)

So even the lowest created thing is attached to God, a principle Chaucer's Parson applies to social orders as well: "God hadde ordeyned that som

men hadde hyer degree and som men lower" (10, 773). In Langland's
*Piers Plowman,* devils populate nature in hierarchal order with Lucifer the
lowest (C-text, *Passus* 1, 126–28). Dionysius the Areopagite's *Celestial
Hierarchy* elaborates a ninefold hierarchy of angels, Hugh of Saint Victor
posits a chain of vices, and Albertus Magnus orders sins according to
the moral weight of their intent.[44]

Sin and virtue, at opposite ends of a moral chain, are centrifugal and
centripetal forces contending for man's spirit. In moral space, man's place
is somewhere between heaven and hell. Plato's Diotima, in *Symposium,*
203a–e, explains that all things reside between poles of perfect good and
absolute evil. By the end of the first millenium, Christian thought had
charted a purgatorial area between them. Egeus, Theseus's father, consoles
his son's thwarted expectations for the tournament by explaining, in
accordance with orthodox Christian thought, that man's life is a purgatorial pilgrimage (1, 2847–48). In Christian geography, purgatory is mediant
between heaven and hell, in eschatology between death and resurrection,
and in morality between good and evil. If man does not complete his
redemption in life, the process continues during the suspended moral
residence of the soul in purgatory. The bond of love stops there, for there
is no chain of created order between purgatory and hell.[45] Down there in
the land of the shades there is *nullus ordo,* as God tells Job (10, 22), for
grace extends no deeper than purgatory, where souls, if they move in
any direction at all, move upward.[46]

By Chaucer's day, on the basis of the writings of the twelfth-century
Platonists, the physical and moral universes were conceptualized in Theseus's terms.[47] The moral and physical universe is spherical, shaped by
the turning of the cone of diffusion about both its central axis and its
apex point. The chain of love, whose motion in every direction about its
highest point describes a sphere, contains at its center a spiritual and
physical point of attraction. For Plato and his followers, the sphere is the
necessary perfection of form to match the perfection of divine thought
(*Tim.* 33b),[48] and its inscribing instrument is the triadic pyramid. Just as
all things in nature are in constant motion away from their physical source
(*Tim.* 81b), man's soul is in motion away from its primal purity, though
it never ceases to incline back toward it. In the physical and temporal
principle of diffusion, sin is the moral force which tugs man away from
God's love.

Mephistophilis describes the organization of elements in motion to
Marlowe's Faustus:

> Even from the moon unto the empyreal orb,
> Mutually folded in each others' spheres,

> And jointly move upon one axle-tree,
> Whose terminal is termd the world's wide pole.
>
> *(Faustus* 2, 2, 39–42)[49]

The ultimate source of this image is the story in Plato's *Republic* (10, 614b-618b), cited by Macrobius in his *Commentary* 1, 1, 9, of the return from the dead of the warrior Er, who tells his listeners that he found himself on a fair field at the center of the universe to which souls from above and below are drawn to exchange accounts of their residence. From that spot, Er saw a pillar of light stretching down from heaven and turned at its extremities by spindles of necessity.[50]

Boethius applies the physics of centripetal attraction at work in these examples to an original location to natural things:

> Repetunt proprios quaeque recursus
> Redituque suo singula guadent
> Nec manet ulli traditus ordo.
>
> *(Cons.* 3, m. 2, 34–36)

[Alle thynges seken ayen to hir propre cours, and alle thynges rejoysen him of hir retornynge ayen to hir nature.] William of Aragon's *Commentary* explains in this context that trees have a natural inclination toward light, animals to kindness, and men to virtue and the good.[51] Animals, argues the Nun's Priest, hold faster to their kind than men (7, 3276), an observation confirmed by Chaucer's Manciple (9, 160–86) and by the narrator of *Troilus* (1. 218–24). Chaucer's Franklin explains the natural attraction of tides toward the moon (5, 1052–53). Even mundane love, like all natural things, sings Guido Guinizelli, has its proper mansion:

> Al cor gentil rempaira sempre amore
> Come l'ausello in selva a la verdura.
>
> . . . . . . . . . . . .
>
> E prende amore in gentilezza loco
> Così propiamente.
>
> ("Al cor," 1–2, 7–8)[52]

[To the gentle heart love always returns, like the bird in the wood to the green. . . . Love takes its proper place in gentilesse.] The lovesick falcon of the Squire's tale, however, ignorant of philosophy, accuses the nature of the false tercelet of a natural attraction *away* from fidelity in love (5, 608–9).

It is in the chains of utterance that the bond of love is most significantly manifest in Chaucer's world. The garrulous eagle of the *House of Fame* applies the principle of plenitude to sound waves:

> Geffrey, thou wost ryght wel this,
> That every kyndely thyng that is
> Hath a kyndely stede ther he
> May best in hyt conserved be;
> Unto which place every thyng,
> Thorgh his kyndely enclynyng,
> Moveth for to come to
> Whan that hyt is awey therfro.
>
> (2, 729–36)

All words, spoken or written, are attracted toward their proper place in the universe. Harry Bailly ordains words to fill the space of the Canterbury pilgrimage. Man's word, whose model is Scripture, is a sensible echo of the inaudible creative *logos* which the Alexandrine schoolmen called *spermatalogos.* Words mediate the mind's desire in the repair of the breach between man and his Maker. In *Ion* (533d–36a) Socrates characterizes the divine power of speaking well as a magnet. If one magnetizes a ring, it imparts its power to whatever ring is touched to it, and so inspired rhetoric is a chain of attraction which is incarnated in the muses. In his *Confessions* 11, 5–6, Augustine speaks of human speech as a link between heaven and earth, and Thomas Aquinas's string of commentaries on patristic texts were known as a *Catena aurea* [golden chain].[53]

In Psalms, 33, 9, David exalts the kinetic force of the Divine Word: *Quoniam ipse dixit, et facta sunt; ipse mandavit et creata sunt* [What is spoken is done, what is commanded is made]. John Scotus Erigena explains the middle term of the Trinity as the Word, which is the active virtue of Christ between God's Principle and the Holy Spirit's power.[54] For Dante in *De Vulgari Eloquentia,* 4, 2, words are the *seme operazione* [seeds of ordinance] of the universe. Poetry, Boccaccio argues in *De genealogia deorum* 14, 8, conveys the high mysteries of divine things in a covering of words. The prayers of charitable friars, boasts the greedy friar of the Summoner's tale, soar like hawks to God's ear (3, 1938–41).

Man's own word moves him toward either salvation or damnation, but in the Man of Law's tale, the circuit of Constance's peregrinations which begins and ends in the City of Love is sustained and completed by God's *sonde* (2, 523, 826, 902, and 1049). In its Chaucerian context *sonde* designates "message," "tidings," or "messenger," though its etymological signification of "sound" is unmistakable. In Chaucer's poetry, *sonde* refers consistently to the bond between man and God manifest in a token of grace.[55] God's *sonde* contrasts with the tidings of merchants who carry tales from one land to another (2, 129–30) and with the fraudulent messages of Aella's mother. It contrasts with the Wife of Bath's *rune* [secret, mystery, whisper] which is the susurrus of dalliance that accomplishes carnal love. Alison accuses one of her husbands of "rowning" with their maid (3, 241), and the hag of her tale saves the life of the knight with a *rowned* answer to the riddle of women's desire (3, 1021).

In the Friar's tale, the fiend who serves God's judgment enforces old Mabely's verbal damnation of the false summoner who refuses to use his own words to repent calumny. In the Summoner's tale, words of anger destroy the bond of spiritual trust between Thomas and the friar; and the squire of the village lord solves the riddle of the wasting fart by designing with words an engine which can capture and distribute this explosive gift of "love." His engine, which like the riddle has ontological being only in a world of word, is a technological artifice for duplicating the Pentecostal descent of the Holy Word to the Apostles.[56] In the Squire's tale the magical gift of the language of birds permits Canace and a falcon to participate in the same world of idea and sensation. The Physician's tale turns about false witness, false judgment, and a plea for grace. The Shipman tells of a trail of words which establish a line of mercantile and sexual credit. In the tale of Melibee, 181 aphorisms guide the hero from hate and vengeance to forgiveness and peace. It is not surprising that the word *sermon* derives from the Latin *series* [chain].

Man's word mediates between intent and deed, though it cozens the deed as well as being its cousin. In the fallen world, as the Pardoner illustrates with terrifying candor, words can make appearances of things seem true. In his *retracciouns,* Chaucer revokes those tales of his which "sownen unto synne," that is, which draw man away from God's love. *Sownen* signifies "to sound" and implies the sweet seductive words of those like sirens who lure man unto shoals of sin. Man is as apt to kill as to create with words.[57]

Soaring higher than words on the chain of love are the purer sounds of music. In *De Musica* 2, 29, Augustine associates the world with *carmina universitatis.* Later in the same tract (5, 17), he describes musical sound, as Grosseteste and Nicholas de Cusa later describe light, as an expansion from a single point into dimensions of length, width, and height that form a spherical geometry of beauty.[58] The single point corresponds to what Theseus calls the Mover's *hool,* his indivisible totality of being. Even cosmic music acquires the weight of disorder as it descends through corruptible elements. In the *House of Fame,* while he is still close to the earth on the back of the eagle, Geffrey hears waves of sound "lyk betynge of the see" (2, 1034); but the higher he soars, the more measured and harmonious is the music that comes to his ear (3, 1395–96). Boethius identifies the musical concord of the earth's motion with the bond of love—*imperitans amor* (*Cons.* 2, m. 8, 15)—and attributes to music the *varietas* of both love and nature as bonds between the One and the Other.[59]

Macrobius's *Commentary,* 2, 3, 7, attributes music to the soul: "Every soul in this world is allured by musical sounds so that not only those who are more refined in their habits, but all the barbarous peoples as well, have adopted songs by which they are informed with courage or wooed to pleasure; for the soul carries with it into the body a memory of the music which it knew in the sky."[60] In the *Parliament of Fowls,* 60–63, Chaucer recalls that Macrobius's Scipio Africanus, rising above the boundary of nature, hears the music which is "in this world here . . . cause of armonye." The Prioress's tale features a song praising the Virgin Mary and her intercession for the soul of a little boy who sings it, though he does not know the literal meaning of his text. Robert Henryson's Orpheus hears the music of the spheres as he sweeps through the sky on his quest for his lost love:

> Quhilk armony, throu all this mappamound,
> Quhill moving cesse, vnvt perpetuall—
> Quhill of this warld, Pluto the saull can all.
>
> (*Orpheus,* 223–25)[61]

Even the mundane music that soothes the savage breast has power to move the soul toward its proper place. Chauntecleer's enticement to love is his song "My lief is faren in londe" (7, 4069) while the Pardoner's is "Come hider, love, to me" (1, 672).

The conventional mythographic figure of music is Mercury.[62] In keeping with the etymological sense in his name (*merx* is the root of *commercium*), Mercury is peacemaker and mediator for the gods. In *De Raptu Proserpine* 1, 90–91, Claudian describes him as *fas per limin utrumque / solus habes geminoque facis commercia mundi* [He who crosses either threshold and is intermediary between the worlds].[63] Pandarus, who crosses thresholds as a matter of self-appointed labors, is Troilus's mercurial intermediary to bring him to his proper place in love, and he is witness to Troilus's consignment of his soul to Mercury (*Tr.* 5, 321–22). It is Mercury who carries the hero to his postmortem residence after his death on the Trojan plain (*Tr.* 5, 1826–27).

Furthermore, each of the "certeyn boundes" which Theseus mentions as a container of things temporal has its *mean.*[64] Dante confirms this by saying that there is a *mezzo stringa* ordained for everything (*Par.* 29, 31–36). Jean de Meun's Faux Semblant identifies the mean (with which he identifies himself) as God's created sufficiency:

> . . . ce sont deus extremités,
> richece et mendacités;

> Le moien a non souffisance,
> La gist le vertu abondance.
>
> (*RR* 11273–76)

The Chaucerian translation in the *Romaunt* is:

> For richesse and mendacitees
> Ben clepid suffisaunce,
> Ther lyth of vertu the abondance.
>
> (6525–28)

Abundance, mean, and sufficiency all pertain to the perfection of a thing in God's design and reflect the stable and incorruptible *mena* that is God himself (*Il Convivio* 1, 4–5). For Chaucer's Miller, sufficiency means *foyson,* the economy of material in the nature with which he associates sexual satisfaction (1, 3165). For the Man of Law, *foyson* is the provisions given Constance miraculously during her long drift at sea (2, 504).[65] For humble Grisilde, it is *habundance,* which is the mean sustenance of nature (4, 202–3), comparable to what might be called today an "ecological balance."

Sufficiency, says Alain in *De Planctu,* 3, in imitation of Boethius's *De Consolatione* (3, pr. 9), is the divine perfection of God's ordained and harmonious joining of things. So his Natura declares: *Eius opus sufficiens, meum opus deficiens* [His work is sufficient, mine deficient]. As Criseyde takes Troilus into her arms for the first time, she whispers, "Welcome my knyght, my pees, my suffisaunce" (*Tr.* 3, 1309). His sufficiency for her is a mean between her private feelings and her public security in Troy. Pandarus, in his jesting bravado, says, "Felicite clepe I my suffisaunce," as a lesson to Troilus how a man may face the loss of his love (5, 763). Boethius extols sufficiency as *perfecta felicitas,* which Chaucer translates as "varray parfit blisfulnesse," along with might, honor, nobility, and gladness (*Boece* 3, pr. 9, 149–52), and all of these things oppose false felicity. Patrick Gallacher has shown how the Wife of Bath pursues a sufficiency of pleasure in the virtuous delight which mediates between the desires of her body and the purveyance of her mind.[66]

The noble Januarie of the Merchant's tale follows the precept that felicity exists in delight alone (*CT* 4, 2021–22). The adjective *noble* is telling here, for Chaucer uses the word most often to identify the perfection or highest order of a thing in its class or kind. The glory of virtue, says Boethius's Philosophia, is higher than nobility of fame (*Cons.* 2, pr. 7, 94–142). In mundane contexts, Chaucer uses the term to designate the highest blood strain or political and social rank. So the Friar is a noble post unto his order (1, 214). The perfection of the referential value of the *noble* minted in Chaucer's lifetime by Edward III is authenticated by the stamped impression of the king. The Miller's Alison is likened to a freshly minted noble (1, 3256).

The perfection of a thing is, ideally, its mean, or medium state, signaled commonly by the word *ynogh,* though even in Chaucer's day that word carried something of the sense "too much" which it has today.[67] When Walter hears Grisilde's first pledge to obey his word in everything, he says "this is ynogh" to signal his satisfaction in her sufficiency of response (4, 365); but, when Grisilde warns him years later not to test his new wife's patience, "this is ynogh" (4, 1051) signals his impatience with her insistence and his desire to have her return to her mean and "perfection" of silence.[68]

Ideally, beauty resides at the mean point between excess and deficiency of qualities. The Physician's Virginia posesses perfect "mesure . . . of beryng and array" (6, 47). Criseyde "mene was of hire stature" (*Tr.* 5, 806), and Anelida is of "mydel stature" (*An.* 79). Moral and intellectual moderation is designated more often by the word *sad,* from Latin *satis.* Grisilde is noted for her "sad" courage (4, 220), and the excesses of alchemists, laments the Canon's Yeoman, are unchecked by any inclination to "wexen sadde" (8, 877). Such terms refer to the stable point where Theseus locates the First Mover. A term equivalent to *stability* is the native English *steadfast,* linked to Grisilde's quality of sadness (4, 564). The Black Knight's lady of the *Book of the Duchess* has a steadfast countenance and a noble port (833–34), as well as sad eyes (859–60). Unstable Fortune, on the other hand, displays only the *hue* of steadfastness, according to the Merchant (4, 2057–64). In "Lak of Steadfastnesse," Chaucer laments man's fall from truth at a time when word and deed are at odds; so, he calls upon King Richard to "wed thy folk agein to stedfastnesse." In matters of language, Dante, in *Convivio* 1, 5, 7, claims that the vernacular lacks the stability of the vulgate: *Lo latino è perpetuo e non corruttibilie, e lo vulgar è non stabile e corruttibilie* [Latin is perpetual and not corruptible, and the vulgar (vernacular) is corruptible and not stable]. These terms do not often lend themselves to irony; but although one can believe that King Cambyuskan's courage is "as any centre stable" (5, 22), one senses sycophantic hypocrisy in Placebo's praise of Januarie's word as "ferme and stable" (4, 1499).

The *otium* of stability is an attribute of the unmoved Mover, while natural things "slide" away from their perfection in mean and sufficiency.[69] Forms of love and speech change, as Chaucer remarks in his discussion of historical change in the *proem* to the second book of *Troilus* (2, 22–28). One may regret Criseyde's sliding courage, as the god of love does in the *Legend,* but her shifted affection toward Diomede is no more than a characteristic of natural change. Understanding this, Pandarus advises Troilus to let time and his sorrow slide away (5, 351–52). Dorigen's anxiety for her husband slides with time (*CT* 5, 924); and later, shocked by a prurience she reads in Aurelius's words, she tells the squire to let his folly slide out of his heart (5, 1002).

Errancy from the stable mean is a movement toward either excess or deficiency, vainglory or wanhope. Pandarus tells Troilus to avoid the extremes of "mistrusten alle or elles alle leve" (1, 688), and Criseyde finds herself later sliding perilously between the extremes of hope and dread, hot and cold (5, 808ff.). The Pardoner castigates the "superfluytee abhomynable" of swearing and the "escesse" of gluttony (6, 471, and 514). The stable point in the space of Theseus's Platonic cosmos is a center toward which all things incline (*Tim.* 33b). Things move toward or away from it without leaving a void (58a–b). The mean point for a human is an ideal location, a center in itself somewhere in the middle of things between the extremes of the One and the Other, between the indivisible and the infinity of divided worlds (*Tim.* 35a). In *Symposium* 203a–e, Diotima identifies this point with the spirit of love halfway between man and God, the exact location of Dante's Beatrice in *Vita nuova*. Diotima's spirit of love is a *daimon* who mediates between good and evil and who carries messages and supplications from man to God. Centers are privileged locations in their significance. The Tree of Life and Tree of Knowledge stand in *medio paradisi* (Gen. 2, 9). The physical center of man's body is his organ of generation, his *kind* or *genitalia*.[70] Macrobius sets the moon in the center of creation, and has its orbit divide air from aether, mortal from immortal realms of being (*Commentary* 1, 21, 53). Dante places in the center of creation the bond between potential and act.[71]

Ovid, following Virgil's example in *Aeneid* 4, 181–84, places Fame in the center of a threefold world: *"Orbe locus medio est inter terrasque fretumque / caelestesque plagas, triplicis confinia mundi"* (*Metam.* 12, 39–40). [There is a place in the center of the world between land and sea and sky, the meeting point of the threefold world.] Chaucer puts the Temple of Fame in the same spot: "Ryght even in middes of the weye / Betwixen hevene and erthe and see" (*HF* 2, 714–15). The threefold world reflects the triple nature of God's ordaining power in the *De Consolatione*: *"Tu triplicis mediam naturae cuncta mouentem / Conectens animam per consona membra resoluis"* (*Cons.* 3, m. 9, 13–14).

Chaucer translates this difficult phrase as: "Thow knyttest togidre the mene soule of treble kynde moevynge al thingis and divydest it by membrys accordynge." He is probably following Jean de Meun's version: *"Tu enlaces et conjoins au corps l'ame moienne de treble nature qui toute chose muet et la devisez par acordables membrez."*[72]

Mercury is not the only voyager across thresholds from one world of being to another. The *daimones* who mediate between man and God are spirits whose trajectories cross the center of things. In a well-circulated myth throughout the Western World, Phaeton drives the chariot of Helios too close to the earth, whereupon Zeus destroys it and casts Phaeton into the sky where he resides as the constellation *Scorpio.* In *Timaeus,* 22c–d, this story is read as an allegory of cosmic disturbances which disturb human life. In *Phaedrus* 246a–48d, Socrates likens man's soul to a charioteer who drives horses of a mortal and immortal mix between heaven and earth. Medieval mythographers read the four wheels of the chariot as the four elements and their spokes as the seasons, humors, winds, weeks, and times of the days.[73] The charioteer passes through four realms: the supercelestial realm of God, the celestial realm of the intellect and the transitory realms of the animate and sensible worlds. Marcilio Ficino's *Commentary* on *Phaedrus* identifies the chariot's ascent with instruction in love of the whole, and its descent with a concern for corporeal things.[74]

The Neoplatonic allegorical readings of such journeys insist upon the one-for-one correspondence between elements of the intelligible and sensible world.[75] Chaucer might well have known Virgil's allusion to the myth of the charioteer in *Aeneid* 5, 104–5, and he certainly knew Ovid's version of it in *Metamorphoses* 2, 31–232. He refers to the story himself in *Troilus* (5, 664) and *House of Fame* (2, 941–59). All such journeys, like Orpheus's search for Eurydice and Dante's for Beatrice, trace a path of love. Troilus's postmortem journey to the eighth sphere (seventh in some manuscripts) gives him a radically different perspective on love. In Alain's *Anticlaudianus,* Prudence journeys to the throne of God, and Guillaume Deguilleville's Grâcedieu, in *Pélerinage de la vie humaine,* releases man's soul to journey homeward to God. Gnostic writings record the downward journey of human souls at birth and their return upward through seven spheres after death.[76]

Chaucer's narrative style gives particular attention to central points and liminal boundaries. Grisilde's inner beauty is perceived in her outer form on the threshold which she crosses to leave her peasant status and become a noblewoman (4, 288–94). John the carpenter of the Miller's tale blesses his house from wights and elves on a *thresshold* just before he is taken in by Nicholas's story of the imminent flood (1, 3478–85). It is across the *thresschefold* (Latin *limen*) of Boethius's cell that the muses retreat before Lady Philosophy. It is while crossing a stile that the Pardoner's three rioters catch sight of the old man who directs their way to death (6, 712); and Sir Thopas pricks over "stile and stone" in his quest for the Elf Queen of his imagination (7, 798). These stiles are boundary markers on a path of love, for death and marriage are but two coordinate steps in the same dance of God's providence. Similarly, dreams are mediant between two states, and pilgrimage stretches between the mundane city and the City of God.

It is a medieval commonplace to conceive of space as three overlapping domains: God, the megacosmos who contains all; the universe which contains man; and man the microcosmos. God is largest, the universe is large, and man is small. The conception is also Platonic, for Timaeus explains that whatever is manifest in the universe as a whole is manifest in man in particular (*Tim.* 39e). Man, says Gregory the Great in *Moralia* 6, 16, is a little world in himself with his own orders of sense and appetite.[77] Saint Bonaventura adds that "the creatures of this sensible world signify the invisible things of God, in part because God is the source, exemplar, and the end of every creature, in part through their proper likeness; in part through their prophetic figuring."[78]

In the design of the universe, man occupies a center point that is the threshold between things corruptible and eternal. His being contains countless triads, each of which is is ordained by the chain of love. Aristotle divides man into spirit, reason, and body (*De Anima* 3, 9, 432a–b), corresponding to the three appetites of imagination, sensition, and nutrition. The exegetes would relate these to irascible, rational, and concupiscent appetites. Plotinus's triadic man consists of soul, body, and *noys,* or the universal intellect which joins them (*Ennead* 3, 9, 1). Boethius divides soul into three powers: one which supports life, one which provides for rational thought and, between them, perception, or judgment.[79] Marius Victorinus makes a nice distinction between man's body, *naturalia,* bound to matter, and his soul, *intelligibilia,* which falls into matter.[80] Wyclif's *De Trinitate* conceives of triune beings of memory, reason, and will in a chain of archetypes stretching from God to the lowest things in the created world.[81] In this triad, God creates but is not created, the universe is created but does not create, and nature (man's body, love, and word) is created and creates. Dante's body contains a heart which senses love, a brain which apprehends love, and digestive organs which weep for love (*Vita nuova* 3, 7). Saint Isidore fractures man's being into a number of parts between the extremes of *spiritus* and *anima* [spirit and intellect], comprising *animus* [will], *mens* [understanding], *memoria* [memory], *ratio* [judgment], *sensus* [feeling], *amor* [love] and *conscientia* [consenting or refusing].[82] Langland reproduces the same list in *Piers Plowman* (B-text, *Passus* 15, 23–39), and glosses *memoria* as man's verbal faculty of prayer.[83] Scriptural story illustrates the triad of *sapientia* (Solomon's wisdom), *fortitudo* (Samson's strength), and *pietas* (David's holiness), which binds the other two in good actions. The fifth point on the star of Solomon that adorns Gawain's shield in *Sir Gawain and the Green Knight* is "pité, that passez alle poyntez" (l. 654).[84] For Dante the three divine emanations contained in man are *potestate, sapienza,* and *amore* (*Inf.* 3, 5–6).

In *De anima* 2, 5–12 (417a–424b), Aristotle describes for the psyche a ladder of values standing on a base of nutritive sense, having ascending rungs of appetite, sensitivity, locomotion and, finally, human cognition (3, 2, 414a). He notes that touch is the primary form of sense since it is shared by all animals, but it is the lowest of the senses in value since it pertains to an organ lower than the organs of sight, hearing, smelling, and tasting (2, 7–123b). In his *Commentary* on Boethius, William of Aragon exposes the way man's physical senses serve reason by recognizing the perfection and deviation of things.[85] Chaucer's Parson lists wits in the order they serve lust: sight, hearing, speaking, touching, and smell, which is the "stynkynge dede of Leccherie" (10, 852–62).[86]

Sight is the highest of the senses, and seeing participates in the thing seen. Sight is responsible for the reading that mediates between a sign and its meaning, as the stories of the martyrs to love in Chaucer's *Legend of Good Women* so amply and ironically illustrate. Timaeus explains that sight of the sky reveals the number and time of the Creator's ordinance (*Tim.* 47a). In his First Mover speech, Theseus exalts the eye as the organ which seizes philosophical truth: "This maystow understonde and seen at ye" (1, 3016), he solemnly affirms, but in the Canon's Yeoman's tale, the cheating Canon tells his dupe priest to "wel seen at yë" (8, 1059) when what is there to see is but an illusion. The current use of *see* to mean "understand" is enduring evidence of the mediant eye between things and their meanings.

The eye is to man's senses what his soul is to his being and what God's purveyance is to creation. In popular thought, only the eye among the senses can cross the limen of the body to exist in both the outer world of appearance and the inner world of form. The eye is a well of love, and it can see love into being. Palamon's eye carries the pain of the sight of Emily into his heart (1, 1096). Chaucer's Thopas, like the Launfal of the English Breton lay, falls in love with a dream image who may have no existence outside of the inner eye of his fantasy. The Prioress's clergeon loves an "unseeable" Virgin Mary.

Though the eye can carry truth to the mind, as Saint Cecilia proves to her husband, Valerian, it can kill like the word. "Ye sleen me with youre eyen Emelye," cries Arcite in the grove in ironic anticipation of the "freendlich ye" which she casts on him the instant before his horse throws him to his death (1, 2680–89). Arcite's mouth and eye are the last organs to quit their mortal functions as he dies (1, 2806–7). The virtue of the eye, as Chaucer's poetry illustrates again and again, is rarely realized. Lady Philosophy recalls to Boethius that "only the lynage of man heveth heyest his heie heved, and stondith light with his upryght body, and byholdeth the erthes undir hym," but man fails to carry his courage and thought upward with his sight (*Boece* 5, m. 5). He is liable to see a good in something which is good only by a feature that is nonessential to its nature, such as estate and array. The "derke membres of the body," says Lady Philosophy, are the cause of breaking the bond between man and God (*Boece* 5, m. 3). Chaucer makes the point in riotous disarray in the Miller's tale, when Absolon sees badly in the dark and misses the desired target of his devotional kiss. The miller's wife in the Reeve's tale stumbles into the wrong bed, feeling but not seeing the location of her baby's cradle.

In effect, Theseus's First Mover speech contains the full panoply of an intellectual anatomizing of the universe. The triune structure of things of which the chain of love is mediant is reflected in the threefold structure of Theseus's exposition: The source of creation, the dispersion of its substance in descent from the Creator, and the returning of things to their source in the Creator's "propre welle" (1, 3037). The return back along the chain of love is explained in terms of the roundness of perfection which, as Timaeus had pointed out, is shaped by a triangle in motion about its apex:

> The heye makere, kyng and lord, welle and bygynnynge . . . yif he ne clepide nat ayein the ryght goynge of thinges, and yif that he neconstreynede hem eftsones into roundnesses enclyned, the thinges that ben now contynued by stable ordenaunce, thei sholden departen from hir welle. . . . This is the comune love to alle thingis, and alle thinges axen to ben holden by the fyn of good. For elles ne myghten they nat lasten yif thei ne comen nat eftstones ayein, by love retorned, to the cause that hath yeven hem beinge (that is to seyn, to God). (*Boece* 4, m. 6, 40–60)

God's love seems to be left behind by man in his erring downward and outward from his created place, but the life of man, like the pilgrimage which informs the *Canterbury Tales,* is a linear trajectory of the body with rounding implications for the spirit. It is a orthoscopic journey of the eye to correct man's Neronian myopia of sight which cannot see forms of beauty behind the entrails of the earth's fair form. As the Canon's Yeoman says with uncharacteristic insight: "If that youre eyen kan nat seen aright, / Looke that your mynde lakke noght his sight" (8, 1418–19). Theseus's exposition of the source and process of things, however, is not just an instruction in the anatomy of the world. The chain of love not only descends from God through his creation, but links the first moment of man's life to God's ultimate purpose. This chain across time is the topic of the next chapter.

# 2

## Love's Progressions and Successions

> You have to proceed from what is already
> there—defined space, a plane. You can make
> something out of something, but you cannot
> make something out of nothing.
>
> —N. Scott Momaday

> There is a special providence in the fall
> of a sparrow. If it be, tis not to come;
> if it be not to come, it will be now; if
> it be not now, yet it come—the readiness is all.
>
> —*Hamlet* 5, 2, 219–22

> Beata l'alma, ove non corre tempo.
>
> —Petrarch, "In me la morte"

THESEUS'S CHAIN OF LOVE HAS A PHYSIOLOGY AS WELL AS AN ANATOMY, for it figures not only the descending bond between God and man but the lateral concatenation of life in God's ordained process. If Homer's chain is a spatial bond between heaven and earth, *progressiouns* and *successiouns* are Theseus's words for its temporal manifestations. *Providence* is not only a blueprint for creation, it is a vector for all things. The *invisibilia* of God's forms includes the imperceptibility of their process. As the vertical chain links God, nature, and man, the horizontal chain links God's *aeternitas* to the temporal shifts of nature and the transitory life of man.[1] For Theseus, at least, time is the *tertium quid* of human life between the poles of Creation and Doomsday.

The narrative context of the Knight's authoritative and eloquent reading of time has Saturn as a cosmological principle elaborating his own power for ruling death and ruin (*CT* 1, 2454–69) and for manifesting his power to harmonize Love (Venus) with War (Mars), while he has Theseus, as a political principle, mediating between Emily and Palomon. The point is that the Knight conceives of cosmic and worldly time as effective

40

masculine concepts. Men in the tales that follow are appropriately garrulous on time, although those tales feature women who, one way or another,
deconstruct male conceptions of time. Time would seem to be a conceptual
principle for men, but a perceptual force in women. I will review this
case very generally in *The Canterbury Tales* as a whole, but with particular
reference to the Wife of Bath's hag and the Clerk's Grisilde. Let me
begin, however, with a brief outline of what the tales reflect of the received
authorities on time before looking at how time shapes story in the *Tales*.
In moving from the one to the other issue I take for granted, of course,
the hermeneutic possibilities that current concepts of time provide us with
for reading the *Tales* back through six hundred years.

In general, in Chaucer's intellectual world, time involves two coordinate
categories of measure, the one objective and physical and the other subjec-
tive and metaphysical. The physical, or linear, measurement of time
locates a period in which events take place: dates, measures, and points
of reference which can be understood within *perdurable,* or perceptual
time, the most significant of which concern the duration between birth
and death.[2] Metaphysical time, which Theseus points to with a surprising
hysteron proteron—"understand and see with eye"—is a conceptual
matching of Chaucer's rationalist and conceptualist style in general.[3] This
time is the hypothetical pattern of things which, paradoxically, since God
exists outside of time, is timeless. The paradox is only apparent, however,
since man is unable to comprehend God's timelessness or, to use a more
Augustinian term, "tenselessness." He can only read God's purpose in
its measured linear progressions and successions seen behind him from
the present moment and assumed before him in a speculative future. Every
moment on the pilgrimage road to Canterbury implies a present concern
with past sin and a yearning for future grace. Every *now* conjoins remorse
and desire.

So, the two times are really one, the physical simply a percept and
rationalization—or humanization, if you will—of the metaphysical. The
urgency to measure time in Chaucer's day derives from a desire to discover
a consoling purpose in its passage.[4] Theseus identifies that purpose anach-
ronistically with *purveiaunce,* the *providentia,* or "provision" for human
life which is the Christian's Providence. In a Christian context, this is
God's chain of love in motion, spinning its conic contours in all directions
outward from its apex in God to describe a time-space sphere. This chain
is the *invisibilia* of God's architectonic *noys* behind the *visibilia* of nature
and God's imperceptible blueprint *catena* for creation's vector. It is the
temporal event-frame for life, but lamely perceived even by Christian
men such as Chaucer's Knight who observes: "Were it by aventure or
destynee— / As, when a thyng is shapen, it shal be" (1, 1465–66). He
is followed by the Pharisaic Man of Law, who says of the cosmos: "no

wight kan wel rede it atte fulle" (2, 713). Similarly, the Merchant admits his ignorance of the cause for May's sudden decision to love Damyan, but avows his certainty that God "knoweth that noon act is causelees" (4, 1975).

God's purveyance is the eternal thought which contains and controls all matter in time. Providence itself is out of time as *logos,* but in time as *actus.* The *logos* has an eternal life before and after time and space, and so *time* is, in this frame of thought, no more than a term designating measure of the duration of matter in motion, two related concepts in the Aristotelian and Platonic physics of Chaucer's day. In the geometries of such measure, privileged scrutiny is directed to the *termini* of beginnings and ends and to the mean sufficiency between them. The termini of the vertical chain of love are God and earth (though the lower end extends to purgatory in the Christian doctrine of grace of Chaucer's day), and the poles of the horizontal chain extend from Creation to Doomsday (though some argue that time originates with sin). The middle of the universe is where Chaucer locates the House of Fame (*House of Fame* 714), and the middle of creation is where Christians conventionally locate the Dome of the Rock in Jerusalem.

Providence is the design of time—what Augustine associates with the sense of time passing and which Heidegger identifies as "temporality"—coexistent with divine being.[5] In 1 Timothy 6: 16, Paul says that God is he, *qui solus habet immortalitatem, et lucem inhabitat inaccessibilem: quem nullus hominum videt* [who alone has immortality and lives in inaccessible light which no man has seen], and, in Colossians 1: 15, he identifies Christ as *Dei invisiblis, primogenitus omnis creatura* [invisible God, creator of all things]. In *Paradiso* 33, Dante differentiates between the imperceptual *luce eterna* of God and the *alto lume* of his creation. Time, like light, has an imperceptible beginning in the stability of that invisible Being which is perfect *privity,* whereas man's time, like Heidegger's *Dasein* and Chaucer's pilgrimage, is a *public* procession. Philosophy makes the point to Boethius another way when she says: "Forthi yif we wollen putten worthi names to thinges and folwen Plato, lat us seyen thanne sothly that God is 'eterne,' and that the world is 'perpetual'"(*Boece.* 5, pr. 6, 97–98). The eternity of God's being falls into nature, motion and time—*aevum*—the moment his purveyance is manifest in creation (*Boece.* 5, pr. 6, 75–83). God's stability is *otium,* or perfection in rest, while rest in the created world is not-being (*Theaetetus* 153a). The concept of God resting on the seventh day of creation joins God's being to the *res* of nature. Chaucer's Merchant parodies God's rest after expenditure of creative spirit when he describes May's four-day repose after her wedding-night ordeal with Januarie:

> For every labour somtyme moot han reste,
> Or elles longe may he nat endure;
> That is to seyn, no lyves creature,
> Be it of fyssh, or bryd, or beest, or man.
>
> (4, 1862–65)

Time, then, is the property of nature, the moveable within eternity which has a birth and a death (*Timaeus* 37d).

After the infinitesmal first instant of creation, all matter is in motion, and all measures of time are functions of man's perception of motion, as Augustine concludes in his *Confessions,* 11. Man has as many pains to see the eternal framework that contains the passing moment as he has to see the forms behind natural appearances. He can only remember the past, sense his participation in the present, and anticipate the future. Like a passenger at the window of a train, he can observe the *seriatim* pageantry of the passing landscape—cows grazing, children playing, women hanging out laundry, men chopping wood—while God, who is high above the train, can scan in an instant sweep of the eye the entire track from its departure point to it terminus. Such a vision, impossible for man, is what Boethius' Philosophy calls the "simplicitie of his [God's] presence" which embraces the "infynit spaces of tyme" (*Boece,* 5, pr. 6, 105–7).

"Fortune" is the name that the man of limited sight gives the service he receives on the track of time, though he should care more about where he is going, according to Lady Philosophy. She explains that it is necessary to appreciate the providential goal in order to disdain the uncertainties of the route. To illustrate this point, she indicates carefully the difference between "foresight" and "provision": "It nis nat yclepid 'previdence,' but it sholde rathir ben clepid 'purveaunce' that is establisshed ful fer fro ryght lowe thingis, and byholdeth fro after alle thingis, right as it were fro the heye heighte of thinges" (*Boece* 5, pr. 6, 109–20).[6]

If God's time is a simplicity of presence, natural time is the "infinit quantite of future and of preterit . . . by successiouns" (*Boece* 5, pr. 6, 75–92). Theseus's mix of pagan myth and Christian thought has Jupiter, or the First Mover, conjoin his purveyance to an ordinance which in Greek story is the power of his father Saturn, who is both Kronos and Chronos, providence and time. As time, he explains: "My cours, that hath so wyde for to turne, / Hath moore power than woot any man" (1, 2454–2455).[7]

The principle of providential time weighs on the conscience of the believing Christian, and it must have weighed very heavily indeed for those who had lived through the Great Plague, the Peasants' Revolt, the Hundred Years War, and the Merciless Parliament. The *carpe diem* and *ubi sunt* conventions of the day consoled man by stressing the infinitude

of eternal bliss (or, alas, wearied him with thoughts of damnation), compared with the brevity of life's sequence of bliss and blunder, joy and
woe. Since time is, then, a point of reference for human activity within
a ordained design, the movement between the terminals of time is progress
toward knowing God and his eschatological purpose. In the learned lore
of Chaucer's day, the first instant of time is realized with the first motion,
and motion has its beginning in the first immeasurable instant of creation,
"whan he *first* made the faire cheyne of love." That moment reifies God's
purveyance into a process, which has a beginning and an end. Time,
paradoxically, is enclosed within timelessness.[8]

Nothing exists before the First Mover. The Primal Love identified on
the inscription above Dante's gateway to the inferno declares itself:
"DINANZI A ME NON FUOR COSE CREATE / SON NON ETTERNE,
E IO ETTERNO DURO" (*Inferno* 3, 7–8) [Before me nothing was created
if not eternal, and I endure eternal]. Plato's Timaeus explains that God
exists always, without a coming into being, while the world is always
coming into being, but never exists (*Timaeus* 28a). What moves exists
in time; what exists in time moves. That which "parfit is and stable"
exists out of time. Boethius's Lady Philosophy refers to Plato's conception
of time as a moving away from God's stability, a falling out of eternity,
and a splitting of God's simplicity into an infinite number of successions
(*Cons.* 5, pr. 6). "By successiouns, / And nat eterne" is Theseus's para-
phrase (3014–15). The vertical chain of love is an organization of substance thrust horizontally through time along God's chosen track, which
Boethius calls "the moevable bond and the temporel ordenaunce of
thinges" (*Boece* 4, pr. 6, 104–6).

"God is the begynnynge of al" recalls Boethius, but Philosophy quickly
adds that he is the end as well (*Boece* 1, pr. 6, 45–49). Stout Harry Bailly
stands at the start of pilgrimage, and the Parson at its end to balance
secular with spiritual interests. In effect, Chaucer's pilgrimage imitates
the course of creation. Its first moment is easy to conceive of but difficult
to measure. It is the immeasurable instant that contrition is activated by
will into motion toward the shrine which figures man's ultimate spiritual
home. That instant imitates neatly the instantaneous *actus* of divine
providence in creation.[9] For Chaucer, it is the moment when "longen folk
to goon on pilgrimages," that is, when mental volition conjoins with
natural processes, the seasonal filling of the air with rain, the land with
verdant growth, and animal life with pricking of *corage*. Within this
general temporal cycle the poet remembers a particular day and place
where he "lay redy" to go on a pilgrimage, like God's thought awaiting
agency and the poet ready to undertake his book. The allusive suggestion
of this fictional context is apt because Chaucer's assembling and describing
of the pilgrims fills the Tabard and the Canterbury road much as the

vertical chain of love fills the space through which it descends with orders of being. Then, after pausing in his story to describe God's human plenty, Chaucer sets it on its ordained track. What God accomplishes in no time takes the narrator much "tyme and space" (1, 35).

Chaucer carefully draws our attention to the niceties of that time and space. Against the backdrop of nature's perpetual vernal rehearsal of God's Creation, he has the pilgrims assemble in a specified place on an unspecified day of the month of April in an unspecified year. He has them quit the Tabard together in random order, it would seem; and since pilgrimage begins for an individual the moment contrition for his sins slants his body toward an authorized shrine, there are as many beginnings as there are pilgrims, thirty or thirty-two in all according to Chaucer's "confused" count.

The duration of the tales told on the way to Canterbury is as inconsistent as the pilgrimage is indeterminant in its temporal divisions. The Knight's performance is almost tedious in its length, the Cook's implausibly brief. The Manciple's early morning performance is short, but the Parson's, which follows late in the afternoon, is long enough to carry through vespers. Curiously, there are no mentions of breaks for meals or for sleep along the way, and from the Watering of Saint Thomas to Boughtonunder-Blean there is no location of performance more precise that "Loo, Rouchestre stant heer faste by!" (7, 1926). In short, despite conventional care for "real" time and space, Chaucer confuses their impressions upon us. Perhaps because pilgrimage is purgatorial, and because there is no measure of the purgatorial space and time spirits move upward through, Chaucer would suggest that there is no calculation possible for the spiritual credit accumulated on the Canterbury road.

Pilgrimage is a celestial track on ties of shame and humility, though we are led to suspect that Harry's and the Wife's pilgrimage conceive of pilgrimage as a spring outing with games that bounce between jest and earnest. After the body is served, Harry turns the feast over to the Parson, who speaks directly for the soul's refreshment. In the temporal structure of pilgrimage there is no need to describe or concern oneself with the return to the dust and heat of home from the sanctity of an instant's grace. Lady Philosophy's reading of the fable of Orpheus, who turns his eyes back to Eurydice,—*perdit dum uidet inferos* [he loses when he looks to hell]—figures the mundane aftermath of all pilgrimage (*Cons.* 3, m. 12).

Pilgrimage is man's staging of what he understands as God's purpose in creation. The invocation to spring which opens the book rehearses creation, followed by Harry Bailly's organization and ordinance of the first movement of the pilgrimage as "Host," an epithet which reflects divine as well as secular mediation. Harry plays the role of Boethius's

God—*Principium, vector, dux, semita, terminus idem* (*Cons.* 3, m. 9, 29)—and the Evangelist's Christ—"the way (*via*), the life (*vita*).and the truth (*veritas*)" [John 14: 6]—as he proposes to be "gyde" (804), provider of a "soper" (815) and "juge" (814) for the pilgrims. That parody extends as well to Chaucer's own anterior design for a book which accords Harry the power to purvey and ordain the action; and, the poet's fictional recollection of a past event is a design for future movement, so that the book is a continuous present, a *tertium quid* between a fictional past event and a real future one. In effect, Harry Bailly mediates the time between a poetic design and its enactment within the fictional context of the *Tales.* For the fictional context of the recollection of the pilgrimage, the role is Chaucer's, who mediates between God's hidden design and a public book which fills our time, just as Harry Bailly's design for pilgrimage is a way of "killing," or "spending" the pilgrims' time.

Furthermore, Harry's demand for obedience at the beginning of pilgrimage, accompanied by an oath on his own food and drink, recalls God's command to Adam, whose disobedience is paid for by Christ's flesh and blood. The straws drawn to establish an order of story is a comic parody of God's ordaining chain of love, though if Harry is performing the carnival trick of getting the short straw into a chosen hand, then he is indeed reenacting something of God's mysterious powers. "Herkneth what I seye" says the Knight, who wins the draw, and with the word "say" pilgrimage motion is conjoined with the time-killing talk whose first verbal instant is *whilom.* These pivotal words mediate between thought and deed. Like the divine *logos,* they mark time.

Measure of time is applied most carefully on the duration of life and death. Just as the exegete pays close attention to Christ's genealogy on the Tree of Jesse—the bloodline descending from David—there is particular interest in the tales in successions of lives, or genealogical strain, though more as a sociological and political status than as providential order. The descent of the blood of Holy Church is a pivotal theme of the Reeve's tale, for example, but lowered to a design for social upward mobility. More urgent is the topical concern with gentility. "When Adam delve and Eve span, / Who was them the gentleman," chanted the peasants going the other way on the Canterbury road to stake their secular claims. In keeping with this ideal, the childless Wife of Bath has her fictional hag argue to the rapist-knight that the chain of gentilesse is distinct from bloodline:

> Heere may ye se wel how that genterye
> Is nat annexed to possessioun,
> Sith folk ne doon hir operacioun
> Alwey, as dooth the fyr, lo, in his kynde.

. . . . . . . . . . . .
For gentilesse nys but renomee
Of thyn auncestres, for hire heigh bountee,
Which is a strange thyng to thy persone.
Thy gentilesse cometh fro God allone
Thanne comth oure verray gentillesse of grace;
It was no thyng biquethe us with oure place."

(3, 1146–64)

The Wife of Bath's hag directs her knight's view of goodness away from the array of youth, good looks, and social estate—that is, away from gifts of nature and fortune—toward the gift of grace. In arguing that gentilesse derives from a bounty that is not part of one's person, her assertion, typical of much the Wife argues, is both true and false. It is true in so far as gentilesse, or *bounty* (etymologically identical with, and semantically associated with *beauty*), as all other virtues, has an ultimate source in God; and it is true also in its claim that gentilesse is not restricted to the higher social estates.

The Hag's statement is false, however, in its implicit assertion that God selects recipients of gentilesse by entering time in order to execute his ordained providence. Christian dogma conforms rather with Ockham's proposition that things moved have no conjunction with their mover after the instant of their propulsion.[10] Augustine had argued that God made all things good initially (including gentilesse, we must assume), and both virtue and sin are expression of man's *will* rather than of his *nature* (*De civitate Dei*, 12,6). Man's will moves his nature freely within time without an interceding divine force. What the Wife willfully ignores is the fact that *everyone* is born with gentilesse, even the knight-rapist who loses it by willing himself away from God.

The point is absolutely essential to deciphering Walter's justification, in the Clerk's tale, of his choice of a "low-born" woman on the grounds that:

For God it woot, that children ofte been
Unlyk hir worthy eldres hem bifore;
Bountee comth al of God, nat of the streen
Of which they been engendred and ybore.

(4, 155–58)

Curiously, this argument has been undermined even before it is pronounced, since the Clerk describes Walter earlier as, ". . . to speke as of lynage, / The gentilleste yborn of Lumbardye" (4, 71–72).

On the other hand, when he introduces Grisilde's father Janicula into the story, the Clerk follows Walter's premise: ". . . hye God somtyme senden kan / His grace into a litel oxes stalle" (4, 206–7). Though a long description of Grisilde's virtuous bounty follows as if to prove the point, the syntax in this passage has God's grace sent to Janicula, who must pass it in his blood strain to his daughter Grisilde along with his social and economic poverty. Although the Clerk would have us believe that the accidence of poverty can hide a form of gentilesse, the cautious condition "somtyme" conceals the obvious truth that God's grace is *always* transmitted *everywhere*. It is man's turning from it rather than God's withholding of it that marks its absence. Only the most intransigent Voluntarist or die-hard Determinist would argue that God selects arbitrarily those to whom he accords grace at their birth. As Boethius's Philosophy puts it: "Alle the lynage of men that ben in erthe ben of semblable byrthe. On allone is fadir of thynges" (*Boece* 3, m. 6, 1–2), which Trevet explains to mean that all men are born with physical and spiritual nobility.[11] What the Wife's hag, Walter, and the Clerk omit strategically from their arguments is that bounty, if it does not come *from* a blood strain, arrives *with* it and is inseparable from it simply because God contains all time but never enters into it. God's gift for Janicula and Grisilde is something sent at the beginning of the world, and the twelve years after the birth of Grisilde's daughter proves the gift of Grisilde's blood despite her social origins. The catena of successive life is the slow and unsteady unraveling of God's providence.

The time span of a single human life is an *aetas* within God's *aeternitas,* one link in the horizontal chain of man's genealogical track through time and space away from the source and moment of creation.[12] Boethius's Philosophy conceives of time as one feature of the chain of being: "This world of so many diverse and contraryous parties, ne myghte never han ben assembled in o forme, but yif ther ne were oon that conjoyned so manye diverse thinges . . . moevynges by places, by *tymes,* by doynges, by spaces, by qualites . . ." (*Boece* 3, pr. 12, 30–42), and the conjoiner of things moves man by his natural inclination to good (*Boece* 3, pr. 12, 89–90).

Man's motion toward good, however, is impeded by the clutter of this world. The horizontal vector of life's concatenation, like the vertical descent of the chain of love, is a progressive diffusion toward disorder. "Disorder increases with time," explains Steven W. Hawking, "because we measure time in the direction in which disorder increases."[13] This is the physicist's thermodynamic arrow, turned into metaphysics by Chaucer's Parson when he says, "Certes, a man oghte hastily shewen his synnes for manye causes; as for drede of deeth, that cometh ofte sodeynly, and no certeyn what tyme it shal be, ne in what place; and eek the drecchynge of o synne draweth in another, and eek the longer that he tarieth, the ferther he is fro Crist" (10, 1000–1001). This is not only true in the life of individual man but in the life of mankind. Sin has its genealogy not in nature but in habit of will, and so sin is correlative with time.

Man's haste to confess before he dies recalls the Host's call for haste in storytelling before the morning passes (2, 16–32). Both calls, one for mundane jest and the other for spiritual earnest, are to "kill" time. The reward for the one is spiritual supping in heaven and for the other a supper in Southwark. In both cases man is enjoined to use time to get back to where he started, though his motion, or "sliding" nature, of which Criseyde is accused,[14] carries him further away. In the geography of Harry's pilgrimage, the turn back is to take place at the shrine of Becket. In man's salvific time, the turn back starts at the moment of Christ's death, when human will is restored with the potential to win God's foreseen feast. The temporal succession of one man's life is one microcosmic piece in the mosaic succession of time between Creation and Doomsday. The natural design of one life reflects the succession of all lives.

The time of one human life is divided conventionally into "ages of man," most commonly into the triad of youth, maturity, and old age whose dominant attractions shift in time through love and war to piety. Four-age schemes associate sociobiololgical change with the influence of the humors. For example, phlegm reigns in children, blood from fifteen to thirty years, choler in the maturity of age between thirty and sixty, and melancholy in later years. Other schemes divide life according to the influences of the seven planets. Shakespeare's Jaques exposes a seven-age scheme in his "All the world's a stage" speech, where the succession runs from infancy to second childhood (*AYLI* 2, 7, 139–60). For the Christian thinker, all things in nature are endowed with a capacity to mount the salvific ladder through each phase of time, with different gifts of nature making the task more or less difficult.[15] The Pardoner may have it harder than the Parson, but all the more merit to his exercise of will if he corrects an innate proclivity to the vagaries of his nature by a willful inclination to God.

The good man is caught ineluctably between two temporal pulls. The first is a desire to travel backward toward his primal innocence and the second to hasten forward toward his future grace. The nostalgic and romantic yearning to retreat from the present course of experience is expressed in the trope of the Golden Age—the historical "firste age of men" which Chaucer describes in his lyric complaint, "The Former Age":

> A blisful lyf, a paisible and a swete,
> Ledden the peples in the former age,
>
> .  .  .  .  .  .  .  .  .  .  .  .  .
>
> The lambish peple, voyd of alle vyce.

(1–2, 50)

This was the time of bliss before the age of Jupiter the lecherous and Nimrod the proud. Boethius calls this *prior aetas* the Golden Age of Saturn and primitive innocence which preceded the Silver Age of Jupiter, when men turned to agriculture and the building of houses, the Bronze Age of possessions which was not entirely bad, and the fourth age of Iron, an era of greed and no justice (*Cons.* 2, m. 5). Chaucer calls the age of Jupiter:

> . . . the tyme . . .
> That men first did hir swety bysinesse,
> To grobbe up metal, lurkinge in derknesse.
> ("The Former Age," 27–29)

The shift to the age of Jupiter brought with it luxury in sexual matters, food, drink, and clothing. It was the first age in which man had time on his hands. "Gold was the first age," says Ovid of Saturn's reign,[16] though it was marked by absence of the metal, and the age of iron, which follows ages of silver and brass, ushers evil into the world. In such schemes of ages, Theseus's identification of Jupiter with the First Mover is curiously askew.[17]

In the eschatological perspective of the Church, the Golden Age is the age of the law of kind, before constraints of lordship and the Mosaic Code. There was no sin then because there was no law.[18] Only once law is laid down can it be transgressed, and man's spiritual history records an accumulation of transgressions. Gower's Prologue to *Confessio Amantis* describes Daniel's reading of Nebuchadnezzar's dream of the statue whose head is of gold, chest of silver, belly of bronze, legs of iron, and feet of clay as an allegory of man's regress through the ages (595–662). "Thus those regions which were once the strongest fall into decay throughout the world and have no center of rest there," says Gower's own gloss to the mention of the Golden Age.[19]

There are crucial points along all successions of time. Just as man has a proper place, a mean location among the created orders, his life span has a mean which is not necessarily its temporal midpoint, but a theoretical point at which man is "most himself," typically at thirty in a human lifetime. At that age, Christ took up his teaching and Augustine realized the truth of Christianity. A significant instant of time, such as the moment of Christ's death, which marks the middle of the curve of salvific time, is *kairos,* a "point in time filled with significance, charged with a meaning derived from its relation to the end."[20] *Kairos* is, to borrow a familiar term from Karl Jaspers, an *axial moment* in time in which one senses change, or, for Hannah Arendt, a moment of *action* distinct from *labor* and *work* in that it provides an identity for the actor, material for story.[21]

Each celebration of the sacraments is a *kairos,* an axial moment when man joins God's chain of love. In the middle of *Troilus and Criseyde* the hero exalts "Love, thow holy bond of thynges" (3, 1261), and in the exact verse-line center of the entire poem he is "bistowed in so heigh a place" (1265). For Troilus, this is a brief instant of grace marking the turn from yearning to achieving. The Canterbury pilgrimage is itself a leaning toward a moment of revealed grace, before man falls back into time and sin, just as Troilus falls away from love.

There is a ripe time for exercises of will in keeping with the age of one's physical and spiritual nature. The ripeness of age for certain turns is a *cursus aetatis.* All things have their proper time, argues the Host as he tries to dissuade the Clerk from indulging in colors of rhetoric; and the Clerk responds with a tale in which a people argue that it is time for their lord to wed, for "ay fleeth the tyme; it nyl no man abyde" (4, 119). Dante finds himself in a dark wood and *nel mezzo del camin de nostra vita* [in the middle of the path of our life] at the beginning of his journey through a threefold universe. Thirty is the just age to wed and to engender children. Walter and Grisilde, Theseus and Ypolita, and Arveragus and Dorigen, though their ages are not given, apparently marry at an appropriate age.

Daun John in the Shipman's tale is thirty (7, 26) but spends his love in an adulterous union. The Merchant's Januarie, who is double thirty years of age, refuses to wed a woman of thirty (4, 1421), and the Wife of Bath, who marries first at twelve, is young for her first three husbands and old for her last two. Excess and waste are prominent in both Januarie and the Wife; and carpenter John of the Miller's tale suffers the consequences of marrying too young a bride. No one describes with more scorn the untimeliness of an old man taking a young wife than the Parson, who compares aged lechers "to houndes; for an hound, whan he comth by the roser or by othere, though he may nat pisse, yet wole he heve up his leg and make a countenaunce to pisse" (10, 858).

Since man's life and his words are *res successiva,* things in succession, the last moment of one event is often the first of another. In the Knight's tale, the sight of Emily in the garden, Theseus's witness of the battle in the grove, and Emily's "friendly eye" at the lists are coordinate axial instants which turn us from one stage of story to another. In the Miller's tale, the kiss in the dark which hits lower than its desired target, coupled with Alison's "teehee" of delight, frame a moment in which Absolon's frail idea of love is shed, and a lesson is learned. From a human perspective, these are "unfortunate moments," bad timing like Aleyn's dark revelation of his "noble game" to the wrong ear in the Reeve's tale (1, 4263), and Nicholas's scream, "water!" overheard heard by John as an announcement of the Great Flood.

Pilgrimage figures an axial turn from sinful engagement in the world to a quest for redemption and itself comprises a number of turns. At the instant its goal is sighted, activity turns from game to earnest, from worrying about a burning blister, a growling stomach, or a torn *overslope* to an urgent longing for penitence. In its full duration, a pilgrimage is a significant passage in the pageant of man's move through life. Its briefest axial instant—the tongue's acceptance of the Eucharist Host—figures the stable eternity beyond life. It is in that essential point that man's temporal nature participates in God's eternal presence. Pilgrimage, as Theseus's father remarks, is a figure of life whose "ende of every worldly soore" is its ultimate axial instant (1, 2847–48). The Pardoner's undying Old Man is not Death so much as he is Time pointing the way toward death, and like time he is exempt from death.[22]

Pronouncements on and measurements of time, as the examples above indicate, are predominantly a male activity. To mock the efficacy of this activity, the narrator-persona makes of the jovial Host a marvelous instance of futile calculation. After the Knight's tale, he "reads" Harry Bailly's mind like a book to record the date, 18 April, and then reproduces the mental calculation Harry would make in order to read the solar clock at ten in the morning before announcing that a fourth part of the day is gone (2, 17).[23] In fact, after fifteen lines, Harry has finally said in conclusion what the narrator offers as his premise—a fourth of the day has passed. There is less "science" behind that observation than playful speculation upon Harry's capacities for playing the pilgrims' "aller cok"; but he is no clock. What is an innkeeper to do with astronomical tables?

Three separate temporal issues pertain to this passage: Chaucer's insight into the Host's mental reckonings, followed by the Host's remarks about the waste of time—which themselves waste time[24]—and the Man of Law's prologue and tale which turn the issue from time to tidings. Harry wants to keep the entertainment on schedule, and his concern with haste is in keeping with the haste in which penitential confession should be performed (10, 998). He is using secular time to thrust his audience toward the spiritual timelessness of grace, but he complicates measure nicely by his comparison of time first with the stream that cannot remount to its source, and then with Malkin's maidenhead, which cannot be repaired. While this mental observation links the physics of gravity with the sexual ripeness of women, the effect is to insist that nature and human age cannot travel backwards through time; and yet traveling backwards toward a grace left behind is exactly what the forward movement of pilgrimage intends. The moral to which these examples point is simply that time should not be wasted, though the logic of his argument is not any clearer than the astronomical lore credited to him. Of course Harry is really thinking about storytelling "to shorte with oure weye" (1, 791), and story can move us backwards to the river's source and to Malkyn before she loses her maidenhead. In effect, story is a pentitential process moving us toward timelessness. Story, like grace, suspends time, and like death, stops it.

As if the substance of Harry's observations is the stuff of story, the Man of Law takes up the issue in both his prologue and tale by conjoining time and story in the single word *tidings,* a familiar word designating what happens *in* time. Story is time, as newspaper titles like *The Times, Die Zeitung, Il Tempo,* and *Tidende* insist, and the Man of Law's tale of Constance is concerned with the power of punctual tidings—rumors of Constance's beauty which reach the Sultan's ear, perjurous testimony about her before Aella's court, lies about her monstrous progeny, etc.— all of which contrast with the ubiquitous and timeless *sonde* [sound] of God's providential signs and messages.[25] If the reader feels that Constance never changes or ripens through time, it is simply that she surrenders herself to timelessness, to "nevere asonder wende" (2, 1157). One sins in punctual time; steadfast virtue escapes time's ravages.

It has been argued that Grisilde also triumphs over time by accepting the will of God.[26] I would say, rather, that Grisilde embodies a *principle* of time. For one thing, her forebearance brings Walter toward an acceptance of change in time in marriage and his children. For another thing, she characterizes her own will as immune to time:

> This wyl is in myn herte, and ay shal be;
> No lengthe of tyme or deeth may this deface,
> Nor change my corage to another place.
>
> (509–11)

The will and courage which is exempt from change is, like Theseus's First Mover, "stable and eterne"; and, indeed Grisilde is characterized repeatedly as one who resists "sliding." In fact, what Walter tempts is precisely her "sadnesse"; that is, her holding firm to her innate sufficiency. As she confesses joyfully to her children, "Youre woful mooder wende stedfastly . . ." (4, 1094), a phrase whose preterit form combines stability of thought—*wene*—with change—*wende.*[27]

This line of exposition suggests a theoretical premise that for Chaucer, pilgrimage, the body of woman, and the body of a book redeem the time that men, like Saturn and Walter who "devour" their children, appropriate and inevitably waste.[28] The Wife of Bath's hag, who slides back time as her knight-husband slides back the bed curtain for the light to reveal a past beauty in a present form, is a complex case in point. Just as the knight retrieves a past beauty out of the present old and ugly form of his wife, the same curtain sliding between bed and chamber light retrieves the honor of knighthood which he shamed when he raped a virgin by the riverside.[29] The hag has mediated his grace, we might say, although we may suspect that only her saying makes it so, for words have the awesome power of making the past present and the present future. Illusion, like dream visions, makes us believe so. Dreams "hold time" in wonderful otium, so that gardens like the *parc de champ joli* of the *Roman de la rose*—where "il n'a pas temporel mesure . . . il n'a futur ne preterit" (20013–16)—and the garden like "verray paradys" of the Franklin's tale (5, 912) are forever green and ripe, just as Grisilde's courage is forever "sad" and ripe. These qualities of women reify what we imagine of God, and both Grisilde and the Wife's hag grant the grace their husbands seek, stability and beauty, respectively. Just as the Wife of Bath vaunts the power to mediate the purgatorial and paradisiacal states of her husbands, the hag of her story offers a reward—as God holds out a promise of grace to man—*before* it is earned, in this case by making a choice betweeen a fair wife of doubtful fidelity and an ugly one of truth. Consider the theological implications of the terms with which she introduces her choice:

> But nathelees, syn I knowe youre delit,
> I shal fulfille youre worldly appetit.
> Chese now . . .
> And take youre aventure of the repair
> That shal be to youre hous by cause of me,
> Or in some oother place, may wel be.
>
> (3, 1217–26)

The point here is that the hag, though she declares her power to save or to damn, knows what the choice will be as much as God knows in what direction our wills bend us. In making herself young she denies "natural" processes, and exempts herself from age; that is, she moves out of time by appropriating something of God's power. By surrendering to her will, her knight achieves grace and redeems sin and time. As if the Wife misses the implications of her story, she ends her tale with the stock formula: "And thus they lyve unto hir lyves ende" (3, 1257).

What complicates the case of the hag besides a gift of beauty which may only reside in her words, is the fact that she, like the Wife of Bath, but unlike Grisilde, does not use time naturally to bear children. Producing children contributes to the genealogical strain which fulfills God's providential design, the ∪-shaped curve of the spirit's process which contrasts with the ∩-shaped curve of the body's.[30] Grisilde mediates Walter's governance by providing him with an heir. A woman holding a child in her womb for nine months before bearing it reflects God's holding the idea of creation in his mind for eternity before reifying it in time. If a mother, like the Creator, initiates a movement toward death, she is herself a principle of time.

Chaucer is certainly aware of this ontology, since so many women in the tales have qualities of the *Deus otiosus*. In the Man of Law's tale, Constance is not only constant in the face of adversity, but the story has her husband and all her friends die (2, 1157), leaving her own death unnoted. Grisilde's father and husband die (4, 1134–35), but her death too is left unnoted.[31] The hag's life of perfect joy comes to an end, perhaps at the end of the world. The Second Nun's Cecilie, like the Prioress's little boy at the limen of his sexual identity, mediates God's Providence. The Squire's Canacee is "ful measurable" when she intervenes for the love-wounded hawk (5, 362), and the Physician's Virgina is a perfection of mean who scorns time's shifts of nature (6, 67–68). Curiously, her own death is perpetrated to prevent a timely movement into sexuality.

Genealogical lines are repetitions of lives. Recording them maps a progress chart toward the timelessness following the ordained and provi- dential end of the world.[32] Records, or books, are *tertia quid* between memory of a past event and its future recollection. The book has the same ontological force, then, as the body of woman. It both makes and redeems time.[33] Chaucer's own sense of book as repetition and temporal succession is urgent in his *retracciouns* at the close of the *Tales*. Here he retraces (not retracts) his poems "and many another book, if they were in my remembrance." Retracing is going back over things, back through time like the Wife's hag, if you will.

Chaucer's "Book of the Tales of Caunterbury," like the tales and Harry Bailly's commentary enclosed within, is itself a retracing which, effectively, spends time, or, if you will, redeems it by "killing" it. He creates an inclusive "now" in which a fictive voice out of time recollects a story of an event which contains stories. He combines the horizontal and episodical links of "historical" or phenomenological time with the vertical and configurative links of all time and any time.[34] That is to say, Chaucer kills time by binding it in a book. Chaucer has effectively deconstructed narrative and its historical time in order to reveal something of the supratemporal flow behind nature and art. In this respect "time" is the dimension of story. As spring repeats creation, story repetition gives verbal form to Providence, emulating the timelessness of God; that is, the story is in time, but does not move with time. Retelling story, like the hag's riddling choice, retrieves the past, so that pilgrimage recollected is grace retrieved, sin and time redeemed.

To understand one's own place in the past is to create in the present the design of the future. Pilgrimage in process and a book in the making are gestations and *inter regna* between two states of being: conception and realization. "Go litel bok, go litel myn tragedye," says Chaucer at the end of his *Troilus*" (5, 1786) in the language of sending a child from his father's lap into the world. "Heere taketh the makere of this book his leve," introduces his retracings. Book is child, child is succession, and both perpetuate life.

The pilgrimage is not completed, as many a frustrated reader laments, nor is the projected series of tales. This is so perhaps because Chaucer would neither close pilgrimage—which, like spring, is to take place over and over again—nor close the process of making, which would mean completion, leaving the labyrinth by"grafting time on the finite structure of being-toward-death."[35] To finish the pilgrimage is to finish the journey toward death which being lost in the labyrinth of art retards. By writing himself out of time, Chaucer writes ahead of himself to speak to us now.

# 3

# Frayed Bonds of Sight and Word:
## *The Legend of Good Women*

To see the World in a Grain of Sand
And Heaven in a Wild Flower.
 —William Blake, "Auguries of Innocence"

I will wipe a litil his eien that ben dirked by the
cloudes of mortel thynges.
 —Boethius, *Boece* 1, pr. 2, 25–26

IN THE LIFE OF MAN, THE CHAIN OF LOVE JOINS IDEA WITH THING, AND philosophical with physical love. As concatenation of word, language attaches the physical form of sound to idea and sensation alike. In *The Legend of Good Women,* Chaucer tests the proposition that sight and word can serve man's ascension on the ladder of love. The fact that each of the legends illustrates breaches of bonds of love suggests that Chaucer wrote the *Legend* either to expose the horror of a world of sight without insight and words without truth, or to put to the proof the nominalist denial of the intrinsic bond between word and idea.

The prologue to the poem sets in place a model of inquisition into the philosophical issue of connections between sight, insight, and language:

> A thousand tymes have I herd men telle
> That ther ys joy in hevene and peyne in helle,
> And I acorde wel that it ys so;
> But, natheles, yet wot I wel also
> That ther nis noon dwellynge in this contree
> That eyther hath in hevene or helle ybe,
> Ne may of hit other weyes witen
> But as he hath herd seyd or founde it writen;
> For by assay ther may no man it preve.
> But God forbede but men shulde leve

Wel more thing then men han seen with ye!
Men shal not wenen every thing a lye
But yf himself yt seeth or elles dooth;
For, God wot, thing is never the lasse sooth,
Thogh every wight ne may it nat ysee.
Bernard the monk ne saugh nat al, pardee!

(1–16)[1]

So Chaucer begins a love poem by reducing the sober thought of the soul's eternal reward into a popular and common speculation on the limitation of the eyes to see things spiritual. In the sovereign realm of language, hell and heaven are linked, however, for English *hell* and French *ciel* are doublets whose root meaning is "hidden, covered." Greek *hades* means "unseen." Since things seen and unseen are concatenate only in the best of worlds, it is the lover's chore to harmonize feelings and thoughts, and the poet's task to forge a bond between those things with audible sound and visible shape.[2]

The informal style of these lines seems to trivialize the complexity of the epistemological issue at stake. It would be a neat cavil to complain that "noon dwellyng in this contree" excludes Christ, who made return journeys from both heaven and hell; Alceste, whose oneiric encounter with the poet is the central topic of the Prologue; Hercules, who sought Alceste in hell; and Theseus, who sought another there with Perotheus. Fiction has its own continuum of reality, one may argue, but how can one measure what can be known through fiction compared to what is knowable through "assay"? Chaucer identifies three epistemological systems here: seeing, hearing what others have seen, and reading what others have written of what they have seen or heard. These are, respectively, knowing by the eye on the thing, by the ear open to an account of a thing, and by the eye on a graphic sign of a thing. All three mediate between wits' apprehension of things and reason's comprehension of their meaning, or truth.[3]

Chaucer's poetic line, however, befuddles the issue in the manner of exposing it. God can neither *forbede* nor *wot*, since he has neither tongue for the former nor eye for the latter (*wot*, from *witen*, signifies a knowing from having seen). The *ysee/pardee* rhyme binds human sense to divine agency, but the *ye/lye* pair puts any truth from sensuous apprehension in doubt.[4] More striking is the amphibology of the last line: "Bernard the monk ne saugh nat all, pardee." Internal punctuation shapes the phrase to mean either that Bernard knew more than what his eyes saw, or that he did not see everything there is to see of the world. Without the comma, *pardee* is an instrumental which has the line mean that Bernard saw more things than God's gift of sight afforded him. At any rate, the top rung of the epistemological ladder of sight is faith's glimpse behind the *visibilia* of creation to the *invisibilia* of its formal idea. It is virtue, says the Second Nun in the *Canterbury Tales,* that allows the eye to see hidden signs (8, 230–31).

Chaucer's scale of sight has at its base the physical eye which sees concrete things, higher is the rational eye which reads the things as signs, and highest is the eye of faith, like Bernard's, which perceives the invisible forms behind things and signs.[5] This is conventional Neoplatonism. Boethius's Lady Philosophy explains a four-rung ladder of perception in *Cons.* 5, pr. 4, beginning with the eye that sees things as matter, followed by the imaginative eye which discerns things distinct from matter, the reasoning eye which sees the species which a subtantial thing represents, and, finally, the eye of understanding which grasps the *forma simplex*. William of Aragon, in his *Commentary* on the fate of Orpheus in *Cons.* 3, m. 12, distinguishes between the imperfect eye, which sees only sensible good, from the better eye, which sees the intelligible good distinct from its substance.[6] This sight is *sovrasenso* for Dante, whose scale of vision moves upward in the *Commedia* in concord with a scale of love from shame through dignity to magnanimity.[7]

A ladder of sight is no guarantee of an ascension, but seeing must be lifted by reason if one would reach to knowing and bolstered by faith if one would reach to truth.[8] The light of the Holy Grail reveals the ideal form of knighthood behind the appearance of all knights of the Round Table.[9] Similitude of things obtained by physical sight alone, warns Augustine, is the matrix of error.[10] Those who see only with their *outter yën* are blind, says Cecile to Almachius (*CT* 8, 498–504). The Pardoner sells a potion whose effect confuses the rungs of sight by having its drinkers believe that which they know is not true (6, 366–71). Januarie in the Merchant's tale achieves the same effect by imbibing May's words. To his expression of shock at what he sees of her struggle in the pear tree with Damyan, she explains:

> Ful many a man weneth to seen a thyng,
> And it is al another than it semeth.
> He that mysconceyveth, he mysdemeth.
>
> (4, 2408–10)

"Allas," laments the poet in recounting the perfidy of Aeneas with Dido,

> . . . what harm doth apparence,
> Whan hit is fals in existence:
> . . . . . . . . . . . . .

> Loo, how a woman doth amys
> To loven hym that unknowen ys!
>
> (*HF* 1, 265–70)

The Squire of the *Tales* makes a comic spectacle out of the people's starring at Cambyuskan's birthday gifts in order to understand their magical properties (5, 189–263). Insufficient sight has the people of the Clerk's tale read Grisilde by her clothing. The victim Priest in *pars secunda* of the Canon's Yeoman's tale sees what is not really there. The bond between the seen and the unseen is an issue that Chaucer treats directly in the *Legend* when he describes Jason's sexual inconstancy in a manner that seems to mock philosophical thought:

> As matter appetiteth forme alwey
> And from forme into forme it passen may,
> Or as a welle that were botomles,
> Ryght so can false Jason have no pes.
> For to desyren through his apetit
> To do with gentil women his delyt,
> That is his lust and his felicite.
>
> (1582–88)[11]

Philosophically speaking, matter is the visible reification of an invisible formative design. Form is Aristotle's *eidos,* the formal cause of creation, whose final cause is *physis,* or nature. It is both an element's intelligible structure and its principle of motion, apprehended by the physical eye and understood by the inner or rational eye. Latin *forma* more often designates "beauty," "outer appearance," and "figure" than either "species" or "ideal."[12] In Scholastic Philosophy, form is *actus* in the world of being, while matter is *possibilitas* in the world of becoming. In Jean de Meun's *Roman de la rose,* Nature is the guardian and continuer of forms (16791–92), and Dante's Beatrice explains that at the moment of Creation, "Forma e materia, congiunte e purette / usciro ad esser che con avia fallo" (*Par.* 29, 22–23) [Form and matter, conjoined and pure, came into being with no defect]. Boethius calls *matter* the visible image of form in *De Trinitate,* II, 10–13. All things owe their existence to form, but God is *uere forma neque imago* (II, 19–20) [true form without image]. Lady Philosophy explains that although the form of a man is contained in divine thought, his figure is contained in nature; if form is difficult to recognize in the figure, it is because the figure signifies the thing, but not the thing which forms it (*Cons.* 5, pr. 4). In his *Commentary* on Cicero's *Somnium,* 1, 11, 11–12, Macrobius describes the process by which souls, or forms, take on bodies. Augustine notes that since it is form that gives matter a visible appearance, things without form are indistinguishable.

Before God's hand touched matter, says Jean de Meun's Nature, there was no order or division of things (*RR* 16747–50).

Chaucer's matter "appetiting" after form reflects Bernard Silvester's description of matter's urgent need for form in *Cosmographia* 1, 1, 35–36. The form that pursues matter is *intelligentsia universalis*. All of this learned lore lies behind Chaucer's image, but in having man-matter pursuing woman-form in an amatory hunt of body for soul, he has reversed the roles of hunter and prey, for, in Scholastic Philosophy, man is form and woman, body. The philosophy of form is central to Chaucer's story of Philomene, who in the Ovidian source, *Metamorphoses* 6, 452, is *divitior forma* [richer in beauty (than her clothes)]. The gap between a thing's formal reality and its casual appearance is announced in the motto which heads the tale in two of the twelve extant manuscripts—*Deus dator formarum*—and which is glossed in the tale's opening lines:

> Thow yevere of the formes that has wrought
> This fayre world and bar it in thy thought
> Eternaly er thow thy werk began,
>
> .  .  .  .  .  .  .  .  .  .  .
>
> Why suffredest thow that Tereus was bore,
> That is in love so fals and so forswore?
>
> (2228–35)

The eternal bearing of the forms of the fair world in divine thought is Theseus's purveyance. Ovid uses the same image of creation in *Metamorphoses* 1, 1–25, and Bernard Silvester in *Cosmographia* 1, 2, 2–23, though Chaucer's immediate source for this passage is undoubtedly Nature's confession in Jean de Meun's *Roman:*

> Cis Diex, qui de biauté habonde,
> Quant il si biau fist ce biau monde
> Dont il portoit en sa pensee
> La bele forme porpensee
> Touz jors en pardurableté. . . .
>
> (16728–33)

[This God who abounds in beauty, when he made this fair world, whose beautiful form held eternally in his mind. . . . ] Jean's immediate source is his own translations of Boethius's *Consolation* 3, m. 9: *tu, tres biaus, portez le biau monde dedens ta pensee et formes cestui monde a l'ymage et a la semblance de celui et commandez que cist mondez parfaiz ait ses partiez delivres et parfaitez.* Chaucer's translation follows suit: "Thow that art althir-fayrest, berynge the faire world in thy thought, formedest this world to the lyknesse semblable of that faire world in thy thought"

(11–14). This is a hefty mass of philosophy laid on the back of a mundane reflection that things would have been better for Philomene had Tereus never been born, but it is typical of Chaucer's style to weight a light remark with heavy reflection and to lighten weighty thought with aery play.

The epistemological quiddity of sight and insight in the opening lines of the Prologue to the *Legend* is a sinuous rhetorical path into the poet's account of his loving adoration of the daisy and further into the dream which it informs. The dream-figure of Alceste is a sign of the daisy's form. The sequence of attractions that leads the dreamer to Alceste describes an epistemological hierarchy. The poet tells us that he disdains books—objects of the eye of reason—for the daisy—object of the physical eye—and both take precedence over the religious devotion which exercises the eye of faith. One is reminded of Theophrastus's notorious argument that love (i.e. marriage) is incompatible with reading.[13] Chaucer's activities run downward in the conventional scale of attractions, but all three sights concord in the poet's recollection of his experience in the meadow; for, although he sees a daisy, he reads it as a book of virtue before which he takes a devotional stance (51–59); and, by describing the daisy as a woman, he links an outer appearance of a thing to its sign of moral virtue. The daisy is a natural, social, and moral emblem of love.[14]

The daisy, then, is an emblem of the chain of love, conjoining in itself nature and spirit, and the adoring poet is a model lover whose affection is for the joined thing and the idea of it. This connection is reenforced by language which aligns the flower with Christ. For example, the poet rises before daybreak to witness the daisy's *resurrection* on the first day of May, the feast of love. Then the poet gives a brief etymological explanation of *daisy* as "ey of day" (184). The day's eye is an image of both the sun and the world.[15] In medieval herbal lore, the daisy is the *consolida media* in a triad of vulneraries which includes comfrey and bugle. It is is both bonewort and bruisewort, a panacea for the health of man's body. The shape of the daisy, a circle with a center dot, is the floral sign of gold and the astrological graph for the sun. Finally, in the stylized conventions of love poetry, the darts of Cupid and Venus are forged with gold.[16]

Chaucer's sensible, erudite, and allusive style describes a quite ordinary experience here, but without implying sensuality. Like Coleridge's secondary power of the imagination which translates what the primary imagination grasps, Chaucer's imagination moves through what is seen and heard toward the ideological intent behind image and sound.[17] He not only recognizes moral virtue in a flower's shape and color, but hears a moral text in the seasonal exuberance of the birds, whose song "The Foweler We Deffye" (138) is a frolicking defiance of corruption and death; and, as if love is confirmed in gestation, each bird couple renews its Saint Valentine's Day vows, swearing upon blossoms to be true.[18] If Chaucer's imagination decodes the sights and sounds of nature, then his art encodes his readings. Fleeting physical impressions are transformed into durable words, and those words seem to have the potential orthoscopic force to set things right in matters of love.

Chaucer's love experience in the *Legend* begins with his attraction to the daisy and then passes into a dream adoration of both the flower and the women who is its sign. Curiously, not only is affection in the dream different, but it seems to belie the knit of love which is the poet's experience before the dream. The dream opens with the poet lying in devotional wonder before the daisy. We do not see what he sees, but we see his seeing and his reading of what he sees. Where the poet in his waking state ranges with full control of his imagination over physical, moral, and spiritual values of the daisy, within the dream he is trapped in a farcical comedy of efforts to understand what is going on before his eyes.

It may be that we are to understand that the grotesque comedy of the dream is informed by the poetic legends which it precedes, or contains, but the dream, no matter how grotesque or comic, is the epistemological source of the stories which follow. It is as if the poet's confusion in his dream engenders the confusion in the stories it incites *after* the dream. The basic confusion, as the opening lines of the poem forecast, is between seeing and understanding. To begin with, at the outset of the dream, the poet spies a woman, dressed in green, wearing a white crown with a gold fret, approaching in the company of a man. The dreamer reads the man immediately as the god of love and reads the array of his "queen" as signs of the daisy, but he has no idea *who* she is. Without worrying about the process of thought by which the poet knows Love, one can wonder why he does not know Love's lady.[19] It is different for the god. When he casts a stern eye on the poet and asks "who kneleth there?" the curt "it am I" (312–14) instantly reveals the poet-adversary of love.[20] In her tardy defence of the poet, Alceste mentions her own name and rank as queen of Thrace, but when Love asks the poet later if he knows who the lady is, Chaucer replies "Nay ... / No moore but that I see wel she is good" (505–6), as if focus on the deeper virtue blinds the eye to its superficial sign.[21] When Love reminds the poet that the lady is the Alceste of Chaucer's books who chose to die in her husband's stead and whom was rescued from hell by Hercules (510–16), the poet recalls the story, her metamorphosis into a daisy and her stellification (517–26), details whose origins seem to be bound to the context of the dream, for they appear in no bookish authority on Alceste.[22]

The process of knowing from sight is an issue in the trial and sentence of the poet for having written of Criseyde so that "men to wommen lasse triste" (333). Alceste, in setting a penance for the poet to write better, notes the ontological incongruity between the poet's appearance and his task: "And thogh the lyke nat a lovere bee, / Speke wel of love" (490–91).[23] Alceste is referring to the popular idea that one must be fair of aspect to be a fair lover, but speaking love, as Cyrano de Bergerac so amply demonstrates, is tantamount to loving. The laws of the *Academie de jeux floraux* in the mid fourteenth century award the title "Fin Amant" to the winner of a competition in poetry.[24] The minstrels at Theseus's court in the Knight's tale compete in speaking "feelingly" of love (1, 2197–2203). Alceste, however, has already accused the poet's verse of being an attraction to love only to "lewed folk" (414–16). Having impugned both his looks and his language, how can she expect him to write better now?

Writing better involves linking the sight of love with an insight into its deeper form. The problem here is that Chaucer and his accusers have rival theories of poetry. For Alceste, true love is loving faithfully until the end of one's life (485), but she is thinking of loving the furniture rather than the Furnisher of Creation.[25] Alceste's theory justifies Love's anger at the poet's depiction of a Criseyde who loses her respectibility by allowing her *corage* to slide from a high to a lower object. Alceste's is, precisely, a theory of social respectibility, whereas Chaucer's own theory, as he explains it in his defence, is a theory of morality in which poetry serves truth by negative rather than positive illustration. He would lead an audience toward virtuous love by exposing lack of virtue in folly, error and vice (466–74), offering the fright of imperfection rather than the comfort of perfection. Chaucer's is a negative theory, a reflection of the Boethian argument that man, unable to understand the perfection of creation, can assume that it exists by his recognition of imperfection.[26] So it is with love. If man is incapable of seeing the perfection of love, he can assume there is one by recognizing imperfection; and if Chaucer cannot write of perfect love, he can at least write of love's failing.[27]

The fragile bond between seeing, knowing, and writing is continually obscured in the poem by the comic confusion between oneiric and waking perceptions of things. Love, for example, chides the poet for omitting Alceste from the list of women whose beauty the poet declares is surpassed by Alceste (537–40). The poet's balade of lovely women, however, is composed *after* the dream in recalling Alceste's dreamed form (247–48).[28] This is a minor complication compared to the major confusion in the missing threshold between dream and waking state at the end of the Prologue. Just after Love has advised the poet to make his examples of true women brief, ". . . with that word my bokes gan I take, / And ryght thus on my legende gan I make" (578–79). While *take* and *make* move us from book source to poem product, the missing *wake* leaves us wondering if the poet is trapped within his dream. This wonderful suspension of dream state is avoided in the G-text of the Prologue: "And with that

word, of slep I gan awake, / And ryght thus on my legende gan I make"
(544–45). While this version wakes the poet, it forgets, however, the
books from which the poet is ordered to make his translations (556–62).[29]
In both versions, nonetheless, the poet ignores his presleep intention to
adore the daisy. In other words, the dream impedes his linking of natural
object with idea in imitation of the chain of love, and sends him back to
translating books to make a synchronicity of old story, that is, to make
old story serve present circumstance.

The stories the poet collects, although they tell the tragedies of women
named in the dream, are related in a manner that clearly undermines
Alceste's and Love's view of love. Having earlier read the figure of
Alceste as a moral virtue, Chaucer tells sad stories of women who exemplify physical and moral waste. The tales repel by their exposition of
pain and destruction rather than attract by examples of fidelity, for their
topic is womanhood wasted by cupidinous love. They impugn the capacity
of women's sight to serve other than personal physical and social interests
as well as the ability of their words to either correct sight or salve love's
harms. For the most part in the *Legend,* love enters the mind through
channels of eye and ear, but is left unrefined by reason. The wounds of
wasted love are kept open by memory, and none of Chaucer's heroines
is able to speak it away.[30] Quite simply, Chaucer's women either know
badly through sight and hearing and speak to no profit in attempting to
mitigate the error of their wits or they are seen and spoken into a poor love.

Despite Love's offhand assertion that no true lover goes to hell
(552–53), none of the women of the *Legend* are wafted to heaven as
reward for their "truth." They suffer a hell on earth without the consolation
of a sight of a future heaven.[31] Not only do these women's words fail to
reduce suffering, the words of their stories fail to mitigate the crime Love
has charged Chaucer with. Whatever consolation these women are given
in Chaucer's source—the book which Love directs the poet to translate—
Chaucer's version deprives them of it. They end in the blunder of fall
rather than in the bliss of ascent. Cleopatra kills herself after declaring
her corpse a text of love: "That shal be wel sene, / Was nevere unto hir
love a trewe queene" (694–95). Thisbe falls in love with what she cannot
see but can only hear through a cracked wall. Her first sight of her lover
is of a dead body, and she kills herself to make of her corpse a testimony
of true love (910–11). Even if sharing the same fate is a sort of fidelity,
there is no consolatory thought that the dead will be reunited in another world.

Dido falls in love with Aeneas's fair form and words (1066–71), and
when he deserts her for the fairer idea of Rome, she writes him a bitter
reproach before she kills herself. Phyllis falls in love with Demophon's
"port and manere" (2453), but fails to read the falsity which runs through

the blood which nourishes them (2394–2400). When he abandons her, she laments her misplaced faith in the public fame of his lineage and in the charms of his fair tongue and then hangs herself.[32] Medea is seduced by Jason's leonine looks and good speech "more than the boundes of myn honeste" (1673). Ariadne does not see the Theseus whose words seduce her, but in return for a promise of marriage she gives him a "clew of twyne" to guide him out of the maze and into her arms (2016). When Theseus deserts her for Phaedra, future mother of the false Demophon, she utters a lament to an empty bed.[33] Hypermnestra, immune to her own pernicious blood strain, chooses to save a husband she does not love rather than serve the evil intent of a father who professes to love *her*. In doing so, she places "wifly honeste" over fatherly love (2701), but her virtue is somewhat sullied by Chaucer's detail of her slowness of foot unheeded by a careless husband in his haste to get away. The consequences of her inagility are not mentioned, but her sacrificial act qualifies her as the only heroine in the collection who emulates the model of Alceste.[34] Lucrece and Philomene, on the other hand, are distinct in neither loving nor being married to the men who abuse them. Their tragedies are not of seeing, but of being seen. Tarquinius's lust is kindled by the combination of Lucrece's beauty and her gestures of wifely virtue. After she is raped, she makes a final gesture of fidelity to her husband's good name by killing herself (1845).[35] The rape of Philomene is incited by her beauty and her mutilation by fear of her unspoken words of blame.[36]

In the stories of the *Legend,* the body's eye and ear conspire in blinding reason to the "truth" of love, while the mouth's language fails to join the body's desire to the spirit's.[37] Nonetheless, in the story of Philomene, seeing, loving, and writing do effect a sort of rebinding of love. The terms of that success, however, only heighten our sense of disgust with a "love" that has neither moral nor spiritual purpose. One can easily suppose that Chaucer inserted this particular story into his collection in order to emphasize a specific point. It is, after all, out of place in the design dictated by Alceste and Love, for, while the other eight stories feature heroines who are mentioned in the balade composed in honor of Alceste's beauty, Philomene is not there. Nor is she among the nineteen attendants of Alceste whom Love indicates as the suitable topics for the book (554–57).[38] Further, she is a heroine who loves no man, while her sister Progne, the central figure in other versions of the story, does *not* love her husband faithfully till the end of her life. In effect, the story of Philomene shifts the focus from women loving to unwanted love, and their goal from sexual and social to familial ties.

Philomene's first words in the story reveal her frailty of words. When she sees the cave, deep in a dark wood, into which Tereus has led her, she asks, "Where is my suster, brother Tereus?" (2315), giving voice to her fear rather than to a need for information. Her language is a desperate attempt to transform the cave into the palace of her expectations and to convert Tereus's obvious design for rape into a kindly gesture. Tereus's lust is corrected neither by the tears he sees nor by the words he hears. Philomene, as her father Pandion and her sister Progne before her, has misread the crooked form beneath the straight appearance of a man, and her words fail to set it straight.

The image of a cave adds to the sense of the futility of Philomene's words. It is not found elsewhere. Ovid locates the rape in a *stabulum* in a *silva obscura* (*Metam.* 6, 521), Chrétien's version, "Et de la hupe . . .," does not mention where the rape takes place but locates the prison in a *maison gaste,* a deserted or ruined house.[39] In Ovid, Chrétien, and Gower's *Confession Amantis* (5, 5715), Philomene's fearful question is Progne's to Tereus when he returns home alone from Athens. Besides this single line, Philomene's only other utterance is her brief outcry to sister, father, and God as she is violated (2328–29).[40] She has no chance to scold her assailant for his infidelity to her sister, for he cuts her tongue out before she can utter a word. No other heroine of the *Legend* says so little, but no other manages to tell so much. Chaucer mentions that she has sufficient food, drink, and clothing, as well as a loom upon which to practice her familiar feminine skill. Further, "She coude eek rede and wel ynow endyte, / But wyth a pen coude she nat wryte" (2356–57). Though this seems excessive detail for such a brief tale, its effects are elusive. "Coude she nat" is curiously ambiguous. It means first that she did not know how to write, following the sense of the first line where "wel" signals a skill and not an opportunity—a disparity between reading and writing talents common in the days of Charlemagne and Alfred the Great, but rare in Chaucer's day—and it means as well that she was prevented from writing because she lacked either a pen or privacy from watchful eyes. These ambiguities are strategic, it seems to me, for they engage the attention of Chaucer's audience upon the indeterminacy of communication.

She could weave and she "waf it wel, and wrote the storye . . . / How she was served for her syster's love" (2364–65) on her journey from Athens to Thrace (the land of Alceste). What sort of text she produced is not made clear. In the fourteenth century, *write* designates the act of making pictures as well as shaping graphs. At any rate, with gestures she directs a knave to deliver her textile, and she adds a ring to authenticate its source. Web, gesture, and ring constitute a text to which her mouth could give no life, and that text traces her journey from her past father's to her future sister's care. It is a text of love which Progne reads well, feigns a pilgrimage—a journey to a shrine of love—and rejoins her dumb sister.

The story ends there, but not the tale. Chaucer adds a moral, not to

praise good women but to warn them against the falsity of men's forms
despite their appearances:

> Ye may be war of men, yif that ye liste.
> For al be it that he wol nat, for shame,
> Don as Tereus, to lese his name,
> Ne serve yow as a morderour or a knave,
> Ful lytel while shal ye trewe hym have—
> That wol I seyn, al were he now my brother—
> But it be so that he may have non other.
>
> (2387–93)[41]

Such is Chaucer's corrective to the tragic fault of trust in what women
see and hear but do not read *aryght*. As a lesson to the heroines of the
*Legend* it is tragically late. It is entirely irrelevant to Philomene, who
neither wanted nor had Tereus true. The moral speaks to Chaucer's fictive
audience, but the tale does not attract men to love by examples of good
women and the promise of rewards of love. Chaucer chastizes all men
as false, except those, whoever they may be, who can have no other.

The moral appended to the tale of Phyllis which follows narrows the
field to its ultimate consituent, the poet:

> Be war, ye wemen, of youre subtyl fo,
> Syn yet this day men may ensaumple se;
> And trusteth, as in love, no man but me.
>
> (2559–61)

Identifying himself alone as a man worthy of trust, Chaucer is authenti-
cating the poet's words as the sole means of grasping the form which is
hidden by appearance. The posture is ironic, since the poet is the one
responsible for exposing the shame of love despite his assigned task to
celebrate love's glory.[42]

In subverting Alceste's and Love's charge, Chaucer has subverted the
authorities of history and human love to produce a poetry of "negative
morality."[43] He converts trust in the truth of love to faith in the power
of the word to reveal what love is not. Curiously, however, Chaucer has
already put that power in question by warning his audience of the malefic
effects of reading such tales:

> And, as to me, so grisely was his dede
> That, whan that I his foule storye rede,
> Myne eyen wexe foule and sore also.
> Yit laste the venym of so long ago,

> That it enfecteth hym that wol beholde
> The storye of Tereus of which I tolde.
>
> $(2234)^{44}$

The notion of pestilent words is a commonplace. The Knight of the *Canterbury Tales* finds disease in the Monk's tragedies (7, 2771), and the Host needs a physic to counter the effects of the Physician's tale (6, 311–13). The power of words to contaminate is an issue that Boccaccio brushes aside in the Epilogue to *Il decamerone* by blaming infection on the body of the reader rather than on the body of the text. If Chaucer means to suggest that poetry violates its readers just as its fictional men violate women, then he is making the same pollution he wrays, and the effect reaches higher than the Temple of Fame right up to the Creator's porch. "Do not read of love," Chaucer seems to be saying, "or you will infect both yourself and those to whom you repeat the story." Foul poetry fouls wits, and by reading her sister's text, Progne is infected with Philomene's harm. What in the opening lines of the poem seemed to be a consideration of the power of poetry to sight love and serve as a balm for the harms of experience shifts into self-contamination.

Were Alceste's story there to complete the *Legend,* a spiritual redress might be gleaned that conjoins all these examples of ill into a final good, and which exposes the means by which failures of physical love are redeemed by a spiritual love. The *Legend,* however, remains an openended text. The redemptive act of poetry which promises to redress the name of woman is never completed, for Alceste is the goal of a penitential task that is unfinished. The Prologue's philosophic premise that there is an insight into the realm of invisible ideas graspable by man is denied by the practice of the tales themselves. Similarly, the philosophical pursuit of an orthoscopic bond between the worlds of visible and invisible forms, between signs and meaning, fails to complete its course.[45]

Philomene's woven text proves more beneficial than the poet's spoken or written words. Its design both tells a story and incites an act of love. The web is a strategem of escape and retrieval, just as Chaucer's *Legend* is a poetic strategem of escaping the strictures ordained by Love as penitence.[46] It can be argued that the passing of a shuttle through a network of threads repairs by reenactment of Tereus's penetration,[47] but one way or another, Philomene's text is a discourse of retrieval as well as a retrieval of discourse.[48] There are other texts in this poem and elsewhere, however, which suffer little to make meaning and have no trouble being read. The chatter of birds in the Prologue renders a text in sounds without words. The song-speech in the *Parliament of Fowls* and the voices of birds in *House of Fame* and in the tales of the Squire, Nun's Priest, and Manciple are signs that blend different epistemological systems into a communicable message.

The silent language of human gesture is a counterexample. May in the Merchant's tale gives directions for adultery in signs. The Pardoner boasts that he can identify people by signs and circumstances without having to use words (*CT* 6, 419–20). Visual hearing and visual thinking are topics of eleventh- and twelfth-century optics, and the extent to which Chaucer's visual images contain ideas has been well documented.[49] The *Legend* illustrates how futile the word is in the service of a form of love unknown or unheeded by the person to whom it is addressed. It is ironic that the two women whose men are most faithful, Cleopatra and Thisbe, seem constrained to make memorial texts of their own dead bodies.

Chaucer's *Legend* and the web of Philomene it contains serve love not by showing what it is, but what it should not be.[50] They display a love that is grounded in the flesh, incited by the wits but unconnected to reason. In her sister, Philomene finds one who can read her text in order to flee sexual love and rejoin a surer bond. Chaucer is looking for a comparable reader. *Writing* well, then, is to write in such a manner, in such a style, that both eye and ear are sensitized to forms of meaning behind forms of appearance. Words spoken "by ordinaunce," says Prudence, citing Salomon to Melibee, "yeven swetnesse to the soule and hoolsomnesse to the body" (*CT* 7, 1112–13), but Chaucer's Philomene represents a victory of the written and visual text over the spoken word.

The stories of Chaucer's *Legend,* in effect, deny the experience of the poet who, in adoring the daisy, conjoins love of thing with love of idea. The old books that the poet turns to for his poem refute nature, and the vicarious experience of old lovers refutes the poet's personal experience in love. In this respect, the poet's service to a dream reflects the Negative Theology which denies man's capacity to know or talk profitably about God. Perhaps the profit of that denial is a greater urge for union with God. There is some irony in the fact that Theseus, one of the guilty lovers of the *Legend,* speaks in the first of the Canterbury tales to assert that human love mirrors the visible form of the cosmos. He is older and wiser then, perhaps, and if his words work there, while the language of women martyrs to love fails, it is because he knows what tasks the tool of word can perform.

# 4

## Word-Chains of Love:
## *The Parliament, Troilus* and the *Knight's Tale*

Out of the dust grew the plants; the plants were
consumed and became muscle and bone; and all the
time, the energy had only been changing form, nothing
had been lost or destroyed.

—Leslie Marmon Silko

Cupide the king ringand ane silver bell,
Quhilk men micht heir fra heuien vnto hell.

—Robert Henryson

HENRYSON'S ORPHEUS, AS BOETHIUS'S, LOSES WITH HIS EYE WHAT HIS
music had won because he looks behind him and downward toward hell
instead of holding his eye upward toward heaven. The chain of love
extends from the absolute hellish disorder of concupiscence to the perfect
heavenly unity of charitable love, from *Venus vulgaria* to *Venus caeles*.
For man, central in the geography of creation, the chain offers paths to
both Satan's snare and God's grandeur. Man cannot avoid strolling along
one or the other; and he may, like Thoreau contemplating a plumbline
through the water of Walden pond, mistake down for up. Virgil explains
to Dante the ineluctability of his choice:

> "Né creator né creatura mai"
> cominciò el, "figliuol, fu sanza amore
> o naturale or d'animo; e tu 'l sai."
>
> (*Purg.* 17, 91–93)

["Neither Creator not creature," he began, "is without love, either natural
or mental; that you know"] Natural love, that which man exercises in the
innocence of Eden, is without sin, but mental love errs when it is fixed
upon the appearances of things rather than upon their forms. No one
expresses this better than Andreas Capellanus at the opening of his *De*

*Amore,* 1, 1: *Amor est passio quaedam innata procedens ex visione et immoderata cogitatione forma alterius sexus* [Love is an inborn suffering which results from the sight of, and uncontrolled thinking about, the beauty of the other sex]; and 1, G. 368: *Quid enim aliud est amor nisi immoderata et furtivi et latentis amplexus concupiscibiliter percipiendi ambitio?* [What is love but an uncontrolled desire to obtain the sensual gratification of a furtive and secret embrace].[1] Chaucer would have seen a version of this in the *Roman de la rose,* 4377–84, which appears in a section of the *Romaunt* not attributed with certainty to him:

> If love be serched wel and sought,
> It is a syknesse of the thought
> Annexed and knet bitwixe tweyne,
> Which male and female, with oo cheyne,
> So frely byndith that they nyll twynne,
> Whether so therof they leese or wynne
> The roote springeth thurgh hoot brennyng
> Into disordinat desiryng
> For to kissen and enbrace.
>
> (4809–17)

Andreas's *forma* [beauty] is also the *forma* that is "idea." Andreas goes on to say that the best love is a *vincula incorporali* [incorporeal cord] that joins hearts (1, 3). The lesser love inclining toward Satan is an excess of feeling for physical things. It is, in Augustinian terms, loving the things of creation more than their Creator, being weighted down by body rather than lifted by thought. Boethius's Lady Philosophy exposes the chain of sensuousness which fetters the human body: " . . . pressus grauibus colla catenis / Cogitur, heu, stolidam cernere terram" (*Cons.* 1, m. 2, 25–27) [His nekke is pressyd with hevy cheynes, and bereth his chere enclyned adoun for the grete weyghte].

Later, *Cons.* 5, m. 3, 12–13, she remarks that *mens caecis obruta membris* [thoughte of man is confownded and overthrowen by the darke membres of the body]. These dark members are what Chaucer calls *wits,* and all of them contribute to the weight of sin, particularly the sin of *luxuria,* as the Parson explains at length (*CT* 10, 852ff.). The idea is commonplace, as an anonymous twelfth-century poet testifies:

> fraude subdola
> subnectendo modula
> manus, sures, oculi
> strenua paci
> uix negant cupidini.

[Sly and deceitful hands, ears, eyes, contributing their nuances, can hardly restrain desire from undergoing hardship][2] The eye which reflects the daisy, the sun and the world, is the principle organ of both transcendental and base love. In the popular optics of Chaucer's time, it not only receives an impression of form, but it strikes that form with its rays.[3] Therefore, as Lady Philosophy reminds Boethius, *Cons.* 5, pr. 6, 2–4, the one who sees is responsible for what is seen: *omne scitur non ex sua sed ex comprehendentium naturae cognoscitur* [alle thing that is iwist nis nat knowen by his nature propre, but by the nature of hem that comprehenden it].

Andreas Capellanus's *De amore* questions whether the blind have any place in the courts of love, since God's gift of sight is necessary for love (1, 6, G, 385). Those with impaired senses are impaired lovers.[4] Chaucer's impaired—the partially deaf Wife, the blind Januarie, the bleary-eyed Canon's Yeoman, the goat-voiced Pardoner—indeed seem deficient of spirit and perverted in love.[5] The eyes' sight provides insight into the "sutile knyttinges of thinges," but as the foolish women of the *Legend* illustrate, reason is "confownded and overthrowen by the derke membres of the body." Alain de Lisle accuses concupiscence of all the senses for the frayed bond between man and God.[6] Man's wits, alas, lack the butterfly lightness to soar upward toward God, for they are elephantine and pressed hard to the ground (*Cons.* 3, pr. 8, 23–27).

Love, Dante's Virgil explains, is both the cause of all sin and the seed of all virtue (*Purg.* 17, 103–5). Right love consists of the primal harmony of intellectual love (*amor animi*), with natural, or physical love (*amor animalis*), and it is to that harmony that the human eye and mind direct themselves. Natural love, Chaucer's love of kind, is ordained by God. His first command to Adam and Eve in the Garden of Eden echoes his first command to living creatures: *Crescite et multiplicamini, et replete terram* (Gen. 1, 22 and 28). Chaucer's Wife of Bath cites that command as authority for her sexual indulgences (3, 28), though she does not mention her own service to multiplying. Prelapsarian natural love is love without lust for the partner's body, but with desire to serve God's providence. One can remain chaste, says the *Glossa Palatina* even when making love.[7] Animals love "naturally" because the physical attraction which brings them together is not attended by thought or complicated by speech. They couple according to a natural attraction which is governed by both season and age. "God tokneth and assigneth the tymes, ablynge hem to hir propre offices" (*Boece.* 1, m. 6, 17–18). Human love, whose natural attractions are supplemented by reason and imagination, connects nature's biological ordinance with social and moral purpose in time.

How human language confounds nature's ordinance is illustrated comically in the *Parliament of Fowls,* a poem whose topic, as far as the poet-dreamer is concerned, is the epistemology of love. Claiming to know nothing of love except what he has gleaned from books, he reads in Macrobius's *Commentary* the exposition of the design of the universe embodied in God's cosmic love. As he arrives at the description of the purgatory in which lechers and breakers of law whirl about in pain (80), the light of day dims and he falls asleep to dream that Scipio leads him into a garden where Nature has gathered the orders of birds on Saint Valentine's Day. Nature is described as:

> the vicaire of the almyghty Lord
> That hot, cold, hevy, lyght, moyst, and dreye
> Hath knyt by evene noumbres of acord.
>
> (379–81)

This is another version of the Theseus's Platonic chain of accord of the elements, but Nature's punctual role here is both creative and providential: to assure continuation of forms, or, if you will, to make sure God's command to the birds to wax and multiply is obeyed.

The operation is frustrated at its inception, however, by a quarrel between three tersel eagles in their claims for the formel eagle who, in deference to her nobility of kind, is the first bird put on the sexual bargaining block. Nature introduces the first claimant as wise, worthy, secret, true as steel, and formed according to her will (395–97); and yet, her will seems to have miscarried, for the tersel's words, as well as those of the two claimants who follow him, are not "natural" at all, but replete with the artifice of the aristocratic courtly code which frustrates natural process. None of them expresses a natural claim to the formel, and Nature finds it necessary to assign the dispute to the election of the other birds, whose speech reveals their particular social and linguistic rungs on nature's ontological ladder.

The contentious babble adds up to little more than reciprocal impugning of each other's grasp of love. The goose suggests that the rejected tersels should look elsewhere (566–67). The turtledove adopts the nobler position that all the tersels should serve the formel whether accepted or rejected (582–88). The duck disdains any notion of the noble joy of suffrance (592–93) and is reproved by the "gentil" tercelet (which one?) for not seeing love any better than an owl sees by the light of day (598–602). The cuckoo, notorious for its unnatural procreative behavior, advises celibacy (606–7).

Nature retrieves her governance with a demand that the formel choose for herself, assuring the formel that any one of the suitors "oughte to been a suffisaunce" (637). Refusing to serve either Venus or Cupid (652), the formel demurs with a request for a year's respite. When this is granted,

Nature's process has been effectively thwarted by a social code.[8] Of course, Venus is the goddess of Rhetoric in the scheme of the Seven Liberal Arts, and her place in the poem is in the Temple of Love, an artifice which contrasts with the natural scene of the parliament. Venereal love opposes kindly, or natural, love as Alain's *De planctu* argues, and the world of art and history in the *Parliament* oppose the garden and its seasonal functions. The comic disorder with which the proceedings end, though the other birds hurry through their choices, illustrates once more the pernicious effects of language on love. Art undoes Nature's accord and confuses both right season and proper time for procreation. In effect, Nature's golden chain has lost its hold on man's sexual and social chain. It is significant that in her reaction to male language of dominance, a "woman" dislodges Nature's hold. In effect, it is Nature herself that is distraught by the artifice of man's language.

Of course, only the human among God's creatures is endowed with the will to wed himself to spirit as well as to body, or *not* to. In the *Parliament of Fowls* the disorder of the speech given birds reflects a human disorder of sense which impedes language from unifying kindly, moral, and spiritual attractions. Pure kindly love, innocent of pursuit of pleasure and selfish profit, is unavailable to man because he is endowed with a reason and language that consent and collaborate with the body's appetites. Man's reason can choose to disdain the things of this world in order to love God, or love the things of this world for God's sake, or love the things of this world for their own sake. In other words, man's reason and its linguistic expression can shift affections toward lower or higher objects but do best when they hold him to those activities proper to time and place in his life. The exigencies of social estates only confuse his options.

Tereus and Jason in the *Legend of Good Women* lower their natures by disdaining reason for carnal delight in their pursuit of women. Grisilde's love of Walter, on the other hand, serves a common profit by begetting children in an act of *honesta copulatio,* without having to lay "a lite hir hoolynesse aside," as the Man of Law says smugly of Constance (*CT* 2, 713). Cecile's Valerian learns to love his wife for the spiritual idea she both figures and teaches. The process of loving in Chaucer's poetry is always a struggle to harmonize the contending demands of genitals, heart, and mind, and it is women who often show the way.[9]

*Troilus* and the Knight's tale illustrate this struggle in different ways, both subtly and tentatively. Both works display attractions of the world that hold man from either seeing or realizing the balance of physical and metaphysical love figured by Theseus's chain. In the Knight's tale, Theseus exposes the image of the chain as a cosmic model for man to emulate in his social and political order, and in *Troilus,* Antigone sings a Trojan song of the powers of love to move man to "flemen alle manere vice and synne" (2, 827–75). Curiously, she attributes the song to "the goodliest mayde / Of gret estat in al the town of Troye" (2, 880–81). Who that is and how a virgin can validate the perfect surety of love are questions Criseyde sees no point in asking, but she might have wondered what virgin could pronounce such an ideal vision of love's good.[10] Nonetheless, for all the blame Criseyde incurs later for her sliding love, her language, in the privacy of her mind or openly before an audience, is careful and moderate, and seems an accurate measure of her feelings. When she sees Troilus riding back from battle against the Greeks, her heart sinks, and in the privacy of her thoughts she wonders, "Who yaf me drynke?" (2, 651). Later, in bed with her knight, she stems the inordinate flow of his words with the speech of quiet control: "Welcome, my knight, my pees, my suffisaunce!"(3, 1309). In neither instance, private or public, does Criseyde consciously belie thought by word. Her care of expression in serious moments reflects her cautious attitude toward love itself. She knows how to express her feelings of love as a social and physical bond, but she disdains from speculating about love as a cosmic bond. Troilus, on the other hand, fails tragically in his language to distinguish between his inner particular feeling of love and the general authority of love's public and universal force. Because of this failure, he makes a tragicomedy out of his attempts to adjust his thought and feeling through the slide of time for either private or public profit. Troilus loves synchronically. His language of love marks his limitations, but it seems as well to be the major cause of limitation.

In *Troilus,* three male voices—the narrator's, Pandarus's and Troilus's—collaborate in a quest for a love which promises neither public nor universal good. The narrator's own posture toward love wavers between Pandarus's game and Troilus's earnest.[11] He breaks into his account of Troilus's sighting of Criseyde at the Temple of Pallas to explain his hero's sudden passion by comparing him with the lead horse of a train who must bear the sting of the coachman's whip should he skip aside to spare his aching hoof the rough stone: "Yet am I but an hors, and horses lawe / I moot endure, and with my feres drawe" (1, 223–24). The analogy compares the gift of nature, which our wills cannot alter, with a social act which our wills, but not a horse's, are free to shape.[12] The law of the horse is the law the coachman has inflicted upon him, but it is no more a horse's "nature" to pull a carriage than a man's to whip a horse. It is, on the other hand, both man's and horse's nature to love, to be attached, if you will, to love's train. As the narrator explains: "That Love is he that alle thing may bynde, / For may no man fordon the lawe of kynde" (1, 237–38).

From a Christian perspective, the law of kind is the law of the first age before the Old Law of Moses was established. According to Saint Paul, this period was an age of death.[13] D. W. Robertson, Jr., refers to it as an age of dull bestiality deaf to both truth and wisdom.[14] From a pagan mythological perspective, the law of kind is the nature of the Golden Age. In the *Book of the Duchess,* Chaucer recalls the pristine ideal of love in the Golden Age "while men loved the lawe of kinde" (l. 56). So it would seem that the narrator is saying that Troilus falls in love with Criseyde because he has reached that point in his life where his feelings have ripened into sexuality. "One must love" is a natural law which acts upon all living things.

This engagement in love, Aristotle explains in *Physics* 2, 1 (192b) is a natural impulse to reproduce one's kind. The impulse is illustrated with comic gusto in the Reeve's tale when the clerks' horse, let loose by the scheming miller, leaves his assigned place to run to the field and frolic with a troop of mares (1, 4064–65). So the law of kind is "love" of kind, the natural emanation of cosmic love on the First Mover's fair chain. Chaucer coordinates cosmic with natural love in the *prohemium* to Book 3 of *Troilus,* where Venus is praised both as the force which moves Jove to ordain all things for love and as the force which incites Jove's love for mortals (3, 15–18). The love figured by Venus holds things in their place in the universe (l. 29), knows all hidden forms of things (l. 31) and sets universal law for man (1.36). This is the Celestial Venus of the mythographers, distinct from the Venus of private and cupidinous love.[15] The narrator of *Troilus,* in the manneristic rhetoric of courtly address, seems to have blurred the distinction between the two, but also between Venus as an abstraction and as a cosmic force. Does Love the god, or love the emotion, bind all things, or both?[16] Either the sensation or the god, or both, makes people worthier and should not be denied (1, 251–52), but none can deny the law of kind that operates on man's body (1, 253–56). In short, the narrator's "Love" is at least three things: nature, a god, and a dart of feeling.[17]

The narrator confuses further the philosophical conception of Venus's bond of love in the opening lines of book 3:

> O blisful light of which the bemes clere
> Adorneth al the thridde heven faire
>
> .   .   .   .   .   .   .   .   .   .
>
> In hevene and helle and salte see
> Is felt thi myght
>
> (3, 1–2, 8–9)

Why, one wonders with patristic spiritual geography in mind, should love's light shine in hell where the bond of love does not extend? In his description of Criseyde however, the narrator indicates that her form, like the form of the daisy of the *Legend,* links a sight of motion with an insight into virtue:

> And ek the pure wise of hire mevynge
> Shewed wel that men myght in hire gesse
> Honour, estat, and wommanly noblesse.

(1, 285–87)

Troilus reads in her sidewise glance a text of reproach (1, 289–92), but her direct look at him kindles desire and affection (1, 295–98).[18] The streams of her eyes, the poet reminds us, are bonds of the god Love (1, 304–5), but we are not sure that Troilus knows this. Later, in the solitary privacy of his room and thoughts, after searching his feelings in a *Canticus* adapted from Petrarch's "S'amor non è," he wonders whether Criseyde is a goddess or a woman.

The poet-narrator confuses the epistemology of love, and so the meanings of his words slide from man's original God-given gift of referentiality.[19] Pandarus has a clear purpose behind his willful adding to Troilus's own confusion, when he instructs his friend:

> Was nevere man or womman yet bigete
> That was unapt to suffren loves hete
> Celestial, or elles love of kynde.[20]

(1, 977–79)

What looks here like an ingenuous distinction between two kinds of love is really two ways of loving: to adore a woman with devotional detachment or to pursue her as a sexual partner. Pandarus is working toward the latter, of course, and he confirms his intent when he refers to his niece's beauty as an inducement for physical intimacy:

> And for to speke of hire in specyal,
> Hire beute to bithynken and hire youthe,
> It sit naught to ben celestial
> As yet, though that hire liste bothe and kowthe.

(1, 981–84)

Whether celestial or of kind, Pandarus's own conception of love does not include the "honest" love of marriage which produces the good of children.

If not celestial, the love Pandarus recommends has its worthy place:

> . . . for noht but good it is
> To loven wel, and in a worthy place;
> The oghte not to clepe it hap, but grace.

(1, 894–96)

The peculiar sense of *grace* here—neither a woman's gift of her attention to a courtly suit nor God's free gift of his own being, but rather a social favor—draws attention to love as a game of amorous pursuit in which the greater reward lies in the nobler prey. For Pandarus, the hunt of courtship is more important than the value of the catch. At any rate, the worthy place is not celestial but carnal. Furthermore, the question touches not only the worthy place for one's love, but its appropriate time and occasion. Would Criseyde be open to Troilus's suit if she were not concerned with her social security after the desertion of her father?

Pandarus's conception of love in Troy is largely a function of circumstance and casual profit. It is his certainty of what love is that incites the energetic mediation for an amorous conjunction of Criseyde with Troilus, who is in dreadful doubt of love's provenance and constitution. Troilus is led to forfeit his private sense of honor by complying with the lie that serves as occasion for the dinner at Deiphebus's house. That accomplished, and the goal of his amorous yearnings within his sight, Troilus listens while Pandarus sits on his bed and reads gravely his own mediation:

> . . . for the am I bicomen
> Bitwixen game and ernest, swich a meene
> As maken wommen unto men to comen;
> Al sey I noughte, thow wost wel what I meene.
>
> (3, 253–56)

He knows where he stands, but holds Troilus in a tantalizing state of bewilderment.

In the private game of *fin' amor* between Troilus and Criseyde, Pandarus is jesting mediator, but the situation is perilous. It is not so much that he worries about exposure of his role as a go-between, but the love affair endangers public security. After all, Criseyde is a hostage in Troy, albeit privately protected by Hector. As the consummation of Troilus's love draws close, the private game is in danger of becoming public earnest. Pandarus's paratactical alignment of women with jest and men with earnest fits what he makes of their sexual roles. While Pandarus plays jesting games in his amorous commerce with a Criseyde who recognizes that the game of love can serve her public surety, Troilus's frantic earnestness increasingly blinds him to the ordinary conventions of society—like marriage—that are ordained for love as a service to social order. In the first full flush of affection, this is understandable; in the continued course of love it is inexcusable.

From beginning to end, the poem traces Troilus's career in love. How much he learns of love before he dies is hard to calculate. If his words are any evidence in the case, he learns little either of the love that is in himself or of the form of womanhood he extols through the exterior of Criseyde's figure and speech. Nothing reveals his ignorance of self and Criseyde better than the comic pathos of his speaking love just before and after its consummation. On the blissful night when Pandarus comes to the patient Troilus waiting in cramped quarters to say the way is clear to Criseyde, the hero pauses to call upon Venus. His apostrophe, using the familiar pronominal form of address (3, 705 et passim), is as inappropriate in its language as is its location of performance in a *stuwe,* or privy (3, 601).

First, he solicits Venus's grace with a reminder that the goddess was in an unfortunate position in the sky at the time of his birth and asks her to intervene with Jupiter to turn that astronomical mishap into good.[21] The confusion of the deity with the planet is a medieval commonplace, but it is, at the least, indelicate to invoke Venus's help "for love of hym [Adonis] thow lovedest in the shaw" (3, 720), an incident which displeased Jupiter's sister-in-law Proserpine. Troilus then calls upon each of the god-planets in order to lend him favor. He evokes Jove first, "for the love of faire Europe," (3, 722) and Mars "for love of Ciprus" (3, 725), an undiplomatic allusion to Venus's own adulterous affair.[22] Then he evokes Phebus, for the love of Daphne, who fled unwanted affection (3, 726–28), Mercury "for the love of Hierse" (3, 729), and Diana (731), though she is the chaste goddess who loves none. He concludes with a call to the fatal sisters to help his work, acknowledging, however, that his destiny has been spun already (3, 733–35).

This is tragicomic waste, if only because it retards a urgent move to Criseyde's bed. More tellingly, it brings to his anticipation of felicity of love detrimental and negative cosmic associations. The gods are unlikely to propitiate Troilus's love by reminders of their unfortunate amorous exploits. Troilus's speech does link cosmic powers with earthly objects, but the associations hardly elevate his earthly affection to cosmic dimensions; they rather color his own desire with rape and adultery.[23] Furthermore, to invoke all the planetary gods except the one whose powers are essential to his pursuit, Saturn-Chronos, undermines Troilus's subsequent desire to extend the moment of love into a timeless present.

The retarding waste of words continues in the fruitless exchange concerning Troilus's supposed jealousy, but it is in response to Pandarus's demand to set Troilus's heart at ease that Criseyde reveals best her own frustration with Troilus's words. While Pandarus settles down by the fire with an old romance, she complains about Troilus's immoderate posture in love:

> . . . for which youre passioun
> I wol nought calle it but illusioun

of haboundaunce of love and besy cure,
That doth youre herte this disese endure.

(3, 1040–43)

This "besy cure" with words continues when he holds Criseyde in his arms for the first time. Pausing in his "good thrift," he speaks to the heaven of her body (3, 1247–51), which should be a path but not the goal of grace, and exclaims:

> ... O Love, O Charite!
> Thi moder ek, Citherea the swete,[24]
> After thiself next heried be she—
> Venus mene I the wel-nilly planete!—
> And next that Imeneus, I the grete,
> For nevere man was to yow goddes holde
> As I, which ye han brought fro cares colde.
> Benigne Love, thow holy bond of thynges.

(3, 1254–61)[25]

After some forty further lines of the same sort of stuff, Criseyde breaks in impatiently to say, "it suffiseth, this that seyd is heere," and then lightens his weighty prologue to love with a curt and succinct invitation to put aside words for love and turn to love's deeds: "Welcome, my knight," (3, 1309).[26] It is perhaps a dilatory complaint that Troilus gives credit to Venus which belongs to Criseyde, but Troilus's speaking to excess and confusion foreshadows his waste of words later when Criseyde is rendered to the Greeks. For one thing, the love that is called Charity, whose mother is Cithera (the Morning-Star, or Venus), is Cupid/Eros, who should not have priority over his mother Venus, who is a more appropriate figure of the charity and love which Boethius cites as coordinate attractions to generation (*Cons.* 3, pr. 11, 170–78). The epithet "welnilly planete" identifies Cithera and Venus as the *Fortuna Minor* of the astronomers whose influence is activated in human affairs by its movement through certain positions in the sky. The praise of Hymen which follows seems premature in accompanying an embrace of nuptial delight outside of marriage, and it sounds inappropriate to the embrace of a woman whose nonvirginal status is known to her lover.[27]

Troilus's claim that he is *holde* [more loyal] than any other man to these powers may be excused by the intensity of his punctual passion, but his devotional posture in more sober moments is before the altar of Apollo, where he prays with more regard to his public status for knowledge of the future progress of the war (3, 540–46).[28] The epithets "benigne Love" and "holy bond of thynges" identify Love (or Cupid), whereas Venus is identified elsewhere with Theseus's fair chain of love. These

epithets foreshadow Chaucer's own invocation to Christ's love at the very
end of the poem, "for love of mayde and moder thyn benygne" (5, 1869).

Troilus's next words continue the reference to Cupid, "Whoso wol
grace, and list the nought honouren, / Lo, his desir wol fle withouten
wynges"(3, 1262–63). This is a translatation of Dante's praise of the
Virgin Mary as man's mediatrix for salvation: "che qual vuol grazia e a
te non ricorre / sua disïanza vuol sanz' ali" (Par. 33, 14–15). Troilus's
typological alignment, however, seems askew. Mary is the mother of the
God of charitable love; Cupid is the son of the goddess who is more
commonly associated with cupidinous love. All this muddle contains a
confused conception of the coordinate pulls of mind and body, and the
hero's inordinate flow of trite courtly terms fails to speak for the specificity of his own love. If the words are not made his *own* in performance,
but remain conventional cliches, they cannot very well make Criseyde
his own.This language is not *his* artifice, but merely *an* artifice. Where
Diomede's words later work individual purpose in brief time, Troilus's
words are, in short, a waste of time.[29] After his ascent to the eighth (or
seventh) sphere where he sees and hears the harmony of the heavens, he
does not speak, but only laughs at his past error of lust (5, 1821–25).

In appreciating the spice that words lend desire in the banquet of love,
one might excuse Troilus for an excessive flow of words which both
retards and interrupts participation in its dessert.[30] He may even be excused
for the stock *aubade,* which curses the day and faults the sun, figured by
Apollo (3, 1450, 1464), whose votary he is; for the desire to hold still
an instant of ecstasy flatters the woman he holds in his arms. It is harder,
however, to excuse his enthusiastic flattery of Pandarus by attributing to
an agency for sexual delight the same powers as Charity: "Thou hast in
hevene ybroughte my soule at reste" (3, 1599). Even Pandarus shrinks
from the implications of this reading of his game as a means of achieving
a harmony of worldly and sexual love in a stable spiritual perfection. To
lighten his own responsibility in leading Troilus so far, he warns him of
the great sorrow which is liable to follow great bliss in the process of
time (3, 1625–28).

For a while Troilus disdains the vagary of time known as Fortune, and
his love moves smoothly across a plateau of happiness, "in suffisaunce,
in bliss, and in singynge" (3, 1716). Sometime during this period, holding
Pandarus's hand, Troilus utters his most expansive and philosophical
exposition of love, one which rivals Theseus's exposition of the chain of
love both in its lyric intensity and diverse imagery:

> Love, that of erthe and se hath governance,
> Love, that his hestes hath in hevene hye,
> Love, that with an holsom alliaunce

Halt peples joyned, as hym lest hem gye,
Love, that knetteth lawe of compaignie

· · · · · · · · · · ·

So wolde God, that auctour is of kynde,
That with his bond Love of his vertu liste
To cerclen hertes alle and faste bynde,
That from his bond no wight the wey out wiste.
(3, 1744–48, 1765–68)

While it would seem that Troilus is expressing here something of his new-found quality of being (3, 1654) after the consummation of love, I see no change at all. While his speech has almost all of Theseus's Platonic underpinings, the comment "al this doth Love, ay heried be his myghtes" (3, 1757) again confuses person with principle, since the pronominal *his* is both masculine and neuter. If love is a cosmic force that orders the material of creation, then the praise is fitting, and prepares us for Chaucer's final call to the God who is "uncircumscript, and al maist circumscrive" (5, 1965); but if Troilus is referring to a personification of sexual desire, then he is tragically wrong.[31]

Pandarus knows how to escape the bonds of such a love, and Criseyde slides out with regretful ease. Praising love's firm hold over the process of creation now, Troilus will rail against love's shift later. His insight is blinded by his affection and made impotent by the courtly language of his noble nurture. Sincere in feeling to a woman and faithful in devotion to an idea of love, Troilus fails to bring his language to a successful merging of the two. If he does not speak his feelings when he sees erratic stars and hears heavenly music after his death, it is not because he has no mortal mouth to sound (he laughs at the woe of those who mourn him), but because, even in his cosmic translation, he does not have words of truth at his disposal.

Troilus's is a tragedy shaped by word and time. In prefacing his reluctant account of a loss of love, the poet laments: "But al to litel, weylawey the whyle" (4, 1). "The whyle" (a faint echo of *wheel*) is under the governance of Saturn, whose rule includes the circumstances that account for Antenor's capture (4, 43–49).[32] One of those circumstances is simply the setting of the sun (4, 48–49), and the Troilus whose aubade who would hold still the sun from rising to turn his night of love to day, would have ten rises and settings of the sun pass quickly to hasten Criseyde's return. In this sense, Criseyde escapes both time and Troilus's arms when she escapes Troy. "Go, litel book," says Chaucer of the text in which he contains her (5, 1786), but Troilus, lacking the right word to either hold or release her, cannot say the same of the text he has made of his love.

The consolation of love which fails Troilus, one reader declares, is pronounced in the Knight's tale by Theseus.[33] While Troilus's attempt to realize a transcendental love is impeded by his nature, unripened by time, frustrated by his words, and unordered by his public enterprise, Theseus's verbal purchase on the universal chain of love is put to profitable public use with nary a nod to private spiritual interests. Theseus is time's darling, even when he seems to be as ignorant of its force as Troilus is. Theseus collaborates with time and love for political good. His First Mover speech brings all three into order. It is not the words alone of his First Mover speech which make it better than anything Troilus says; it is what he does with them. Before he brings Palamon and Emily together, the order he seeks in his governance of things is repeatedly subverted by incidents that escape his control. Although he is indefatigable in the exercise of arms and tongue to govern, the wild disorder of reason and affection in the rivalry between Palamon and Arcite threatens his rule.

Views of love in the Knight's tale come also from three masculine perspectives: the two aspirants for Emily's grace, Theseus, and the Knight-narrator of the tale. Palamon and Arcite are neophytes in love compared with the experienced Theseus, who has loved Helen, Ariadne, Phaedra, and Hippolyta. Though unexperienced in love, the knight-cousins know the language of *fin' amor*. When Emily's song in the garden strikes Palamon's ear as heavenly music out of the mouth of an angel (1, 1055), he wonders, as Troilus had, whether the stimulus to his senses be woman or goddess (1, 1101). The speculation sounds conventional rather than personal and spontaneous.

In his turn, Arcite looks, sees, and complains in the hackneyed terms of the courtly code that he will die unless he have her mercy and grace (1, 1120). Both seem to be "putting on" their affection, for one loves by being seen as well as seeing, and Emily seems untouched by their gazes. To Palamon's surprised reaction to his sworn-brother's words, Arcite drops his put-on mannerism to ridicule Palamon's: "Thyn is affecioun of hoolynesse, / And myn is love, as to a creature" (1, 1158–59). He then lowers his terms to mock both love celestial and of kind:

> Wostow nat wel the olde clerkes sawe,
> That "who shal yevere a lovere any lawe?"
> Love is a greater lawe, by my pan,
> Than may be yeve to any erthely man;
> And therfore positif lawe and swich decree
> Is broken al day fro love in ech degree.
> A man moot nedes love, maugree his heed;
> He may nat fleen it, thogh he sholde be deed,
> Al be she mayde, or wydwe, or elles wyf.

(1, 1163–71)

This is a far more pernicious view of the love of kind than anything Pandarus showed himself capable of. Arcite flouts both the social ordering of love and nature's procreative design. The rhyme scheme makes the rub of casuistry and cynicism grate all the more. *Heed* implicates both the reason in one's head and the care in one's heart, and its rhyme with *deed* frames an assertion that the need to love can be controlled neither by reason nor care nor even death! The list of objects subject to this ineluctable urgency of love is as shocking as Troilus's thoughtless offer of his own sister to Pandarus as reward for services rendered (3, 409–10). For Arcite, fornication, adultery, and deflowering of virgins are natural manifestations of love "as to a creature."

The old saying of clerks is common in texts from Augustine to Boethius but nowhere cited with such vehement scorn for sexual discipline.[34] The narrator-knight makes a comparable remark about love in an apostrophic aside on the fratricidal combat between Palamon and Arcite in the grove:

> O Cupide, out of alle charitee!
> O regne, that wolt no felawe have with thee!
> Ful sooth is seyd that love ne lorshipe
> Wol naught, his thankes, have no felaweshipe.
>
> (1, 1623–26)

Typical to his tautological style, he repeats the sense of the first couplet in the second, but the Knight at least keeps Cupid and charity at words' length here, and his use of *felawe* suggests pertinently the Northern English sense "law of goods," that is, equal share of property. The Knight errs, however, from the conventional uses to which the aphorism is put by old authorities. Chaucer would have known Ovid's *Ars amatoria* 3, 564: *amor et majestas non coniuerunt* [Love and majesty do not accord],[35] and he might have known of William of Malmesbury's citation of that maxim in a warning to rulers that personal lust has a bad influence on public rule.[36] It is certain that Chaucer knew Jean de Meun's description of the Golden Age, when kings knew how to keep *amors et seignorie* [love and lordship] at a distance (*RR*, 8451–54). Nevertheless, the negative particle which the Knight inserts between love and lordship makes all of a difference: "*Neither* love *nor* lordship will share its rule" is quite distinct from "Love does not convene with lordship." The Knight implies to the contrary that lovers, like kings, do not share dominion.[37]

When Theseus decides to go hunting on the same morning, he comes upon the two cousins fighting in a grove. His initial anger is mollified by the women in his hunting party, and he decides not to kill them. While tossing about in his mind for remedies for breach of order, he reflects on the folly of lovers which he experienced in his own youth:

> And yet hath love, maugree hir eyen two,
> Broght hem hyder bothe for to dye.
> Now looketh, is nat that an heigh folye?
> Who may been a fool, but if he love?

(1, 1796–99)

What Theseus means by "love" here is the feeling which disturbs reason for the time until man matures.

In setting a contest in the lists for Emily's hand, Theseus may suppose that one of the contenders will either be killed or return to exile in Thebes and so in any case resolve the disturbance. Theseus conceives of himself as the executor of destiny, of that which is to come to pass for his own good (1, 1841–42), but the change of rules concerning weapons which he announces later to protect life are of little avail. Arcite suffers a fatal accident at the very moment Emily fixes an affectionate eye upon him (1, 2680), and it is only on his death bed that he is able to speak to Emily, and then only to commend Palamon's virtues and to commit his own soul to Jupiter (1, 2786–92). For the funeral pyre, by tearing up forests and forcing their inhabitants to flee, making the ground "agast . . . of the light" (1, 2931), Theseus despoils the nature he later honors in his First Mover speech.[38]

It is curious that Theseus should argue an order of the universe as a bond of love after having destroyed its natural order. That Theseus should be so undone by Arcite's death, which eliminates the threat of a losing claimant for Emily's hand who might have borne a grudge and led an army against Athens, can be attributed to pride of word. He had intended to award Emily to the winner of a battle, but the winner's death obviates the gesture. Finally, with time as a balm for his wounded pride, and "by processe and by lengthe of certeyn yeres" (1, 2967), he seizes upon the occasion to strengthen his political power by giving Emily to Palamon.

In the tradition of old authority, Theseus puts philosophy to work for political order.[39] The summary conclusion of his First Mover exposition before the couple is that one should make a virtue of necessity (1, 3042), that is, profit by whatever happens. In this context it suggests that Arcite's death can be turned to a good.[40] Arcite, before he sees Emily for the first time, consoles Palamon with a comparable resignation to things: "We mooste endure it; this is the short and playn" (1, 1091). For Boethius, "necessity," like "fortune," is but another word for the "purveiaunce" man cannot comprehend (*Boece* 5, pr. 4, 66–72). Theseus uses the term for *what has happened,* and his pragmatic use of the aphorism flatters the deceased Arcite with the virtuous hap of dying while his fame is at its apogee. The virtue is also, of course, the political profit that can be made of his death.

The coda to his long argument is a surge of optimism whose terms turn back to the qualities of the chain of love:

> I rede that we make of sorwes two
> O parfit joye, lastynge everemo,
> And looketh now wher moost sorwe is herinne.
> Ther wol we first amenden and bigynne.

(1, 3071–74)

A new beginning out of the chaos of sorrow is a fine prospect, but the transformation of social and natural cycles of order and disorder into a perfect and eternal joy is well beyond Theseus's ordaining powers. Palamon and Emily submit tacitly to the marriage project without commenting on the philosophical idea it fulfills.

Critical opinion is varied on the political wisdom of Theseus's speech, with the scorners gaining on the praisers.[41] No one can ignore the overt political purpose of the speech which the text amply acknowledges (1, 2970–76 and 3076), but is the argument that marriage imitates God's cosmic order necessary to his urgency to fix a political alliance? Probably not, but Theseus would have his word, or ordinance, authorized by its reflection of divine ordinance. The uncertainty of that reflection, however, casts doubt on the surety of the bond he is forging with Palamon and Emily. One has the impression that he is repeating what he has heard without knowing what it really means.[42] While Theseus's exposition can be glossed—as I have done earlier—to reveal its exposition of the received science of Chaucer's day, his particular style unsettles them.

The one issue which continues to puzzle me the most in his exposition is the idea of time as the ordinance of Jupiter, Prince, and Mover. The phrase "certeyne dayes and duracioun" (1, 2996) looks at first sight like two equivalent ways of saying that human life has a biological limit, but the two may be quite distinct measures: the "dayes" of a person's life and the "duracioun" of the life accorded the human species. The added qualification that engendered things may abridge their days (by suicide or accident?) lowers the conception out of the context of a providential design into a banal truism that, while man can not live longer than the biology of his kind permits, he may fail to reach that limit. Theseus's disdain of authority for this point suggests that what he tells us we are expected to know already.

The insistence that only a fool does not know that every part, including the parts of *aetas,* derives from its whole, neatly avoids explaining the difference between the part and whole, that is, between God's eternal and his creature's transitory being. The appeal to the authority of one's senses—"this maystow understonde and seen at ye" (1, 3016)—further confuses what can be seen with what can be known. Does one see to understand, or understand to see? Perhaps it is the *potestas* behind the words rather than the sense in them that persuades.

The "thou" of "maystow," if pronominal number means anything here, gives Theseus's purpose away. Even if others are present—"hust was al the place"—his words are for the couple alone, and the "thou" points to Palamon, the only target of an argument for the marriage that is to be the phoenixlike virtue arising from the ash-necessity of Arcite's death. Emily needs no persuasion, having neither will nor voice to protest. The naming of Jupiter as the prince and cause of "alle thyng" (1, 3035–36) is also puzzling. Of course, Jupiter is a figure of the Creator for the medieval mythographers,[43] but he is not so in either the pagan mythology of Theseus's pre-Christian world or in the mythological system of the Knight's fictional world in which the pagan gods speak and act. Jupiter and Saturn are Olympian counterparts of Theseus and Egeus, and as Jupiter is given powers belonging properly to his father, Theseus's right to title and rule belong rightfully to his living father. Curiously, Theseus's reference to Jupiter is in many ways more Homeric than Platonic, in that the chain is a figure of imperial power rather than a bond of love holding diverse things together. It is Jupiter's power in the *Iliad,* not his love, which stills the strife between the other gods.

In effect, Jupiter is a poor choice as a figurative source of cosmic love in this particular context. In the mythology Chaucer knew well, his rule ends Saturn's Golden Age by ushering lechery into the world.[44] He is the most notorious of lover-gods, changing into bull and swan to exercize a lust for earthly women. Though stories of his sexual escapades are absent here, the character of Jupiter in the Knight's tale is far from a First Mover or a cause of all things. He is even incapable of settling the petty strife in heaven (1, 2438–42), accomplished by his father, Saturn, who has the art to please all parties, even if it is against his "kynde" (1, 2443–52).[45] In effect, the Knight's Saturn executes the providential design of the son Jupiter, whereas in the Neoplatonic Christian scheme the First Mover's chain belongs to the Son who executes the design of the Father. In fact, the Knight's Jupiter is but a name in the mouths of others, whereas Venus, Mars, Diana, and Saturn speak; and when Saturn speaks to Venus, he exposes a providential control over the process of things:

> I slow Sampsoun, shakynge the piler;
> And myne be the maladyes colde,
> The derke tresons, and the castes olde;
> My lookynge is the fader of pestilence.

> (1, 2466–69)

What Saturn controls are phenomenological events occurring in time ordained by Boethian *purveaunce.* For the exegetes, the death of Samson fulfills a scriptural prophecy which foreshadows the redemptive self-sacrifice of Christ. Saturn rather than Jupiter, then, is the appropriate Christian figure of God's ordaining power. It is not Jupiter who is both prince and cause, but Saturn who converts all according to his *welle,* "from which it is dirryved" (1, 3037–38).[46] It is Saturn-Chronos who controls the process and "lengthe of certeyne yeres" (1, 2967) who finally unites Palamon and Emily. It is Saturn who numbers the "certeyne dayes" of Arcite which end with the hero "siker of his goode name" (1, 3048). Finally, it is Saturn who adjudicates the outcome of the trial in the "noble theatre" of the world (1, 1885).[47] The infernal fury of Pluto sent at Saturn's request (1, 2685–85) is death: "I slow Arcite, foundrynge his hors" is an understood anaphoric extension of the exposition of his force. Theseus acknowledges it unwittingly when Palamon is captured in the lists: "Arcite of Thebes shal have Emilie, / That by his fortune hath hire faire ywonne" (1, 2658–59). Fortune, remember, is the word for providential time in the mouth of those who can not see through events to their order and governance in the process of all things.

In brief, Theseus's attribution of the "faire cheyne of love" to Jupiter accords with Platonic *allegoresis,* but not with the world of the Knight's fiction. Though the flow of the plot suggests that Theseus might be moving from scorn of foolish love toward praise of divine love, his claim that Jupiter's cosmic design may be seen by the eye arouses our suspicion that any appeal to the world of ideas is but a means of securing political order.

Perhaps it is asking too much of Theseus to have him sincerely concerned with a chain of love binding punctual politics with the providence of divine thought. After all, Theseus's plans for the things of this world depend upon an authority for order, and Jupiter, rather than Saturn, is that figure. Theseus has no stake in the philosophical implications of the chain of love, but only in the order they can help him impose. If there is any lesson to be learned from the unfortunate death of Arcite, it is not that life reflects a body of ideas, but that ideas can be rearranged to fit the circumstances of life. There is something of the nominalist cynic in Theseus.

Both *Troilus* and the Knight's tale repeat the threefold process of amatory possession—visual, verbal, and physical—which characterize the stories in the *Legend of Good Women.* Speaking love fills time between seeing and consummating love. The Parson explains lechery later as a process in time, beginning with the eye seeing and ending with *factum,* in which the mouth speaking love is the median activity after seeing and hearing, and before touching and the "stinking deed" (*CT* 10, 852ff).[48]

In *Troilus,* Pandarus moves the word through time and space to deed, and Theseus does the same for Palamon in the Knight's tale.

Speaking love serves both the body's and the soul's quest for grace. Man's word reflects God's *logos,* the latter giving life and the former destroying it. The Parson reminds his listeners that the confession which conjoins contrition to satisfaction requires speech. Only the mute can confess without oral utterance. *Ex verbis enim tuis iustificaberis et ex verbis tuis condemnaberis* [By your words you will be acquitted and by your words condemned] says the evangile (Matthew 12, 37). Troilus wins Criseyde with privy words, not all his own and not all out of his own mouth. He is trapped in the language of the code of love and to leave it would be to lose the devout feeling it expresses. Neither Pandarus nor Diomede *need* the code, and neither love as Troilus does. Troilus loses Criseyde because of the public force of Calkas's words to the Greeks in concert with the force of Diomede's privy words. Troilus fails, perhaps, because he cannot put language to public purpose no matter how sincere and elevated his idea of love.[49] Theseus succeeds in the short run, no matter how devious his thought, for he knows how to use words to hide disorder. "Philosophy," goes an old adage, "is a retrospective rationalization of failure."

In the world of the *Legend,* Theseus wins Ariadne's body with words. In the Knight's and Chaucer's worlds, man's words cannot by themselves win grace, but can only plead for the grace which is the free gift of another. So Chaucer sends forth his little tragedy to mediate between himself and God (*Tr.* 5, 1786–87). Man's word is like Adam's limp hand in Michelangelo's Sistine Chapel creation mural, stretched out toward God's vivifying finger. The gap between them is bridged only by the spark, the poet's *scintilla,* of God's love. Alcuin reminds his audience that Christ is *unica lingua Dei* [the unique tongue of God][50] and, for Dante, the word reflects Christ whose referentiality as coin is validated by the Moneyer.[51]

At the beginning of *De vulgari eloquentia* Dante calls Christ *Verbo aspirante de caelis* [the breathed word of heaven]. So man's word rehearses God's *logos* as much as the sweet breath of Zephirus rehearses in annual succession God's inspiring spirit. The word encloses time, and the Knight's Saturn contains the events he speaks. As mediators between man and God's fair chain of love, human speech and writing move man toward his designated place in both the vertical and horizontal space of creation. Man cannot rewin his original place by his own efforts, but he can, by trying to regain it, solicit a grace God has already foreseen.[52]

Theseus is a tyrant, and although pity runs in his gentle heart, he demands respect rather than affection. He is firm on the question of order but weak on the question of humanity. Were he concerned with the courtliness of love he would, I should think, ask Emily just once what is in *her* heart.[53] Pandarus and Troilus are less successful than Theseus in achieving goals because they direct their words to private rather than public good. Troilus's words waste time and love, and when he loses his temporal and spatial proximity to Criseyde, the quality of his love plummets from the heights of *amore d'animo* down past *amore naturale* to the hate his last frantic madness in pursuit of vengeance exercises.[54] "Lo here, thise wrecched worldes appetites!" says the narrator of the tale, having directed his book upward to the Maker to mediate his own soul's sake. Ironically, though Troilus conceives of his love for Criseyde as an exercizing of his participation in the cosmos, he cannot hold to the idea and let the body which mediates it go free. Though love should join him to eternal bliss, he is held to the ravages of time.

# 5

## Economies of Word as Bonds of Love: Dorigen and Grisilde

It is indeed a base, ugly and contaminated wit that is constantly and curiously obsessed with the beauty of a female body.

—Giordano Bruno

The work of art is an interplay of vision and thought. The individuality of particular existence and the generality of types are united in one image. Percept and concept, animating and enlightening each other, are revealed as two aspects of one and the same experience.

—Rudolph Arnheim

AT THE HEIGHT OF HIS ACHIEVEMENT OF LOVE, TROILUS HAD EXULTED love as the power that holds all nature in its proper place:

> That the se, that gredy is to flowen
> Constreyneth to a certeyn ende so
> His flodes that so fiersly they ne growen
> To drenchen erthe and al for evere mo;
> And yf Love ought lat his bridel go,
> Al that now loveth asondre sholde lepe.
> And lost were al that love halt now to-hepe.

(3, 1758–64)

His images of the bridle and leaping love, however, not only diminish the *idea* of love by placing it under the horse's law of emergent sexuality (1, 223), but they foreshadow his own surrender of Criseyde's bridle to Diomede, who knows very well the difference between horse's law and the linguistic artifice which commands it. Troilus's pronouncement on love's service to man (and it is difficult to read his "al that now loveth" in this context as an allusion to *all* animate things) denies the providential force of *love* which includes precisely the letting loose of Noah's flood.

The source of Troilus's image is the untutored Boethius's doubt concerning man's place in the ordained harmony of creation in *Boece* 1, m. 5, 33–35, "O thow governour, governinge alle thinges by certeyn ende, whi refusetow oonly to governe the werkes of men by duwe manere?" and his concluding appeal to God to slake the tempests of nature, *Rapidos rector comprime fluctus* (*Cons.* 1, m. 5, 46), which is translated by Chaucer into a figure of fortune: "O thow, whatsoever thow be that knyttest alle bonde of thynges, looke on thise wrecchede erthes! We men that ben nat a fowle partye but a fayre partye of so grete werk, we ben tormented in this see of fortune. Thow governour, withdraweth and restreyne the ravessinge floodes, and fastne and ferme thise erthes stable with thilke bonde by whiche thow governest the hevene that is so large." Wondering at this stage in his instruction if God's bond descends through *all* natural things, Boethius recognizes, at least, that it is not only a bridle of senses. The rest of *De Consolatione* is devoted to Philosophy's exposition of all those other things which the bond is.

The pagan Theseus knew the Boethian model, and his confident "understonde and seen at ye" challenges Palamon to read all created things as "cantles" of the universal chain of love. The Christian Dorigen in the Franklin's tale, however, looks out at the sea off Brittany's Côte Sauvage and reads the jagged black rocks as signs of those same loosed constraints to which Troilus refers. Echoing Boethius, Troilus, and Theseus, she complains to their Maker:

> Eterne God, that thurgh thy purveiaunce
> Ledest the world by certein governaunce,
> In ydel, as men seyn, ye no thyng make.
> But, Lord, thise grisly feendly rokkes blake,
> That semen rather a foul confusion
> Of werk than any fair creacion
> Of swich a parfit wys God and a stable,
> Why han ye wroght this werk unresonable?
> For by this werk, south, north, ne west, ne eest,
> Ther nys yfostred man, ne bryd ne beest;
> It dooth no good, to my wit, but anoyeth.
> Se ye nat, Lord, how mankynde it destroyeth?
>
> . . . . . . . . . . . . . . . .
>
> Which mankynde is so fair part of thy werk
> That thou it madest lyk to thyn owene merk.
> Thanne semed it ye hadde a greet chiertee
> Toward mankynde; but how thanne may it bee
> That ye swich meenes do no good, but evere anoyen?
>
> (5, 865–84)

Then, lamenting the rocks as impediments to her husband's safe return from abroad, she concludes with a call for redress: "But wolde God that alle thise rokkes blake / Were sonken into helle for his sake" (5, 891–92).

Unlike Boethius, Dorigen has no teacher at hand to explain God's providential design, and so she holds perversely to blaming God for having untied the knot of "greet chiertee" with which he bound creation.[1] Denying God's purveyance is blasphemy, and Dorigen has been credited with being the first to so impugn God's good in Western literature.[2] Boethius is taught that God did not create evil, though he created man capable of seeing it, for evil is but an illusion caused by an imperfect accord between sight and insight.[3]

Dorigen's friends take note of her despair, and on the sixth of May (the Feast of Saint Prudence) they bring her into a garden so craftily made by man's hand that to sight and smell it seems second only to the true Paradise (5, 906–12). The redressing of God's nature by human art is but one tip of the tale's ontological teeter of word and wit. Imitating God's architectural design is often a satanic enterprise, and the garden, though it is a redress of the disorganization of creation evident in the rocks, can only *appear* to be paradisiacal. All these understandings "at ye" recall Theseus's exposition of the fair chain. The rocks which merit hell and the garden which mirrors heaven are readings of nature and art mediated by uninstructed sight. Whereas Theseus in the Knight's tale imposed his own view of love upon the course of events, first Dorigen and Arveragus, then Dorigen and God, and later Dorigen and Aurelius, funtion as joint foci in a series of elliptical circumscriptions of love in the Franklin's tale.

The first act of shared centricity in the tale involves the first of a series of riddles: how to balance a husband's surrender of private will with his wife's promise of humility and obedience (5, 745–51). In effect, Arveragus renders to his wife a natural superiority of reason in exchange for a public deference to his superior gifts of nature and fortune—sex, rank, and marital title—and so seeks to join a courtly lover's deference to a husband's mastery, a natural to a social ordinance.[4] In return, Dorigen offers wifely humility and truth (5, 758). Where Theseus's concern was public array, and Troilus's was private affection, Arveragus and Dorigen aim at the best of both in a balance of public and private, or visible and invisible forms of love. Their story records the swings of that balance.

The teller of the tale applauds this contractual artifice with an aphorism closer to the Wife of Bath's husbandry than to Theseus's philosophy:

> Love is a thyng as any spirit free.
> Wommen, of kynde, desiren libertee,
> And nat to ben constreyned as a thral.

> (5, 767–69)

*Free* means "unrestrained" in this context, though it carries etymological suggestions of "love," "nobility," and "generosity" with it. The demeaning qualification that women "of kynde" desire liberty lowers them to the level of the Manciple's cat, who stalks mice despite his master's care, so much "appetit fleemeth discrecioun" (9, 175–82). The Franklin's praise, unwittingly or no, confuses the honor of a courtly vow with a quality of horse's law reminiscent of Arcite's unbridled lust (1, 1165–68). In effect, there is neither order of mastery nor bond of love to hold the union of Dorigen and Arveragus in place.

Their vows are wistful words of intent, and like Theseus's grand exposition of the cosmos, the proof is in the profit. The first element to slide from their loose knot of love is Arveragus himself, who quits Dorigen's side to enhance his honor in foreign service. We are not told if his call to a public exercise of his degree suits her will, but Dorigen is left alone regretting her husband's absence. Her consoling pillars of ease— patience in love and self-governance (5, 771–90)—are insufficient to protect her from a dark fantasy (5, 844). Leaving the privacy of her chamber to look at the black rocks which jutt up from the sea, she impugns the principle of plenitude which asserts that everything in the world has its proper place.[5] It would seem that she would have her words, quoted above, expunge her fantasy, but the words provide her with no window to God's providence, and so the good she cannot see in God's design she attributes to his blindness (5, 876). In effect, the rocks that figure her despair are spoken out of herself and unto God. Though she disavows God's creative *logos* manifest in the rocks and all created things, she implores God to reorder nature. Her almost obsessive yearning for collaboration with God displaces for a time her thoughts of collaboration with Arveragus in her marital contract. Nonetheless, what Dorigen seems to see is a nature that denies God's love for the creatures in it, and, if her words cannot alter the landscape, they work like a charm on herself. Having packed her dark thoughts into words, she seems to be rid of them. Her mood brightens and she quits her private despair for public pleasure in play with friends in the beautiful garden of fair forms, colors, and odors. The manmade *locus amoris* is a refuge from God's disorder where she frolics and lets her sorrow slide (5, 924).

It is in the garden that she meets Aurelius, the best singer and dancer "sith that the world bigan" (5, 930–31). He is a wise and virtuous servant of Venus who has loved Dorigen for over two years before he declares his love to her in the modest and humble language of the courtly code, concluding with the conventional request: "Have mercy sweete, or ye wol do me deye!" (5, 978).[6] Whatever the intent crouching behind these fumbling but apparently sincere words, Dorigen takes the request as an invitation to adultery, and she replies without an instant's delay with a

verbal parry out of measure with Aurelius's modest and conventional
thrust, but one which asserts her continuing faith in the bond of love:

> "Is this youre wyl," quod she, "and seye ye thus?
> Nevere erst," quod she, "ne wiste I what ye mente,
> But now, Aurelie, I knowe youre entente,
> By thilke God that yaf me soule and lyf,
> Ne shal I nevere been untrewe wyf
> in word ne werk, as fer as I have wit.
> I wol been his to whom that I am knyt."
>
> (5, 979–86)

Just as she had read the rocks, she reads her own fear and perhaps
something of her desire in Aurelius's words, though we cannot be sure
she reads the intent in them. It is rather as if the mention of her husband's
absence in the mouth of her suitor (5, 969–70) disturbs her much as the
rocks had. In a sort of Freudian concatenation of association, she judges
his intent with the same carelessness with which she had impugned God's.
Now, as well as the black rocks, Aurelius is a threat to her patience and
self-governance. Her hasty oath on the God whose creation she had earlier
doubted is but a figure of speech, but it intensifies her carelessness of
language to the point where her own intent is put in doubt. Not only is
her word *untrewe,* but she agrees to an infidelity of *werk* by vowing to
be Aurelius's love "by heighe God above" if he makes the coast so clean
that no rocks will be seen (5, 989–98). She reads an intent never expressed
and offers a reward never solicited: "Thanne wol I love yow best of any
man; / Have heer my trouthe, in al that everre I kan" (5, 997–98). The
contract to render her love to him who removes the phalliclike rocks is
not really a "rash promise," as many critics would have it, for her oaths
which authenticate it lend the contract an awful seriousness. In terms of
current speech-act theory, she has no power over the meaning her words
obtain in context. They are empty of her intended referential value. So
are Theseus's, one might argue, but Dorigen, if only because she is a
woman, has no control over the awful social power words can provide.

The words have almost magical effect in shaping a cosmos of desire
for two inhabitants. First of all, regardless of the condition under which
she proffers her body, her words commit her solemnly to *love* Aurelius
best of any man, should he remove the sight of the rocks. Secondly, they
bind her love to a natural, or preternatural, occurrence. Finally, in offering
her love as a reward for a task she deems impossible, she incites a desire
in Aurelius to achieve it. This is a cruel tease, but the words have a force
independent of their intent and meaning, a force somehow connected
with the hidden form of her own desire. In other words, Dorigen's language
drifts far from the bond of referentiality into a paradigmatic dimension.

It is not the referential content of Aurelius's plea, but an associational meaning that Dorigen assumes is a sexual intent not spoken, and in turn she offers in return a sexual deed which is clearly not intended.[7] Like her appeal to God's reason to remove his unreasonable work, nothing *real* is expected beyond the relief of having spoken it. Her promise to Aurelius is a riddle, inviting her suitor to act according to either what he *hears* her say or to what he *knows* she means. He chooses the former, though he understands right away that her challenge is a cruel refusal of grace, crueler than any courtly assignment of difficult tasks whose accomplishment would prove the suitor worthy of his lady's grace. The task she assigns is to all appearances impossible.[8]

Why should Aurelius strive to win a prize he knows is not sincerely offered? If the meaning of Dorigen's words depend not upon her intent but upon her audience's economy of understanding, then Aurelius can ignore the source and context of her discourse and respond to the words alone. That is, he can simply ignore the linguistic complicity between two people who share a common understanding of what words mean, and assume a referentiality in her words which she herself denies; but what can he gain by doing so? Dorigen's words have touched Aurelius not so much by their sense, independent of relevance, as by his own desires. Speaking the impossible makes it possible, and renders the task of achieving it irresistible. She may have sacrificed something of her power of word to save her husband, but her willingness to surrender her love (body?) to clear the sea for her husband's safe return cannot entirely salvage her intent, for she does not promise just to be Aurelius's love, but to love him "best" above other men. She has not only asked for the impossible, but promised a reward out of reason's control to deliver.

If the rocks had already disappeared from her mind once she had spoken them to God, how did she retrieve them to rid herself of them once more? It may be simply because Aurelius brought them back into her mind by mentioning her husband's absence (5, 969–71). The culprit is now Aurelius, and the issue is more complex, for not only her husband's safety is brought back to her attention, but with them a desire for the love she misses. In effect, Dorigen compensates for the loss of one love by speaking another. Speaking adultery saves her for the time being of doing it in *factum*.

Speaking idle love is dalliance, what the Parson identifies as the third finger of the devil's left hand (10. 855). In civil law, adultery is theft, the misappropriation of another's property. *Avowtrie,* Chaucer's Parson reminds his audience with a view of the word's etymology, is a breaking of faith (10, 874–76); and, Dorigen has sworn faith to Aurelius by High God. A woman may love a man best by loving God more, but never by loving another man. The phallic black rocks are removed as easily by

words as her temptation to love another man; and her words, no matter
how distant their sense is removed from her intent, seem to restore
Dorigen's peace of mind. We hear nothing further of her until Arveragus
returns and she finds herself once more in bliss (5, 1090).

Her role in the story becomes passive for a while after she speaks the
black rocks out of God's and her responsibility and into Aurelius's. She
had seen the rocks as impediments to her love; Aurelius now sees them
as impediments to his. The psychic shift is what Freudians call counter-
transference, the transformation of a subject from the one who announces
it to the one who receives it.[9] Aurelius is now trapped in the web of those
words, and he lies in bed for two years in languid torment (5, 1102–3)
before his brother brings him to the magician at Orleans.[10]

The Franklin explains at length that natural magic is illusion,[11] and we
see that illusion in words. Magic, illusion, and word are all names given
to mediations implicit in Theseus's chain of love, and indeed the Orleans
magician's art mediates Aurelius's desire. Mouth and hand are his tools
of trade, and the Franklin mentions that the source of magical skills is
books (5, 1205–14). Words can befuddle sight, but man's words, unlike
God's timeless *logos,* require time, and the magician awaits the right time
and tide to make it *seem* that the rocks are away, at least for a while (5,
1296). His magic consists of making a visible item in nature invisible,
and so reverses both God's creative process of reifying form in matter
and man's efforts to read through visible things to their invisible forms.

Ironically, time mocks Aurelius's effort, for Arveragus has already
returned from abroad when Aurelius goes to claim his due from Dorigen.
Neither the rocks nor absent love are problems for her now, but Aurelius,
though the husband's return has removed the original purpose of his
courtly suit, is still caught in the steel trap of her words. When he meets
Dorigen to claim his due, he rehearses her contractual terms accurately
(5, 1329), including the oath to God above, and then announces with
careful equivocation that "I woot the rokkes ben aweye" (5, 1338). *Witen*
suggests knowing by sight.[12] Though Dorigen had pleaded with God to
remove the rocks because they are an "unreasonable" work, now she
objects that this "merveille" is against the process of nature. Of course,
what she had set as Aurelius's task requires just such "merveille." In
effect, she apes God the principle, while Aurelius apes Christ the agent.

It is poetic justice of sorts that she is cozened by words, for he has
not claimed that the rocks *are* gone, but only that he *knows* them to be
away. Dorigen misses the nuance and responds to a supposition. She hears
and believes her ears, but does not go to confirm with her own eyes what
has happened. She turns homeward, "a sorweful creature" (5, 1346), and
indeed a *creature* Dorigen has become, for the moment, in the economy
of Aurelius's courtly word.[13] Caught in Fortune's fetter, as women are

prone to be (1, 2681–82), instead of being wafted aloft on love's chain (5, 1356), she contemplates suicide, a worse crime against God's process of nature than practicing magic. Alone in her house, she turns over in her mind stories of women who kill themselves rather than be "defouled with mannes foul delit" (5, 1396). Her examples are symptomatic of her problem in finding a verbal charm which can free her from dark thoughts of unreasonable worlds. No story she can think of fits her predicament. Of the women whose tragic stories she considers, several are virgins rather than wives. Others are wives who die with their husbands or avenge them. Unlike Lucrece, who kills herself to spare her husband's good name, Dorigen thinks only of her own name (5, 1361–62).

Her "allas that ever was I borne!" exclaimed to her husband when he returns home (5, 1463) is a careless blasphemy against God's providence, but Arveragus provides the words which restores order. First, he threatens to kill her if she makes her vow to Aurelius public; and in the middle of the threat, which itself is an assumption of sexual mastery, he shifts out of the formal and into the familiar second-person pronoun. Then he orders her to hold to her word, advising her that "trouthe is the hyeste thng that man may kepe" (5, 1479). Arveragus is referring, of course, to Dorigen's sworn word, but her word to Aurelius did not and does not mediate her true intent, while her sworn word to her husband to be true does (758). Hers is not a word of honor, but a story whose meaning pertains only to her own desperate and fantastic world.[14]

There is an underlying irony behind her lament and consultation with Arveragus, for while the Franklin abridges her confession to her husband by saying to his audience that she "toold hym al as ye han herd bifore," we are not sure what words she used, and not sure what Arveragus makes of them. What Aurelius had carefully reminded her is that she pledged to love him best of all, but Dorigen and Arveragus seem to assume that she has pledged her body. Were it within her power to direct her love, as Christian man has the power to love God best of all things, she could certainly love Aurelius "best" without committing adultery, though perhaps not in the Franklin's particular fictional world.

Arveragus sends her off under guard of a squire and a maid, but that protection is only symbolically appropriate, for while they may guard her body, they have no power over her word or her intent. When she meets Aurelius, she announces simply that she is there to hold her truth (5, 1513). This is enough, apparently, to shift the balance of words back in her favor. The complexity of the contractual bond increases with each verbal exchange. Now, what is Aureilus to understand of what her "truth" consists? She is not coming to announce that she loves him best, and Aurelius again knows that her words hide truth. He courteously responds to the gentilesse of Arveragus rather than to her words (5, 1527); and, having shifted his attention from *her* truth to her husband's, he is loosed from the obsession to possess her grace, as well as the body he never asked for.

In this world of wonderful words, Aurelius has won only what he has sought in the first place: words. He no longer wants the body they speak for, if he ever wanted it. The series of releases from bonds are a third riddling act in the tale: Which is more real, love or the words which express it? Aurelius does not fumble for words. He releases her from her debt with astonishing ease, but is left again with the debit of his own word of financial credit. The magician has it just as easy later to release Aurelius from a debt so openly acknowledged.

Words are the currency of the Franklin's illusory world. In the end, nothing really changes, for words cancel words' debts. The tale reduces God's creation and its formative *logos* to dalliance, and Dorigen's body, like all the verbal acts of the tale, is but a text that changes hands, if a bit too freely. In the end her body mediates the rote rehearsal of a code of gentility between three estates. Whereas Theseus in the Knight's tale had deployed his stock of words for a public good, the words of Arveragus, Dorigen, and Aurelius are exchanged for private ends. There is no indication that they bear profit. The end of the story brings us back to its beginning with Arveragus and Dorigen in a position to repeat their vows, but there is little evidence in the text that new words could mean more this time.

Dorigen's eye and mouth may not have served reason, but the confusion she caused turned a potential tragedy of spirit to a comedy of verbal commerce which kills time in a male-bonding sport of competing gentilesse. That in itself, however, has certain significance, for Dorigen's inconsiderate words are occasion for three men to move their own spirits higher on the chain of love. In this respect, the body of a woman has served as a *tertium quid* between man and his sexual, social, and spiritual goals. She figures the earthly matter of the cosmos, and man its aery form. In the oversimplistic ontology of popular thought, men write books in imitation of the *logos* while women bear children in imitation of nature. The sexual superiority that permits Arveragus to dictate conduct to Dorigen is natural to the principle of plenitude and to the practice of his social role. On the whole, men project visual, linguistic, and sexual energy, and women receive it. Man more easily lowers his nature to the sensuous mean of woman than woman raises hers to man's intellectual mean; but this is just and right, for God created the sexes complementary rather than distinct. In fact, it is a conventional notion that fallen man must solicit the mediation of woman in order to regain the fullness of being he lost in Eden. Boethius's Philosophy, Alain's Nature, and Dante's Beatrice mediate intellectual and spiritual knowledge. Christ mediates

universal redemption as a "maid."[15] Pandarus often plays a female role
with Troilus in the course of his sexual commerce, and while the Wife
of Bath usurps a man's role, the Clerk, whom the Host compares to a
"mayde ... newly spoused," replies to the wife by speaking from a
woman's point of view.

Man loves woman best when he loves the universal bond of love her
being figures and the holy spirit it encloses. It would then seem that
women should love men in return for loving the best in them. In the *Book
of the Duchess,* White rejects the Black Knight's suit with its promise
to be faithful and true (1243) but accepts it when he promises to honor
her name, the outer sign of her inner beauty (1259). Dido laments that
man needs three women: one for fame, another for friendship, and a third
for delight (*HF,* 301–10), but she omits the one who mothers his children.

Loving a woman is a means for man to honor his bond to his Maker,
for woman's body is a vessel of grace identifiable with Holy Church.
Protection of a woman's body mirrors the defence of Holy Church because
*Virgo Maria est ecclesia* [the Virgin Mary is Church],[16] and both the
body of the Church and the womb of the Virgin Mary are vehicles of
salvation. The bond between husband and wife which produces offspring
is *honesta copulatio,* and the childbearing bed is an image of the church
altar.[17] The womb that carries life attracts particular attention, then, for
Christ, borne in an obedient woman's womb, redeems the sin of Eve,
born of Adam, the first disobedient man. Only the womb of woman can
accomplish God's first charge to Adam and Eve in the Garden of Eden
to wax and multiply.[18] For this reason Bernard de Clairvaux praised
Mary's womb as the *hortus conclusus* [enclosed garden] of Canticles 4:
12; and woman's womb is reflected by the allegorical garden of the
*Roman de la rose.* The womb of the Virgin Mary is a *claustrum,* the
bond which holds together the *trinam machinam,* or threefold world. The
Second Nun reproduces this image in her prefatory praise of the Virgin:

> Withinne the cloistre blisful of thy sydis
> Took mannes shap the eterneel love and pees,
> That of the tryne compas lord and gyde is,
> Whom erthe and see and hevene out of relees
> Ay heryen. . . .
>
> (8, 43–47)

Mary is unfallen love and redeemed womanhood, and her womb's
acceptance of God's spirit is a model for all women. Chaucer praises the
Virgin's round of perfection in his "La priere de Nostre Dame" (or "An
ABC") as the intermediary for man's salvation. Each strophe is a link
in a chain of praise stretching from A to Z. The first strophe opens with

"Almyghty" and the close of the last—"able, Amen"—turns us back to the beginning. The middle strophes praise Mary's motherhood as "tresoreere of bounty to mankynde" (107) and as "vicaire and maistresse / Of al this world, and eek governouresse / Of hevene" (140–42).

Mary is a model for the Wife of Bath, who refers to her own womb as a "chambre of Venus" (3, 617), a term borrowed from Jean de Meun's La Vieille (*RR*, 13336). In his *Ars versificatoria*, 1, 57, Matthew of Vendôme calls the womb of Helen of Troy *Veneris delicios domus*.[19] The chamber of Venus dedicated to what the Wife calls "ese" (3, 127), rather than to physical and spiritual fruits, is the waste counterimage of Mary's womb and a dark reflection of love. An elegant example of it is the doubtfully impregnated womb of May in the Merchant's tale which Januarie strokes affectionately after he has seen it serve another's desire. May, the Wife of Bath, and La Vieille are "modern" women, whose forms of love Jean de Meun contrasts with the love practised in the Golden Age when

> Sanz rapine et sanz convoitise
> S'entrecoloient et baisoient
> Cil cui il geu d'amors plesoient.
>
> (*RR*, 8432–34

[Without rapine or greed, they would embrace and kiss, those who were pleased by love's game.][20]

Though woman's womb mediates Providence, it is the basest of human organs according to the Parson's scale of lechery (*CT* 10, 862). The wombs of Chaucer's Wife and Jean's La Vieille are not engaged in the *honesta copulatio* of the *mediatrix* mother, but rather with the lechery of the *meretrix* prostitute, whose sexual activity, like her cosmetics, counter nature.[21] The whore utters words of deceit, and her seductive song, like the music of the sirens, leads to man's destruction.[22] Boethius's Philosophy must banish the *scenicas meretriculas* [strompettis of the theater] from her ward's cell before she can instruct him (*Cons.* 1, pr. 1, 49–50). Peter Damian compares monks who care more for the rules of Donatus than for the Rule of Benedict with husbands who leave their chaste wives in the nuptial bed to visit prostitutes.[23] Prostitutes lure men downward from his proper place on the chain of love, whereas the conjugal good of *honesta copulatio* draws him upward.[24]

The womb of women mediates God's providence because the life it yields serves both the process of natural time and the progress of redemptive time. If the Wife of Bath's chamber of Venus serves her private desire, there is public profit in the children born to the Clerk's Grisilde. Her child-producing womb is central to the Clerk's tale because it is the means by which the private good of Walter and the public good of his people are brought into accord. At the beginning of the tale, Walter is shaken loose from his *otium,* or his slothful indulgence in the present without regard for the future (4, 78–80) by his people who implore him to marry:

> Boweth youre nekke under that blisful yok
> Of soverayntee, noght of servyse,
> Which that men clep spousaille or wedlok.
>
> (4, 113–15)

*Yoke* here figures the beneficial bond of marriage, but its bestial suggestions of a fetter of man's spirit to his flesh are inescapable (*Cons.* 2, pr. 1, 280; 2, m. 7, 570, et passim). Although "lok" derives from Old English *lac* [gift], in this context rhymed with *yok,* it suggests a moral "lock" which holds fast a *wed,* or pledge. The people simply wish to assure their own future with their lord's heir. They scoff at Walter's choice of a wife until they see her dressed in queenly array (4, 372–85) and think less of her years later when they see the regal array of Walter's new bride (4, 981–94). In short, the folk fail to grasp the invisible forms of virtue beneath outer wrappings of physical bodies.

Walter is what his name signfies: Old High German *walt* [ruler]—English *wielder*—and *heri* [people]. He rules and the people are ruled, but Grisilde is his intermediary agency in the performance of justice, "so wise and rype wordes hadde she" (4, 438). *Rype* signals the right word in its proper time. Earlier in the tale the adjective joins with *sad* to mark the sufficiency of *corage* with which she cares for her old father (4, 220). On the one hand, Grisilde is a bond connecting stable Walter with his unstable people. On the other, she is the means by which Walter can achieve his desired *otium* of "reste and pees" (4, 487). She brings his people to "reste and ese" (4, 423) by serving "the commune profit" (4, 431), while she is herself in a proper stable condition (4, 663). On his behalf she evokes God's grace to provide Walter with "plesance ynogh unto youre lyves ende" (4, 1036).

The friction between Walter's concealed private concerns and his outrageous public treatment of his wife is caused by the break in his lethargic existence. In marriage he falls out of his own sense of measure, and the process of the tale traces Grisilde's moving him toward a truer measure. The perversity of his testing is not so much in the cruel form he gives it, but in his willful effort to destabilize his wife in order to feel more secure in himself:

> . . . I have doon this deede
> For no malice, ne for no crueltee,
> But for t'assaye in thee thy womanheede.
>
> (4, 1073–75)

What exactly does he mean by "womanheede"? On one side of its semantic range is a set of invisible virtues proper to a woman, of which patience and steadfastness are but two.[25] On the other side is the popular secular convention of the social behavior of women—chiding, lying, impatience, and all those negative qualities Theophrastus lists in his *Golden Book of Marriage*. If a test tries virtue, and a temptation prompts sin, then Walter has indeed tempted his wife's patience and steadfastness.[26]

When her children are taken away,[27] she remains patient, and even fails to react to the sergeant who comes to take away the daughter and whom the Clerk calls suspect of face and word and suspicious of fame (4, 540–41). Grisilde appeals to him as "worthy gentil man" (4, 549), and so he is in his service to Walter. As he comes later for the son, the Clerk calls him ugly, but his appearance seems to have no effect upon Grisilde, and her resistance to deceptive appearances is a feature of her steadfastness.

The narrator insists more upon her bounty, that combination of beauty and generosity of spirit which Walter praises early in his somewhat pompous declaration to his people: "Bountee comth al of God, nat of the streen / Of which [children] been engendred and ybore"(4, 157–58).[28] Of course, the bounty which is not invisible grace is a gift of nature, and all are born, as Boethius argues, with nobility of character. Besides public and private appearance, Grisilde's bounty is her childbearing power. Walter's argument about blood needs proof not only in the social graces which belie her base social heritage, but also in the children she brings into the world. (The case would be stronger for Walter's argument if Grisilde were the daughter of a liar or a horse-thief; but her father's virtue, which Walter is glad to acknowledge, makes her birth "low" only in respect to social degree.)

When she is forced to return to her humble beginnings, Grisilde resists displaying her womb before the people, not only, I suppose, because of shame to her modesty, but because of the people's inability to read her virtue beneath her exposed flesh.[29] They are quick to judge array but incapable of perceiving the virtue it covers. So, divested of her regal estate, she begs Walter for her old smock:

> Ye koude nat doon so dishonest a thyng,
> That thilke wombe in which youre children leye
> Sholde biforn the peple, in my walkynge,
> Be seyn al bare. . . .
>
> (4, 876–79)

Her womb is her private vessel, her hidden form of womanhood, while her clothing—the array by which she is too hastily judged by the folk—

is her public appearance. Her womb is her bounty, if you will, and her appearance is her beauty. In her, of course, the two are one, but Grisilde would not expose to the people a sign they cannot read. Her stripping and asking for her old clothes is a clear renunciation of Walter's array and an assertion of her "real" self. In effect, his testing has brought forward her natural power as a woman, that previously invisible form of her beauty which is bounty. The Wife of Bath would understand the point though she means something different when she quotes Saint Jerome: "A womman cast hir shame away / Whan she cast of hir smok . . ." (3, 782–83).

The Friar's tale also associates womanhood with the emblem of a smock, a garment so called because it is pulled over one's head rather than buttoned or tied (Old English *smugan* "to creep into").[30] Grisilde reminds Walter that she came to him in marriage with the triple dowry of faith, nakedness, and virginity (4, 866), whereas Chaucer's Latin, Italian, and French sources mention only "nakedness." Reunited with Walter after being forced to acknowledge the beauty of her own daughter, she achieves the three goods of marriage that Augustine lists in *De Bono Conjugali:* fidelity, offspring, and permanent union.[31] In her obedience to her lord, in sacrificing her son, and in maintaining herself in a state of patience and moderation, she reflects the Virign Mary. Like Mary, she mediates a private purpose of her lord's which serves the public good of the people. In short, her perfection is confirmed in an obedience which bears fine fruit.[32]

The tale is not so much an allegory as it is an exemplum. Its "Envoy" challenges us to read Grisilde as a Marian model of woman and an *integumentum* of the truth of womanhood lying beneath the surface of a fictional character.[33] It concludes with a curious allusion to the issue of reading true values beneath deceptive array:

> If thou be fair where people are in presence,
> Show thou thy visage and thyne apparail;
> If thou be foul, be free of thy dispence;
> To get thee friends, always do thy travaille.
>
> (4, 1207–10)

This advice to wives, spoken in woman's voice, is an obvious response to the Wife of Bath's ironic "benediction" which calls upon Christ to shorten the lives of husbands who are "nygardes of dispence" (3, 1263). *Fair* is "beautiful," but the apparel that displays or conceals it is bought and not born. A smock, on the other hand, is homemade and is akin to the true word, whose value is not adulterated either by fit or appeal to the eye. "Fair" is a judgment of the viewer, and its truth depends upon a quality of the bond between sight and insight. To be "free" of dispense is to be generous in paying others to tolerate what might be perceived as foul, and "dispence" signals the Wife's sexual and commercial interests.[34] "Friend" and "free" are both associated with root words for "love," and "travaille" is the pain of bringing children into the world (*OED* definition 3).

One ironic thrust of the "Envoy" is its specious distinction between fair and foul, comparable to the specious distinction which Dorigen makes between the hellish black rocks and the paradisiacal garden; for the former hurt her not at all, but the latter presents the temptation to be false to her husband. The distinction between the outward show of the fair and the foul alludes to the Wife of Bath's hag, who claims that she has the power to be ugly or fair, and faithful or fickle, though she does not reveal what common *inner* form lies beneath both shapes. Another ironic thrust of the "Envoy" is its verbal excess after the already supernumerary "But o word, lordynges." Both carry the story too far, just as Walter had carried his tests too far. The Clerk's speaking too much both apes the Wife's earlier rhetorical preamble—which incites the Friar's and Summoner's dilatory exchange (3, 831–38)—and neglects Grisilde's telling example of moderation of speech.[35]

Dorigen is rewarded for all her errors with a return to domestic order, perhaps as a sort of providential gift for her noble intention to be true despite a moment of verbal weakness. She incites three acts of gentilesse with personal and private consequences. Grisilde's silent submission to her husband's word and her begetting of a girl and boy have public and political consequences even more telling than Theseus's verbal mediation (which one can only hope will provide a common profit of political order, if not a Theban succession somewhere beyond the story). Grisilde produces gentilesse out of her womb, and out of her bounty the rest and peace her husband so urgently insists upon. She is the means by which an idle life sets itself on a track toward a future good higher on the chain of love.

# 6

## Aping God's Chain of Love: The First "Fragment"

Love is humility rising; humility is love descending.
—Attributed to Saint Francis de Sales

As all is woven together in one whole
Each works and resides in the other.
As heaven's might goes up and down,
It reaches the golden bucket to each!
On scented wings from heaven down
To earth below flies the harmony
Which rings through all created things.

—Goethe, *Faust*

WALTER'S SECOND "THIS IS ENOUGH, GRISELDE" IS AN AXIAL EXCLAMA-
tion which leaves behind both test and shifts of array for the sufficiency
of felicity in marriage and parenthood. A comparable moment occurs in
the Canon's Yeoman's tale, when the Canon announces that a marriage
of elements has been accomplished whose issue is a "teyne of silver fyn"
(8, 1240–41):

> . . . and glad in every veyne
> Was this preest, whan he saugh that it was so.
> "Goddes blessyng, and his moodres also,
> And alle halwes, have ye, sire Chanoun.
>
> (8, 1241–44)

The alchemist's crucible is a marriage bed where life is conceived,
and the priest's blessing evokes God's mother as the spiritual cause of
the operation. Crucible and crosslet are *testes* in the language of the
alchemical arts (8, 818),[1] whose mediator is the *privee stoon* (8, 1452),
a nice term for God's secret artifact (8, 1472–74). *Stone* is a common

107

term for testicle (*OED* def. 11, from the twelfth century), and it is
appropriate that "privee stoon" should be an oblique allusion to the
*spermatologos* of God, the spirit which is Word. The Yeoman quotes
Plato to the effect that Christ so loves the stone that he will reveal it to
some while denying it to others. The stone, then, figures God's gift of
grace, and the Yeoman's collocation of Plato and Christ recalls the end
of the General Prologue where Plato and Christ are cited as authorities
on the use of the word: Christ for simplicity of style and Plato for subtlety
of thought (1, 739–42). It is love, claims the false Canon appropriately
if insincerely, that incites hands to work wonders (8, 1153–55).

Crucible, crosslet, and testes are images of matter awaiting the engen-
dering form of word. They figure the parched earth of March in the chain
of being awaiting *licour* to infuse nature's veins. Comparable images of
the fair chain of love can be found throughout the tales. Many of them
are comically incongruous, such as the pear tree in Januarie's garden into
which May climbs to couple with Damyan, and the stairs leading to
the merchant's counting room in the Shipman's tale, whose ideological
reflection of heaven is evoked by the wife's call through the door, "Peter!
It am I" (7, 214), after coming up from the *hortus amoris* where she had
contracted an exchange of love for money with Daun John. In the General
Prologue portraits, the curious pin of the Monk which contains a love
knot is an image of the chain.

The most telling artificial representation of Theseus's fair chain is the
rosary of the Prioress, who is herself a figure of the Church, which
mediates between man and God. Chaucer's description emphasizes her
worldly concerns for pets and her refectory manners with meat and wine
rather than with the flesh and blood of the sacristy, but the final detail of
her array illustrates wonderfully her combined worldly and spiritual office:

> Of smal coral aboute hire arm she bar
> A peire of bedes, gauded al with grene,
> And theron heng a brooch of gold ful sheene,
> On which there was first write a crowned A,
> And after *Amor vincit omnia.*

> (1, 158–62)

With her prayer beads connecting her arm to an inscribed *Amor,* the
Nun is as much an ambulant emblem of the cosmos as Alain's Nature,
Boethius's Lady Philosophy, Holy Church, and the Virgin Mary. The "A"
of *Amor* identifies Christ, the God of Love,[2] and each green coral bead
is a prayer (Old English *bed*). The crowned [flat-topped] "A" is also
"alpha," or creation.[3] The inscription which follows glosses it as *Amor,*

but the "A" is as stubbornly polysemous as Hester Prynne's scarlet letter: Angel, Able, etc. As the first letter of the alphabet, "A" stands for preeminence and perfection of kind. In Chaucer's "An ABC," it is Almighty queen. In *Troilus* it qualifies Criseyde's beauty: "Right as oure firste letter is now an A, / In beaute first so stood she, makeles" (*Tr.* 1, 171–72). Though that particular "A" may be an oblique reference to Richard II's Queen Anne of Bohemia, the conjuncture of the graph with the adjective *makeles* [mateless, matchless] recalls the Virgin Mary of the lyric "I Sing of a Maiden." The green of the coral and the gold of the brooch are combined colors of fecundity in the chromatic scale of Christian iconography. Chaucer's audience would have no trouble seeing in *Amor* the City of Love *Roma,* a trope for the earthly paradise of Jerusalem, itself an anagogic figure of the City of God. The shrine of Becket at Canterbury is an obvious figure of all of these things.

The inscribed text *Amor vincit omnia* is ubiquitous in the Middle Ages. If its source is Virgil's *Eclogues,* 10, 69, its literary peregrinations move through secular to religious contexts. Virgil's line reads: *Omnia vincit Amor, et cedamus Amori* [Love conquers all and let us give ourselves to Love], but the third-person singular indicative form *vincit* is an inflection of both *vinco* control, master" and *vincio* bind, limit." "Love binds all" is an equally accurate translation. Chaucer may have changed the word order for the sake of his rhyme, but he would have come across the saying in other orders elsewhere. The *Carmina Burana* "Ianus annum circinat" has: "Vincit amor omnia, / Regit amor omnia."[4] [Love conquers/binds everything, love rules everything]. Chaucer's word order has the initial letter-sequence *AVO,* whose first and last letters are Alpha and Omega, beginning and end. The *V* between them is the conventional Latin abbreviation for both *vir* and *urbis.* In effect, the Prioress's strand of beads and brooch is a catena conjoining spiritual form with worldly process.

More remote, but undoubtedly known to Chaucer, is the scholastic play on the Virgilian word order. *OVA* is "eggs," which figure the world in Neoplatonic commentaries. An anonymous French dialogue "Placides et Timeo" explains: *La coque, c'est le firmament; la peau blanche par dessous, c'est la terre; le blanc, c'est l'eau; le jaune, c'est le feu* [The shell is the firmament, the white membrane is earth, the white of the egg is water, and the yellow is fire].[5] All four elements are bound together in the Cosmic Egg, just as Plato bound them in a fair chain of love. The conception was known in England well before Chaucer's time. The Alfredian translation of Boethius inserts it into meter 20, lines 169ff., in describing the earth as the yolk of an egg, though Boethius's *De consolatione* has nothing of it.[6]

The flat-topped "A" is interpreted by Joachim of Fiore as an *elementum triangulatum,* whose flat top is the Father and whose two legs of the graph are the Son and the Holy Spirit.[7] That "A" also contains a shape of Omega, and thus it encodes the procession of the Holy Ghost from God and Son. Though this may seem a long extension of the implications of the Prioress's chain, it is not easy to fix the limits of its semantic parameters for Chaucer's day.[8] At any rate, what any survey of its meanings should not fail to take into account is its pertinence to the Prioress's office of mediation between two worlds, no matter how heavily grounded her appetites are in the array and comforts of her secular estate.[9]

In the Knight's tale, even before Theseus exposes the fair chain of love, he illustrates its principle in the "noble theatre" (1, 1885) that he designs to mediate the destiny of Palamon, Arcite, and Emily. The theater is an image of the world, the ordered combat in its lists reflects God's ordinance, and Theseus, who creates the theater, is "trewe juge" (1, 2657) of its ordained process. The wonder of it is, the Knight says: " . . . Swich a place / Was noon in erthe, as in so litel space" (1, 1895–96).

Theseus himself orders the design and construction of the temples of Mars, Venus, and Diana. Since the idols in those temples mediate the desires of Emily, Palamon, and Arcite, it is effectively Theseus who mediates the power of the gods those idols incarnate; that is, Theseus himself plays both Jupiter and Saturn even before he rationizes that play into a philosphical scheme. Theseus's power over the theater, then, figures the cosmic chain of love with which he compares marriage in his First Mover speech, but in the next tale on the Canterbury road, the Miller tells a tale in which the Knight's pagan philosophical scheme takes on different substance in the Christian here-and-now of fourteenth-century England. That difference is represented by an elaborate artifice which reifies the chain of love.

Before he tells his tale, however, the Miller, like the Knight's Fortune, disturbs established plans of procedure. In this case they are Harry Bailly's rules of governance, his ordinance for this particular pilgrimage. The Host had called upon the Monk to follow the Knight, probably in deference to high religious rank after the performance of someone of high secular rank. The things of God are rendered after those of Caesar, but the Miller, pale with drink, inserts himself in the hierarchal order, saying: "I kan a noble tale for the nones / With which I wol now quite the Knyghtes tale" (1, 3126–27). This verbal irruption into the Host's concatenative design for order contains a link of its own to the Knight's story. The word *noble* echoes the Knight's diction in his tale of noblemen told in a noble style. *Noble* designates an ideal and a superiority of kind, or blood. The gold coin Edward III minted was called a noble in deference to its perfection of referential value authenticated by the image of the king himself, and it remained so until Henry VIII replaced it with the sovereign almost two hundred years later. *Noble* is a word used typically by the Knight to signal the perfection of Theseus (1, 873, 998, 2569, 2715, and 2975). The Miller applies it later to his own mediatrix of love, Alison, "ful brighter . . . than the noble yforged new" (1, 3255–56), an apt image for a woman of great natural beauty who passes through many hands without, in the end, appearing to have lost any of her own referential value. The Miller's use of the word in his interruption of the Host, however, mocks its semantic resonance, for his tale features nobility neither of style nor of character. The lovesick Absolon puts on "noble" airs, in keeping with his hair which shines like gold (1, 3310), but his noble amatory ambition turns to sensuous confusion. The effect of the Miller's riposte to the Knight is to lower the notion of noble governance to an anarchy of art, science, and nature.

Nonetheless, although the Miller's lewd pragmatism counters the Knight's Boethian world picture, as readers are quick to appreciate,[10] his tale builds much of its sense out of a store of popular scriptural imagery which recalls Theseus's chain of love. To begin with, the plethora of images with which Alison is described in the tale identify her with nature's *foyson* (1, 3323–49), the material bond of nature between God and man. Nicholas's hands follow his mouth's dalliance to reach with a tactical *nexus* on her natural good (1, 3276). Since Alison belongs in marriage to an old carpenter named John, Nicholas imitates the secret God whose word impregnates the womb of Mary.[11]

Another example is the song *Angelus ad virginem,* which Nicholas is wont to sing before sounding out the "kynges noote." The two pieces of music balance heavenly and worldly order (1, 3216–17). Although the latter has not been identified, in Chaucer's day the "Angelus" was a popular celebration of the Annunciation, the announcement of an angel to Mary of the arrival of the Holy Spirit into her womb.[12] The Annunciation marks Mary's acceptance of God's spirit in her body to mediate man's redemption, and it is typically respresented in medieval iconography by a cord of light connecting heaven with Mary's bower.[13] The song is appropriate in the mouth of a clerk, but comically incongruous as musical enticement for an adulterous love which breaks the bond of holy matrimony.

The parish clerk Absolon competes for Alison's love with his own music. While she lies in Nicholas's embrace, Absolon stands beneath her casement window and pleads in the poetic idiom of the Canticles—read by the exegetes as Christ's call to Holy Church into his embrace—for her to pass a token of grace past the wall-limen of her house. After he kisses her "nether yë" instead of her lips, Absolon goes off to prepare his vengeance while the cuckolded husband sleeps "abidyng Goddes grace" (1, 3595) in the form of a flood. In the role of the Christ who is to return at the Second Coming, Absolon returns as a thief in the night

(1, 3790–91) with judgment made and punishment at hand.[14] He announces to Alison that he has brought her his mother's gold ring, another sign of love's bond,[15] but carries in his hand a coulter, or plowshare, the popular emblem of the preacher's chastizing tongue.[16] To the request for a sign where she is, Nicholas answers Absolon with a fart. *Sicut audio, iudico* [As I hear, I judge] says Christ (John 5, 30), and Absolon applies the red-hot coulter to his rival's *towte*. Nicholas screams "Water!" John hears the cry as an announcement of Nowell's flood, cuts loose his bucket, and plummets down with an arm-breaking crash. All of man's senses are brought into the parodic play, and the bodily channel from a kissing and crying mouth to an eructating anus is a cruel parody of love's chain.

This comedy of word and deed is a vivid reflection of the spiritual mediation of Mary and her Son for man's grace, but that which best represents Theseus's grand exposition of the fair chain of love is Nicholas's construction of a *locus amoris* built according to Theseus's blueprint for the cosmos. Displaying clerkly wit, Nicholas concocts an elaborate if dilatory strategy of convincing John that heavenly signs reveal "Goddes pryvetee," his providential design for an impending flood (1, 3658). Nicholas convinces the gullible carpenter to play *artifex* and construct a threefold world of large tubs suspended from the rafters with sufficient sustenance for "oure purveiaunce" (1, 3566). This architecture of salvation corresponds to Theseus's threefold world of God, man, and a bond of love between them. The roof is not quite the sky and the tubs not on the floor, but the cords are ways both up and down. As an ostensible means for saving life, Nicholas's scheme is a design of providence, but its underlying intent is fornication, a perversion of God's conceiving of life.[17]

During the portentious night of the predicted flood, Nicholas and Alison quit their cramped salvific quarters for the greater prurient comfort of a mundane bed. "Every soul is either an adulteress with the devil or a spouse of Christ," says Thomas Brinton,[18] and Alison choses the former in the guise of the latter. Meanwhile, the exhausted husband remains alone in suspense. The purgatorial suggestion of his place is pertinent to the diabolical image of the lower bed of lust, toward which the thwarted Absolon moves to speak his love.

This threefold world of actors—husband above, lovers below, and Absolon still lower in the street—reflects the heirarchy of the four elements. There is the upper air in which the tubs hang, and the lower earth upon which the bed of love stands. Then, when Absolon kisses an organ of waste instead of the organ which pronounces grace, he fetches a fiery coulter whose application causes an urgent cry for water. The air is not only the space above the bed, but the speech of the lovers and the fart which attracts the fire exploding the cry for soothing water. Nicholas's fart is also a parody of the divine afflatus of the Holy Spirit which descends first to Mary's womb and then to the tongues of the Apostles. Nicholas's threefold world, held in place by ropes of deceit, is a parody of Theseus's love-bound cosmos and the word which binds a couple in marriage. In the Miller's arena of action, the marriage bond is fractured rather than bound.

The Miller's tale of lewd experience in a world of discordant scriptural typologies quits the learned authority of the Knight by unveiling before the pilgrim audience an experience whose play of wit and word belies the design which engenders it. Theseus's theater of the world contains a public spectacle whose play serves the common good. John's house is a private arena in which the *pryvetee* of God is acted out in the secrecy of a woman's amorous play. Woman shadows God's invisible and mysterious being, suggests the Miller in answering the reeve Osewold's fear that fiction skirts close to fact:[19]

> An housbonde shal nat been inquisityf
> Of Goddes pryvetee, nor of his wyf,
> So may he fyne Goddes foyson there.
>
> (1, 3463–65)

This grammatical amphibology identifies God's wife with John's. A comparable coupling of the enduring world of noble ideas with the sordid arena of punctual experience is, in the end, the achievement of the Miller's performance, for the Miller's quiting of the Knight subverts the implicit values of the Knight's noble pagan world, whose authority rests largely upon a learned pagan philosophical base figuring the Knight's own Christian world. The Miller's tale tests the idea of the fair chain of love in current experience, where Christian and Platonic lore tumble into *lewed* confusion. The Knight's celebration of the transformation of pernicious private desire into public good is tranformed into a mockery of the *derne* love which results in public spectacle.

The Reeve follows with a tale that extends the parody into the temporal implication of Theseus's chain as *successiouns* of the species. Though his announced intention is to quit the Miller in turn, the Reeve tells a story which builds upon the implications of both preceding tales. He repeats something of the Knight's concern with law and the plenitude of creation as well as something of the Miller's comic Christian culture, all within an anecdote from current life near Cambridge. The central concern of the tale is, in Platonic terms, the descent to corruptibility of things as they move down and away from their perfect and stable source. What is precisely at stake for the miller of the tale is the bloodline into which he has married and to which he has contributed by fathering a daughter.

The daughter's grandfather is the town parson, who intends to make her his heir,

> Bothe of his catel and his mesuage,
> And straunge he made it of hir mariage.
> His purpos was for to bistowe hire hye
> Into som worthy blood of ancetrye;
> For hooly chirches good moot been despended
> On hooly chirches blood that is descended.
> Therfore he wolde his hooly blood honoure,
> Though that he hooly chirche sholde devoure.
>
> (1, 3977–86)

The scriptural source of the Parson's thought is Saint Paul's words to the Ephesians 5, 32, which Chaucer's Parson explains tersely in his discussion of lechery: "Trewe effect of mariage clenseth fornicacioun and replenyssheth Hooly chirche of good lynage" (10, 920). There is comic incongruity in the Reeve's exposition of the zealous grandfather's thought in his lowering of the terms "good" and "blood" from a spiritual to a secular context. His possessions are the goods of his office which he would leave to a granddaughter in whose veins runs *his* "holy" blood.

Since clerical celibacy was Church policy after the Third Lateran Council (A.D. 1179), Malyn's grandfather should be a spiritual rather than a biological father. In the logic of his intentions, however, the wealth of the Church should pass down to the benefit of children of the clergy, and he will honor his daughter in marriage even if he need devour (rob?) the Church. This genealogical chain of "love" descends, then, from a Parson, whose epithet of office is "Father," to a granddaughter Malyn, whose mother, the miller Symkyn's wife, is the connecting bond.[20] The repetition of the phrase "hooly chirche" to characterize Malyn's blood strain associates her with the Virgin Mary, who is the supreme female figure of *Ecclesia.*

Malyn's virginity, a negotiable material and spiritual commodity for both father and grand-father, is spent in a secret act that parodies Mary's secret and miraculous impregnation. Both philosophically and religously, the integrity of that descending bond of love counteracts the corruption and diffusion of human values away from their source in God. The scriptural model of the bond of love which is man's genealogical strain is the Tree of Jesse, Christ's mortal bloodline. In the less spiritual environment of Trumpington, Symkyn, his wife, and her father conceive of lineage as a ladder of social mobility. The Reeve measures the mother's social pretensions against her character:

> . . . somdel smoterlich,
> She was a digne as water in a dich,
> And ful of hoker and of bisemare.
>
> (1, 4963–65)

The social opprobrium of the circumstances of her birth are more than compensated for by the social rank of her father, and she displays more pride than humility in her lineage.[21]

Some time later along the Canterbury road, the Host repeats the overworked observation that society should profit by the Church's biological blood strain rather than, as Saint Paul had argued, have the Church profit from society's blood:

> Religioun hath take up al the corn
> Of tredyng, and we borel men been shrympes.
> Of fieble trees ther comen wrecched ympes
> This maketh that oure heires been so sklendre
> And feble that they may nat wel engendre.
>
> (7, 195458)[22]

The punctual image of the parson's sexual nature unbridled by Church rule is the clerks' horse, let loose to run across the fields after mares, crying joyfully "weehee" (echoing the ecstatic "teehee" Alison giggles in wicked delight after Absolon had kissed lower than he had sought).

Symkyn's own expectations for his daughter are disappointed when he discovers that Malyn's flower of virginity has been robbed in exchange for the flour he had taken from the clerks. He promises vengeance on the perpetrator of the deed:

> Thow shalt be deed, by Goddes dignitee!
> Who dorste be so boold to disparage
> My doghter, that is come of swich lynage?
>
> (1, 4270–72)[23]

The genealogy of the parson descends, indeed, to the *corrumpable,* though one may hope that Malyn is impregnated by this servant of Holy Church. Malyn does not fare badly. In fact, she makes of her dark trial a mediation for grace. When Aleyn quits her bed, he utters for her, in what seems to us cruelly and perversely ironic for the occasion, a brief *alba,* or *aubade:*

> . . . Fare weel, Malyne, sweete wight!
> The day is come, I may no lenger byde;
> But everemo, wher so I go or ryde,
> I is thyn awen clerk, swa have I seel!
>
> (1, 4236–39)

This sounds as hypocritical as Dorigen's promise to Aurelius, but Malyn seizes upon the words as an abridged but sure bond of love and replies in kind with a brief adieu that opens with "deere lemman" and closes with "goode lemman." In the middle of her touching and seemingly sincere response, she reveals the location of the stolen flour, whose substance has been transformed into the accident of a cake, just as her invisible but real virginity has been transformed into a real but invisible womanhood. Where Aleyn's aubade was but a flowery excuse to quit her bed to get some early-morning sleep, Malyn's blend of courtesy and information is an occasion to grant a gift of grace not asked for. In effect, the victim's words convert a rape into a courtly encounter. They make a virtue of necessity.

It is neither attractions of wits nor feelings of affection that had prompted Aleyn's assault upon Malyn, but a point of law which he explains to Aleyn much in the spirit of Arcite's explanation of love's force to Palamon:

> For, John, ther is a lawe that says thus:
> That gif a man in a point be agreved,
> That in another he sal be releved.
> Oure corn is stoln, sothly, it is na nay,
> And we had had an il fit al this day;
> And syn I sal have neen amendement
> Agayn my los, I will have esement.
> By Goddes sale, it sal neen other bee!
>
> (1 4180–87)

This is a making a law of love out of a love of law; but, as is so often the case in such serious pronouncements, the words enclose a plenitude of unordered meanings. *Los* means "reputation" and "honor" as well as "loss." Wondrous is the recourse to a woman's body—chaff—to compensate for loss of corn—fruit. To the old clerk's saying that love knows no law, Aleyn would reply that law, however, knows love.[24] *Esement* designates the sexual as well as the legal relief Aleyn contemplates as compensation. *Sale* is even broader in its semantic reach.[25] First of all, in prosodic performance the word would be monosyllabic (to accord with the phonological convention of final vowel elision before words beginning with a with a vowel, and to keep the line length at ten syllables, though both features are flexible). Benson's glossary has *sale* as the Northern form of "soul," but the usual Northern form is *sal*. To the ear, the word is homophonous with the Northern modal *sal* "shall," which Aleyn employs regularly. *Sale* is the Northern form of "sole," the North Sea delicacy. God's sole would be a curious allusion to the *Icthys* who is Christ. In Chaucer's own London dialect, *sale* is Modern English "sale," the giving of something with expectation of return. God's sale would be an appropriate designation for a gift of grace as well as an apt term for a legal balance of accounts: the use of Malyn's virginity for a portion of flour.

The real fun comes about in the commutative movement in the dark through the strait space of the miller's house which he challenges the two clerks to amend:

> Myn hous is streit, but ye han lerned art;[26]
> Ye konne by argumentes make a place
> A myle brood of twenty foot of space.
> Lat se now if this place may suffise,
> Or make it rowm with speche as is youre gise.
>
> (1, 4122–26)

The challenge to make real space out of words recalls the Word of God whose language does indeed provide sufficiency. Clerks are figures of that divine force. The furniture in Symkyn's chamber—three beds, two of which are ten or twelve feet apart, and a cradle—recalls an order of plenitude, but their disposition in this dark microcosm is uncertain. The room is also filled with a plenitude of sounds, for the miller snorts and farts like a horse, while his wife and daughter snore in a cacaphony that Aleyn compares ironically with the last sung religious service of the clerical day (1, 4171). No music of spheres this, but the little room is indeed a little threefold universe in the image of Theseus's grand design; and the acts of love it contains in its move through space invite comparison with the tight world of Nicholas, Alison, Absolon, and John in the Miller's tale. Like the carpenter, the husband-father rests in stillness while his wife accepts the embrace of another.

Despite Symkyn's satiric challenge to the clerks to make the *invisibilia* of number into real space, the microcosmic order of the room, unlike the three-tubs-and-a-bed amatory universe of Nicholas, is alterable, or commutative. The three beds remain in place, but the cradle at the foot of one is slyly shifted out of its proper place to the foot of another. Where Nicholas had plotted shifts from two tubs to one bed to fulfill an amatory purveyance, in the Reeve's tale, one clerk moves to a bed of love while the other changes the design of things to have an object of love move to him. Strait may be the gate, but the mansion of the father has sufficient room for all sorts of love.

The darkness not only takes away clear sight, but it muddles memory and reason.[27] After the wife rises to relieve her bladder, she returns to a different bed, fooled by her touch of the misplaced cradle. Then she mistakes John's touch for her husband's and is pleased at its newness;

and while Aleyn is robbing Malyn of her virginity, John commits the theft of adultery on the body of Symkyn's wife. In the confusion that follows, the wife cries out *"in manus tuas,"* the Latin version of Christ's words uttered on the cross as his soul strains toward reunion with his Father. The wife's heart is broken, and her womb and head are assailed. In short, her rational, animal, and sensible souls are in simultaneous disarray.[28]

Disarray and confusion of ordained structures are the Reeve's counter to Theseus's metaphysics of order. The private and imperceptible acts of love in darkness have public consequences of altering the purveyed descent of the blood of Holy Church. Malyn's disparagement discounts her marriage value. The body of a clerkly figure of the Church undoes her grandfather's identification of her body with Church; and so like the Miller, the Reeve undermines the ideological authority of the Knight and his hero's philosophical conception of a fair chain of love binding all things.

The Cook's brief fragment of a tale does not carry far the possibilities of another contemporary image of the threefold world bound together by love, but the ingredients for another assault on the bonds of love are there. The tale has two thieves and a mediant wife. Her shop, which is but a countenance for the activity which produces her sustenance, is a *locus amoris.* The prostitution in which she engages, as Chaucer's Parson later explains, is a mockery of the proper worship of God (10, 902). It imitates the act of creation without either its intent or effect. On a scale of love, the sale of one's body is no lower, perhaps, than robbing a virgin of her *centissimus fructus,* an act the Parson compares with a beast's breaking of his enclosure (10, 869–70), or, if you will, a horse breaking horse's law. Prostitution is a baser form of love than stately marriage, or frolicking natural sexual energy, or confused but enjoyed dark encounters. So, while the three earlier tales relate public exposures for good or ill of private or hidden manifestations of love, the Cook's tale arouses expectations of a story of love which remains, by its occupational design, a hidden activity.

Few readers do not respond to the riot of disarray and destabilization in the three tales which follow the Knight's performance. That riot is foreshadowed by the confused mêlée in Theseus's lists, but whereas Theseus continually restraightens order, there is no artifice of reorder in the closure of the other tales, though there is in each a suggestion of repose after activity. The difference of closure derives from the difference between the grave and learned authority of the Knight concerning the distant past, and the comic and lewd "realities" of the present.[29] The track of both time and value leads away and down from the speculative *in illa tempore* of the Knight's golden past to the *hic et nunc* of the rusted metal of present-day England.[30] The chain of love stretches, as Mark Twain's Connecticut Yankee would see it, all the way from Camelot to Bridgeport; but, even Camelot is suspect: "'Camelot—Camelot,' said I to myself, .... 'Name of the asylum, likely.'"[31]

# 7

## Quests and Parodies of Quests for the Chain of Love

The law was ordained by angels through the hands
of a mediator. Now there can only be a mediator
between two parties, and yet God is One.

—Galatians 3, 19–20

Love refines
The thoughts, and heart enlarges, hath his seat
In Reason, and is judicious, is the scale
By which to heav'nly Love thou may'st ascend,
Not sunk in carnal pleasure. . .

—*Par. Lost* 8, 589–93

WORD AND IMAGE ARE MAN'S WAYS OF EXPRESSING HIS PERCEPTION OF love's bonds and of inciting virtuous acts of love. Malyn's last words to the man who disparaged her blood—"good lemman, God thee save and kepe!'" (1, 4247)—redeems a guilt and converts a victim's shame of rape into a magnaminous granting of grace. Words nourish mind and spirit, and words of one sort or another, as Geffrey learns in his dream in the *House of Fame,* fill the space between man and God. Like the Prioress's beads, they mediate man's grace.

Man's word of mouth collaborates with visual image to move him toward either salvation or condemnation. In the Merchant's tale, May's "writyng to and fro, / And privee signes" proffer grace to Damyan (5, 2104–5) and her sign language directs her lover up into the pear tree where the two consummate their love before the blank eyes of Januarie (5, 2209).[1] Chauntecleer's enticement to his flock is the song "My lief is faren in londe" (7, 4069), and the Pardoner's is "Come hider, love, to me" (1, 672).[2] Like the Wife of Bath and the Canon's Yeoman, they display bodies as corraborative texts.

The pageant of Chaucer's pilgrims as they move toward a shrine which contains the body of the Christ of the English folk, England's particular spiritual patron, is a visual text which collaborates with speech and spiritual intent. Pilgrimage provides the means for the mouth to exercise the body's part in the threefold penitential process of contrition, confession, and satisfaction, or thought, word, and deed. It is a parabolic motion toward love, located on the *mappa mundi* as Rome, and on spiritual charts as Heaven. In the process of pilgrimage, confession is the earnest sound which mediates man's desire for grace, while swearing and telling ribald tales are jesting sounds that mediate pleasurable participation in social company.

The quest for either spiritual or physical love is mediated by words. Words serve reason, but on a lower rung of the ladder of the senses the mouth serves the stomach's appetite. Although eating is somewhat below song and speech on the ladder, it reflects just as well the chain of love. Accordingly, it has its virtuous mean. "Attempree diete" is the poor widow's physic in the Nun's Priest's fable (7, 2838), and the Physician's Virginia keeps her mouth free from the mastery of Bacchus (6, 58). On the other side of the balance is the gluttony that the Pardoner exclaims: "O cause first of oure confusioun! / O original of oure damnacioun" (6, 499–500). Eating is coordinate with speaking in raising man's soul toward God, or lowering it away. Just as the ingestion of the Host in the rite of the Eucharist joins man with God for an instant, man's eating sustains the body which contains his soul. Chauntecleer comes face to face with the fox at the moment his own eye is on the dainty morsel of a butterfly, an emblem of nothingness; and his paltry reason is no match for the cunning, voracious, and wordy fox. The Pardoner's demand for time to drink a draught of ale while he thinks about some honest thing to tell (6, 328) enacts a conventional association of drink with poetic inspiration. The Host's call for some moist and corny ale to head off a heart attack, so strong is the effect of the Physician's tale (6, 315), evokes the medicinal power of drink to counter the infection of word.

Wine and distilled alcohols are more powerful than ale on a scale of liquid virtues. Distilled beverages, a relatively recent addition to the liquid menus of Chaucer's day, were considered to possess preternatural force. Distillation, from Latin *distillare* "to drop, trickle down," is an alchemical process to isolate the Pythagorean *quinta essentia,* the fifth element which combines the other four. Quintessence is the purest effusion of a substance.[3] Though not quite the quintessence, alcohol was assumed to be an impure form of it, for its burns while wet and warms while cold, thus exhibiting the properties of three elements. This *aqua vitae* also protects organic materials from corruption, and so involves the fourth element.

Chaucer alludes to distillation in his description of the Canon who rides so hard his forehead drops sweat "as a stillatorie" (8, 580). When Troilus considers his loss of Criseyde, in him "teris gan distille, / As licour out of a lambic ful faste" (*Tr* 4, 519–20). There is a far more significant allusion in the opening lines of the General Prologue which mention the "swich licour / Of which vertu engendred is the flour" (1, 3–4). This is the liquid upon which the *spiriculam vitae,* or breath of God, moves (Gen. 8: 1).[4] Lydgate, in "The Flower of Courtesy," 35, 3–4, calls the inspiration of the muses "lycoure swete," and Caxton's *Book of Courtesy,* 333, honors Chaucer as the fulsome fountain of "lusty liquour." As for wine, the Wife of Bath is an authority on its effects on love:

> And after wyn on Venus moste I thynke,
> Fro al so siker as cold engendreth hayl,
> A likerous mouth moste han a likerous tayl.
> In wommen vinolent is no defence.
>
> (3, 464–67)[5]

As if mimicking the Wife, the Pardoner exclaims that he will "drynke licour of the vyne, / And have a joly wenche in every toun" (6, 452–53).

Wine, like love, is an agent of accord. For example, when the Cook has had too much to drink, the Manciple forces him to drink again, "up peyne of deeth" (9, 86), and ". . . of that drynke the Cook was wonder fayn" (9, 92). We need not wonder about the illusion of sudden sobriety as a symptom of revived wholeness, but the Host who is expert in tavern matters seizes upon the occasion to publicize his trade as a service to love:

> Where that we goon, good drynke with us carie;
> For that wol turne rancour and disese
> T'acord and love, and many a wrong apese.
> O thou Bacus, yblessed be thy name.
>
> (9, 96–99)[6]

Harry's jest contrasts with the digusting reality of the immeasured gluttony which the Pardoner preaches for his own interests, and of which the Manciple accuses the Cook:

> Hold cloos thy mouth, man, by thy father kyn!
> The devel of helle sette his foote therin!
> Thy cursed breeth infecte wol us alle.
>
> (9, 37–39)

The breath of disease, like the infectious stink of alchemists, is the malefic counterpart of the redolent breath of Zephirus which quickens life. The latter figures God's privy spirit which inspires life in matter, but the breath of alcoholic spirits floats from the throat that is man's privy (6, 527).[7] The Canon's Yeoman's breath, which is an instrument in the alchemical transformation of matter, is also a reflection of the divine breath whose worldly residence is the elusive philosopher's stone. Similarly, the Word of God, which is a gift of love and life, has an ironic reflection in the poetry which, like Chaucer's tale of Tereus and Boccaccio's of Madonna Oretta, infects its hearer. Alcohol, then, is another emanation of the fair chain of love, transporting man either upward with its spiritual vapours or downward with its ape-wine dregs. It is, then, quite appropriate that the pilgrimage to restore spirit should be guided by a restorer of man's body in the figure of an innkeeper whose tavern reflects the tabernacle. It is equally appropriate that it should end in the Eucharist where wine in a chalice becomes Christ's blood in the mouth.

Pilgrimage is a quest for restoration of both body and soul in the form of a journey in search of a specific token of health. Among the tales told by the pilgrims, only three have quest structures: the Wife's, the Pardoner's, and Chaucer's tale of Sir Thopas. Each of the three recounts a search for an element whose physical form figures spirit. In the Wife's tale, the quest is to save a human life; in the Pardoner's, it is to kill the destroyer of life; and Thopas's pursuit of the elf queen is a quest for an idea of love itself. In the first, sexual appetite is at stake. In the second, the stomach's appetite is crucial, and in the tale of Thopas, the arming of stomach prepares the conquest of spirit.

The Wife's tale is set in the days when the invisible form of the elfin queen of the otherworld takes on visible appearance at times. The knight who rides from the river arrives from a common boundary between two worlds; and, like otherworldly kings of the ilk of Jupiter, he rapes a virgin.[8] Rape is tantamount to murder, for one who rapes a virgin, Chaucer's Parson explains, casts that woman out of the "hyeste degree that is in this present lif, and bireveth hire thilke precious fruyt that the book clepeth the hundred fruyt" (10, 868–69). The knight is sentenced by law to lose his *heed* for having violated a *maydenhed* against the maiden's *heed* (3, 887–92). The homophony fits the punishment to the crime nicely. The law of equity, however, is tempered by grace when Arthur grants judgment to Guinevere (3, 891–98), who sets as a penitential task for the knight the discovery and public revelation of what women most desire, as if knowing women's eroticism redeems acting out men's.[9] He sets off on a quest to find an intangible and unknown thing whose public exposure will earn the grace of Guinevere's female court. It is, essentially, a quest for right words which will save the knight's body.

The body of a woman has damned him, and now the body of a woman sets his penance. He gathers many responses and knows intuitively that they are wrong until he meets the foul wight under a forest side—another limen between two worlds—who offers him a lifesaving response in exchange for a marriage vow.[10] So the judgment of Guenevere mediates between a theft of a young woman's virginity and the gift of a male body into an old woman's keeping. Neither maid nor hag is an object of the knight's love, but both serve the physical interests of his body. The hag whispers the answer in his ear, as if she were divulging a divine privity that the trees must not hear; and he returns to court with her to expose with manly public voice her counsel before the court (3, 1036–40). None of the three estates of womanhood—wife, maid, and widow—contradict him, and so his words make him worthy to have his life (3, 1045). There is some irony in a woman saving a knight from certain death, but the customary fit of sex to social function is one of the Wife's narrrative targets.

The saving words, however, are the hag's and not yet part of the knight's thought. When she claims her contracted reward, the knight resists and once again the court constrains him to accept his due, so he and the hag are married *prively* (3, 1080). At this point, the tale has turned from a knight's quest for information to a hag's task of imposing her lifesaving authority upon the conjugal bed. Her chances of success are hinted at in her declaration that any grievance he has concerning her may be amended. In the nuptial bed, it is the wife who turns to the groom for a kiss. When he recoils from her, citing her age, foulness, and low birth, she gives him a lesson in gentilesse which is, essentially, instruction how to read beneath the appearance of things to the perfection of forms behind them. Where he had imposed his sexual will upon the virgin despite her heed, the hag imposes her body upon the knight against his will. Where he had misused the physical force of his sex, the hag works with the sensible force of her mouth. Her pillow-talk is a verbal bond of love to direct his vision to a loftier view of love, but one wonders if his fatigue and mental dullness succumb to the weight of her words before his reason submits to the surety of her logic.

It is hard to know what the knight learns, but his reward is purveyed even before he is tested. For him is ordained what the hag has decided before his will enters the matter: "But nathelees, syn I knowe youre delit, / I shal fulfille your worldly appetit" (3, 1217–18). It is only *after* her promise of reward that she poses her riddle-choice between a foul and true wife and a fair but uncertain one. The knight's surrender of the choice back to whom he now calls "lady, love and wife" (3, 1230) wins him both beauty and truth, and the couple live out the rest of their lives in the felicity of worldly appetite (3 1257–58).

This radical reversal of worldly roles has the hag the pursuer and the knight the pursued in the hunt of love. On the figurative level of the philosophic chain of love, she appropriates for herself the divine role of purveying and ordaining. Her gift of grace reflects God's free gift that does not require man's "earning," but does require the free admission of God's power to grant it. Her choice between foul and true or fair and doubtful is a choice between salvation and damnation. "My love? . . . nay my damnacioun!" cries the knight when she says she would not exchange him as her love for any metal or *oore,* i.e., gold/grace (3, 1064–67), though he does not realize yet that she has the power to provide him with both one *and* the other. Furthermore, the hag foresees that the knight will have his grace—his appetite fulfilled—even before he exercises his will for it. When she draws back the bed-curtain to reveal the truth of her multiform self, she offers to his eye a vivid illustration of a bond of love joining superficial and essential values, that is, beauty and bounty. The ultimate irony of the tale is that the real riddle is not what women most desire, but what men most desire; for, what women most desire, finally, is the power to grant what men most desire. The hag knows this and exercises her mastery to deliver it.[11] The Wife knows it, and reveals in her prologue how she used her body to mediate her husband's desires, all of them except, apparently, the enigmatic fourth husband. If the Virgin Mary mediates man's spiritual needs, the Wife and her hag mediate physical needs.

It is not surprising, then, that the shape-shifting of the hag reflects Satan as well as God, no matter what the knight takes her to be. Just as the summoner in the Friar's tale makes a contract with a yeoman whose diabolic identity he does not take seriously, the Wife's knight contracts a marriage with a being who has only the *appearance* of her sex. A fairy wight, like a magician from Orleans who converts things from foul to fair, only *seems* to be able to knit discordant things with bonds of love. The fair is foul which is not true.[12] When the story concludes with the knight's exuberant pleasure in the sight of a fair and young thing in his arms, we are not invited to suppose what is liable to come after the bath of bliss he will experience for a time. The hag, like the Wife herself, can provide, perhaps, only the *semblance* of a hell, purgatory, or paradise for the man she dominates.[13] The temporal closure of narrative saves the knight, and saves us.

The Wife's tale, then, poses as an allegory of grace,[14] though the literal figuration lacks a certain justice. The fortunate knight is absolved of a heinous crime and obtains the felicity of amorous grace without having either expressed contrition or performed more than token satisfaction. He does, however, do the one thing which is *sine qua non* for grace: acknowledge the power of its provider.[15] That the knight appears to be the target of the hag's private design for her own sexual authority and pleasure makes her, finally, more diabolic than divine.

The Pardoner's tale of the three young rioters is a parodic reflection of the Wife's allegorical quest as well as of the particular pilgrimage which is the occasion to tell it. His tale takes the Wife's as its thematic pretext, just as her exposition of her five marriages is the Pardoner's avowed pretext for disdaining marriage (3, 163–69). The thematic issue of his story is the reading of signs. The rioters swear a pact to kill death after they are told that a "privee theef . . . clepeth Deeth" has killed one of their fellows with a spear (6, 675–77) which recalls the love-shaft of Emily's eyes which slay Arcite. They understand this death to be a person and set off on a quest to find and destroy him. Of course, to destroy death, of which John Donne makes much poetic capital, consists paradoxically of dying into an eternal life. Allegorically, then, the rioters are on a quest to ascend the chain of love from the lower rungs of mortal life to its eternal spiritual apex.[16] They are searching unwittingly for what the hag's knight was sentenced to discover: knowledge of the privy and invisible forms behind things of this world.

The old man they meet as they cross a stile is taken by them as Death, though he claims to be searching for a death which eludes him. When he directs them toward their goal, he reflects the the Wife's hag as mediator of bodily interests which figure interests of the soul; and, like the Wife's Hag, he provides what they most desire. In leading the rioters toward death he guides them toward eternal life, even though theirs is a quest to prolong their mortality. The gold they find under an oak tree is a form of death they had not expected, though it causes the death it figures. Gold is another form of God, though they miss that insight by more than an ell.[17] Their "literalist" reading of the gold as Fortune's grace (6, 779–83) instead of the root of all evil, is the cause for the axial turn from a collaborative and public quest to kill death toward privy schemes to kill one other. The rioters find a different form of death than that which they hunted, but only after having renounced the search.

The telling difference between the Wife's hag and the Pardoner's old man is in their quest directions. The hag turns a individual quest to preserve life into a joint effort to satisfy the knight's sexual desire and her own marital interests, while the old man turns quest away from his own figure to a figure of the rioters' own damnation.[18] The Wife's comic affirmation of a quest for love is countered by the Pardoner's caustic denial of its possibility. Her celebration of wit and reason as mediators for sexual good is answered by an example of the deficiency of wit and reason to mediate either worldy or spiritual desires. The rioters' quest with its exercise of gluttony, hazardry, and swearing reflects the cupidinous occupation which the Pardoner attributes to himself in the professional use of his mouth. The rioters' drawing of straws to designate which of them will fetch provisions reflects Harry Bailly's straw-drawing to designate the first teller of tales (both drawings seem to be fixed). The swearing and drinking with which the Pardoner mimics the Host (6, 309–15 and 320–22) link the performative context of the tale with the tale itself. Finally, the rioters' last supper foreshadows the prize promised at the end of the tale-telling which figures Christ's Last Supper. The Pardoner's tale figures the very pilgrimage in which he and his audience participate.

From another perspective, the tale is a spitting out of personal venom, what the Pardoner's own moral stomach has composted of its natural nourishment (6, 421–22). In concert with the grotesque revelation of person before the pilgrims, his verbal display is a scornful challenge to their reading of appearances, particularly of his own. The rioters of the tale are the pilgrims themselves who can read neither the signs along their way nor understand what the goal at the end of their road portends.[19] The Pardoner's moral tale is pernicious of intent, even if "under hewe of hoolynesse" (6, 421–22); but, who among his pilgrim-companions can read the tale's sense any better than he can read the shape and hue of its teller? The Host's scurrilous attack on the Pardoner's gifts of sexual nature at the close of the performance only confirms the tale's implication that the pilgrims can read neither the truth behind outer array, nor the *sententia* behind the letter of a text, nor the essential spiritual truth contained in the conventional appurtenances of a holiday cruise to Canterbury.

The Pardoner gives his lewd audience his own reading of pilgrimage in both his "history" of self and "story" of others.[20] Like the Wife's hag, he knows something of the true and enduring forms behind the pageantry of quest. As the hag figures herself as God, so the Pardoner makes of himself a figure of Christ the mediator. He cites 1 Timothy 2:5–7 to the effect that Christ is the true soul's leech (6, 916), and he identifies his mediation in his sermon text from 1 Timothy 6:10, *Radix malorum est Cupiditas* [the root of evil is cupidity]. That popular saying is taken out of the context of Saint Paul's broad attack upon the preaching which pleases an audience to loosen its purse strings. The evil consequences of the cupidity against which Paul inveighs is neither murder nor theft, but false instruction in spiritual matters. The Pardoner, then, hides his spiritual malice of false instruction—for Augustine the most sinful of all lies[21]— by vaunting the material cupidity which he claims is his constant theme.

Whether or not the Pardoner cares if his audience can grasp the sense of his moral tale in the specificity of its pilgrimage context, it would appear that later performances respond purposely to it. For one, the pilgrim Chaucer's tale of a comic amatory quest refigures the Pardoner's tragedy of spirit and adds a different twist to the sense of the Wife's quest story. Chaucer's first tale, like the Pardoner's, takes material from

128 CHAUCER'S CHAIN OF LOVE

the Host's terms of introduction. Harry begins by demeaning the unnamed
pilgrim directly:

> "What man artow?" quod he;
> "Thou lookest as thou woldest fynde an hare,
> For evere upon the ground I se thee stare."
>
> (7, 695–97)

Then, turning to the pilgrims, Harry displays Chaucer's figure:

> This were a popet in an arm t'embrace
> For any womman, smal and fair of face.
> He semeth elvyssh by his contenaunce,
> For unto no wight dooth he daliaunce.
>
> (7, 701–4)

This bit of dalliance on Harry's part provides two services for the designated teller of the next tale. First, it saves the performer from exposing
his own body, as both Wife and Pardoner had done for themselves.
Secondly, it provides essential material for the tale of Thopas, just as
Harry's invitation to the Pardoner had provided images of hazardry and
gluttony for his tale.

In this case, the reference to hunting the hare reappears in Chaucer's
description of the forest full "of bukke and hare" through which Sir
Thopas rides on his quest for the elf queen (7, 756).[22] The term "elvyssh"
with which Harry pokes fun at Chaucer's figure provides Chaucer with
his tale's quest topic while carrying a number of related associations.
Middle English elf and elfish suggest notions of secrecy, sex, and magic.[23]
The marriage of metals is described by the Canon's Yeoman as an "elvysshe craft" and "elvysshe nyce lore" (8, 751 and 842). In the Man of Law's
tale, Donegild's false announcement to Aella of the birth of a monstrous
son (2, 754) accuses Constance of being an elf; and the Wife recalls the
pre-Christian past when elves walked where friars now tread (3, 873–80).
The hag of the Wife's tale seems to be herself an elf queen who dances
on the green (3, 860). So the Host's elvyssh singles Chaucer out as one
who rides alone and—typical to the Host's reading of human shapes—
draws attention to his sexuality or, by ironical implication, his lack of
it. The dalliance Chaucer lacks is both public banter and derne love-talk.

Chaucer responds to the expectations this description might raise with
a tale that shapes its images into story. In effect, he "translates" himself
into a tale of a quest by a hunting knight for an elf queen; and, as if to
underline a dalliance appropriate for his tale, he performs it in an irregular
metrical romance verse form that is more an unsteady trot than an amble.[24]
Like the knight of the Wife's tale and the Pardoner's three rioters, Chau-

cer's hero goes in search of something he has never seen; but, where the Wife's knight had met an elfin queen whose being he could not comprehend, and where the rioters meet an old man they could not read, Thopas pursues a body he has only caught furtive sight of in a dream.[25] When Thopas is struck with love-longing, he cries out "O seinte Marie, *benedicite!*," aligning paratactically the invisible object of his love with the Virgin Mary and himself with the religious fervor of innocent youth. He is every-pilgrim in search of the invisible mediatrix of his spiritual desire.

The cavalier Thopas echoes and apes the Pardoner's confidence-man speech. Where the Pardoner had sworn that he would have "licour of the vyne" at the moment his mouth is full of beer (6, 452–56), Sir Thopas swears an oath on ale and bread while he is drinking wine (7, 872 and 851). The three rioters meet the old man as they are about to tread over a stile on their hunt for death (6, 712), and Thopas pricks over "stile and stone / An elf-queene for t'espye" (7, 798–99).[26] The Pardoner's hair is as yellow as wax (1, 675) and Thopas's hair and beard are like saffron (7, 730).

This imitative style evokes the Wife of Bath as well. Thopas's face is white as *payndemayn* (7, 725), a detail which recalls the Wife's characterization of virgins as bread of pure white seed, while wives are barley bread (3, 144–45). Alison's tale features a queen as the authority for the knight's quest to redeem himself from a sexual crime, whereas Thopas's authority is an elf queen he has met in a dream. The quest of Thopas, like that of Alison's rapist-knight, leads directly toward women. While the rapist finds a fairy wight who awards him the grace of bliss, Sir Thopas pursues on the *gras* [grass] a *gras* [grace] which rhymes with his own name (7, 830–31).[27] When he is finally armed for his decisive combat, he "gooth an ambil in the way" (7, 885), which suggests the Wife's rather than a knight's horsemanship (1, 469). Whereas Alison's knight has to learn the painful lesson that human love involves more than bestial assault, Thopas's sexuality is in search of a physical object to match the *invisibilia* of his imaginative erotic assault. Where the Wife's knight, as well as the Pardoner's rioters, lacks self-reflection, Thopas's love-longing is autistic, for he loves what is only, for the narrative span of the story, inside himself.[28] Of course, in the conventions of *fin' amor,* a lover like Troilus is liable to love his private imaginative text of a woman more than the public text of her womanhood. Consider all those who fall in love through words without sight: Henryson's Erudices and Chaucer's Man of Law's sultan come quickly to mind.

In all three tales, the quest is joined by someone who offers a certain insight into the nature of his search. The Wife's hag joins the rapist-knight to turn his search from the authority of women's words about desire to the proof of his own experience with them. The Pardoner's old

man turns the rioters' quest from a literal to a figurative reading of death.[29]
The profit of the hag's lesson is her appearance of beauty and promise
of fidelity. The waste of the old man's lesson matches his wasted age.
In the tale of Thopas, the diverter of quest is the three-headed giant
Olifaunt, whose instruction, like the old man's, is in his figure as well
as in his words. Many-headedness is explained in the Parson's tale with
an oblique reference to the Wife of Bath: "If a womman hadde mo men
than oon, thanne sholde she have moo hevedes than oon" (10, 922).
Boethius's Philosophy explains the giant's name in terms which implicate
the Pardoner's cupidity, since *Olifaunt* [elephant] is the weight of earthly
goods which counter man's attraction toward heavenly goods (*Cons.*
3, pr. 8, 23–27).[30] Olifaunt both threatens and enlightens Thopas. The
tricephalic giant threatens to kill the hero's horse unless he leave the
giant's haunt, and in the same breath he confirms that the queen of fairy
lives there with music and symphony (7, 2000–2006). Finally, he drives
Thopas back with stones "out of a fel staf-slynge," an engine with obvious
sexual overtones.

The quest of the Wife's tale is achieved in a bliss not sought, and the
quest of the Pardoner's tale in a death not sought. Sir Thopas's quest is
unachieved, not because of any lack of virtue in the hero, but because
of his maker's failure to finish the story. Olifaunt retards Thopas's progress, but the villain who blocks it permanently is Harry Bailly, who
interrupts the quest by stopping the tale just after the hero has armed
himself with food and harness to battle for his lady's love.[31] The words
of one ontological level of narrative reality suddenly dominate those
of another.

The pilgrim Chaucer then saves his own "quest" in narrative perambula-
tion by continuing it in a direction away from the blocked frame of his
doggerel rhyme. First he refits himself with the polished armor of a lesson
to Harry Bailly on how to read texts before taking to the narrative road
again with another tale. His rhetorical armor is intricate and ornamented
with more devices than either Thopas or Olifaunt carry into the field:

> . . . Ye woot that every Evaungelist
> That telleth us the peyne of Jhesu Crist
> Ne seith nat alle thyng as his felawe dooth;
> But nathelees hir sentence is al sooth,
> And alle acorden as in hire sentence,
> Al be ther in hir tellyng difference.
> For somme of hem seyn moore, and somme seyn lesse,
> Whan they his pitous passioun expresse—
> I meene of Mark, Mathew, Luc and John—
> But doutelees hir sentence is al oon.
>
>                                                     (7, 943–52)[32]

One implication of this passage is that the same quest story may be told in different ways, so that the wearisome verbal effort of Prudence to convert her husband to peace in the tale he is about to tell carries the same message as the tale he has just been prevented from continuing.[33] The passage also draws attention backward to tales already told. The authority of the scriptural versions of the Passion invests the tale of Sir Thopas with a *sentence* that may not have escaped everyone, but it certainly escapes the Host.[34] There is a telling difference between the sound of Chaucer's quest story and the discursive styles of the Wife and Pardoner, while the *sensus,* a critique of pilgrimage and its participants, is *oon.* There is even a subtle suggestion in the allusion to the Gospels that *Sir Thopas* might be a different style of figuring the Passion.[35] Chaucer the reporter makes a comparable alignment of the *Tales* with scriptural style earlier in the General Prologue when he excuses the language of the tales to come on the grounds that "Crist spak hymself ful brode in hooly writ" (1, 739).

All these points are pertinent to Harry's conduct as guide and governor, for, as if he had foreseen the imminent interruption of his tale, Chaucer describes Olifaunt in terms that could portray the Host himself. Furthermore, the ending of the tale of Thopas figures incomplete pilgrimage, while Thopas's preparations for his quest for the invisible queen figure the tale-telling "nonsense" which fills time but holds back the penitential moment of grace at its end.[36] Chaucer's tale neither espouses the Wife's metaphysical optimism for love nor condones the Pardoner's caustic scorn of spiritual quest. It constitutes one more stylistic rendering of pilgrimage, and its abrupt close and shift to yet another style implies that while interruption may end a quest, it does not end questing. Even the subversive art of the Pardoner is matter out of which God makes good.[37] A giant, as well as an ugly hag and an old man with a walking stick, can figure mediation for grace, and a foppish knight as well as a rapist and three rioters can figure those whose purpose on the road to Canterbury is seasonal and sensual rather than festival and spiritual. It is a neat and clever scheme to have the Wife's tale of a surrender of domestic mastery seized upon by the Pardoner as the pretext for a tale of a quest which illustrates the tragic waste of pilgrimage, itself seized upon by a pilgrim-poet who poses as a muddling minstrel to tell a story whose eschatological contingency redresses both the Pardoner's and the Wife's conceptions of pilgrimage.[38] One need not seize the hidden form of an artistic intent to appreciate its product.

The tale of Melibee with which Chaucer fulfills his task is an earnest corrective for errant questing. It offers another way of looking for the invisible form behind creation and another view of pilgrimage. Where Thopas searched for the body of an idea, Melibee is led toward the idea behind body, both that of his wounded daughter Sophie and of his own damaged spirits. Sophie is weakened knowledge of self and the world under the assault of sin. Sophie's name echoes *Hagios Sophia, logos* in the Orthodox Church's Trinity. She is, like Christ, the sacrificial means by which man is enabled to work for his redemption. Melibee, "A man that drynketh hony" (7, 1410), is one intoxicated with delights of the world and word. He cannot retrieve the bond of love until instructed by Prudence, who can accord the past and present with the future. Prudence is the power of confession which moves man toward reunion with the body of Christ, figured by Melibee's daughter. The allegory reaches in several directions. As man's search for the judgment which *prudence* mediates, it is an allegory of pilgrimage. At the same time, the tale denies allegory by a literality of style that has Prudence utter the *letter* rather than the *spirit* of truth. She and her husband make of words a world, and of the world nothing but words.

The incompleteness of the tale of Thopas figures the incompleteness of the pilgrimage and of its book, while the completeness of the tale of Melibee is an emblem of the completeness of God's design which one is liable to read as confusion. The tale of Thopas looks to the pilgrimage actors and their tales, while the tale of Melibee looks past this particular rehearsal of man's quest for grace to its end. Harry Bailly can only block what he reads as a misdirected narrative amble and only praise what he reads as an example of domestic harmony; but his praise of the story of Melibee as a reflection of his own family reveals an allegorical reading for all the pilgrims:

> Al be it that I dar nat hire withstonde,
> For she is big in armes, by my faith:
> That shal he fynde that hire mysdooth or seith.
>
> (1920–22)

Harry is speaking here of his wife Goodelief, but with her he identifies Holy Church, the Virgin Mary, and the chain of love. Her name *Goodelief* can signify "Love for God," "Love for goods," "Belief in God" and "Belief in goods." All is for our doctrine.

The concatenation of quest tales stops after Thopas, but the point that pilgrimage is a verbal as well as a spiritual quest has been well made in each of them, and the pilgrim Chaucer concludes the series with sublime humor. Thopas the hunter is a hunter for souls as well as for wild deer, but the Monk who is invited next to tell a tale, though he is a hunter by taste, does not seem to get the point, or does not wish to pursue it. Instead, he asserts the guiding force of Fortune in a sequence of brief tragedies which the Knight blocks because of their lack of "joye and greet solaas"

(7, 2774). The Host agrees with the Knight "by hevene kyng" (7, 2796) and calls for a hunting tale. The Monk cannot seize the occasion as Chaucer had to make narrative capital of the interruption, and surrenders the stage to the Prioress's Priest, who tells a tale in comic array, of many hunts which adds a different twist to the Wife's and the Pardoner's critiques of pilgrimage.

With the talk of hunt in the air, an avian love and chase tale is particularly apt. Harry Bailly, by now as is his unwitting wont, informs both genre and theme in his flattering introduction, not of the Priest, however, but of the Monk somewhat earlier:

> Thou woldest han been a tredefowl aright,
> Haddestow as greet a leeve, as thou hast myght,
> To parfourne al thy lust in engendrure,
> Thou haddest bigeten ful many a creature.
>
> (1945–48)

In regretting that the spiritual vows of monks abrogate their natural potential, Harry impugns the lack of a harmony between the two, for religion has "take up al the corn / Of tredyng" (7, 1954–55). Jokingly, Harry disdains the spiritual fruit of grace for the natural fruit of the womb. The Monk fails to satsify the Host's expectations as well as the tastes of the Knight, who would have preferred a tale of one who "clymbeth up and wexeth fortunat, / And there abideth in prosperitee" (7, 2774–77). The Nun's Priest shapes his tale out of words to the Monk, seizes upon both Host's and Knight's imagery of avian lust, fall and climb, and tells the tale of a treadfowl who flies up out of the mouth of misfortune into a tree where he abides in prosperity. If the fox's mouth, like the devil's, is the furnace of hell (10, 856), Chauntecleer's escape is a climb up the chain of love.

The Nun's Priest packs his tale with philosophical and cosmic signs of the cock's qualification for that flight. Chauntecleer is described as the best of his kind, a paragon among readers and speakers of the natural process of time (7, 2850–58). His physical array combines four colors— black, azure, white, and gold—and he governs seven hens (7, 2860–67). The fairest, as the sun is fairest among the seven planets in the sky, is Pertelote. In short, Chauntecleer's body and his farmyard are a cosmos in small. He himself is its harmonizing bond of love whose natural power of song reflects the music of the spheres in general and the church organ in particular. Thus, by his natural office he links the world of flesh with the world of spirit. The song he and Pertelote sing together, "My lief is faren in londe!" (7, 2879) infuses the world with love.[39] What is amiss in Chauntecleer's microcosmic world is the otherworld threat of the fox to his body and the innerworld menace of appetite to his reason. The internal danger is illustrated in the dream which drags on so long that he fails to awake to perform his naturally ordained office. The dream, according to Pertelote (whose name rhymes with *throat*), is caused by a misbalance of his humors,[40] while the widow who rules the macrocosmic universe of the tale is a figure of stability and moderation of diet, in keeping with her place: "No deyntee morsel passed thurgh her throte" (7, 2835).

Chauntecleer's dream is of a thing like Thopas's elf queen, never seen except in a dream. Where the notion of the aery elf queen quickens love in Thopas, the beastly apparition inspires fear in the cock (7, 2906); and where the doughty swain sets forth on a quest to realize his dream, the cock descends from his perch to dispute the epistemology of dreams with his hen. Ceding a natural superiority of reason to a natural affection for his paramour, Chauntecleer concludes:

> . . . *In principio,*
> *Mulier est hominis confusio—*
> Madame, the sentence of this Latyn is,
> "Womman is mannes joye and al his blis."
>
> (3163–66)

The Latin here is as deceptive in form as the shape of the dream fox, and those who are quick to find fault in the translation are liable like Colfox to lose their prey. In the first place, the translation fits the fact of his sensuality. In the second place, even taking *confusio* at first English sight as "confusion," the translation carries that sense into a sensual context, for the bliss and joy of a woman's body is indeed often a man's ruin. Thirdly, *confusio,* as the Priest would know, if not his cock-hero, has a primary meaning of "connexion, or bond," and woman is indeed man's bond of bliss. Chauntecleer's surrender of his reason to that bliss foreshadows the corruption of his paradise by the fox who is the dynamic *confusio* in all its senses.

Having restored domestic harmony with his words, Chauntecleer descends from his perch, finds a corn for breakfast, then supplements the needs of his stomach with those of his genitals. He exercises his sexual rule over the hens of the coop before calculating prime similarly "by kynde" rather than by lore (7, 3196). In other words, everything for the moment seems to be in natural order until his eye falls upon a butterfly in the foliage where Colfox lies in wait (7, 3273–74). The conjuncture of the butterfly and the fox is ominous. They often share the same colors, but the one is light and aery in flight and the other cunning on the ground. A butterfly is a sign of nothingness.[41] Chauntecleer's natural appetite for the butterfly, though he seems to have had already his gastronomic fill, corresponds with the fox's own natural appetite for the cock. Nonetheless, Chauntecleer is protected by a "kindly" urge to flee (7, 3279):[42]

> For natureelly a beest desireth flee
> Fro his contrarie, if he may it see,
> Though he never erst hadde seyn it with his ye.
>
> (7, 3279–81)

Chauntecleer recoils from the sight of a natural enemy with an onomatopoeic cry which identifies his own kind: "Cok! cok!" The fox who, like any pilgrim competing for a feast by telling tales, shapes his words to achieve his goal. Like the Nun's Priest and Chauntecleer, Colfox is out to serve his appetite; and, just as his prey is a silly cock looking for a butterfly of a meal for himself, the Nun's Priest's target is his pilgrim audience competing for a prize meal.

The logomachy of the confrontation of fox and cock is the Priest's parody of the tale-telling contest.[43] Who are the foxes and who the cocks among the pilgrim audience are open questions. At the moment, however, the fox has the upper word, and he uses it to talk Chauntecleer out of his proper nature and into trust of a word whose intent is to serve a stomach:

> My lord your father—God his soule blesse!
> And eek youre mooder, of hire gentilesse,
> Han in myn hous ybeen to my greet ese.
>
> (7, 3295–97)

A pretty amphibology this, but Chauntecleer can neither make it out with his gallinaceous ear nor foresee the consequence of the flattery which persuades him to close his eyes altogether as he counterfeits his father's skill.[44] With one mouth crowing, the other seizes his repast. At this point the narrator pauses to invoke the goddess of love:

> O Venus, that art goddess of plesaunce,
> Syn that thy servant was this Chauntecleer,
> And in thy servyce did al his poweer,
> Moore for delit than world to multiplye,
> Why woldestow suffre hym on thy day to dye?
>
> (7, 3342–46)

There is no calendar on the henhouse wall for Chauntecleer to note the propitious date of his fate, and the law of kind contains no statutory distinction between delight and multiplication. An animal's delight is his instinctive enticement to serve God's purpose. It is the man and not the beast in Chauntecleer which exercises a will to exceed or waste the mean nature of his body. It is not bestial but human love which is to harmonize reflex with reflection, but even this point is confused by an earlier statement that "thilke tyme ... beestes and briddes koude speke and synge" (7, 2880–81). Does possession of speech raise animals to the spiritual status of man on the hierarchal chain of being and give them free will?

Caught in the fox's maw, Chauntecleer figures the innocent pilgrim trapped in the verbal distraction of tale-telling. Words waste wits. Words also save, and it is by words that Chauntecleer extricates himself. When Colfox, in the excess of his pride, agrees to defy the chasing mob (like the birds of the *Legend* who defy the fowler), his opened mouth is Chauntecleer's avenue of flight to a tree for his body's salvation out of a vulpine trap. It is the fox's opening his jaws to say "In feith it shal be don" (7, 3414) that releases him.[45] "Brynge us to his heighe blisse!" (7, 3446) are the Priest's releasing words from his tale, but whether or not the pilgrims understand the pertinence of the Priest's exit line or the relevance of his tale to pilgrimage is left an open question. Fox and Harry alike are representatives of the world, the flesh, and the devil.

The Priest's tale impugns the collaboration of mouth and eye in search of sexual and gastronomical surfeit. In deceiving his prey, Colfox had hidden his hunger of eye with an appeal to his appetite of ear:

> I am nat come youre conseil for t'espye,
> But trewely, the cause of my comynge
> Was oonly for to herkne how that ye synge."
>
> (7, 3288–90)

This deceit is confirmed by the illogical and undetected claim for his eyes' authority in the matter of Chauntecleer's voice (7, 3300). The lack of harmony between the functions of eye and mouth is critical for Chauntecleer, whose dream vision keeps him sleeping beyond the time to sing the dawning. Like his father, he closes his eyes to danger while opening his mouth to pride of song. The necessity to harmonize one's wits is the lesson Chauntecleer seems to have learned by the end of his adventure: "For he that wynketh, whan that he sholde see, / Al wilfully, God lat him nevere thee!" (7, 3430–31) In chorus, Colfox adds that man should hold his peace rather than jangle.

The parodic possibilities in the tale seem endless. The example of Chauntecleer is a warning to the pilgrims to be wary of mouths like the Pardoner's which consign them to the slaughterhouse of the body instead of to the high bliss of the spirit. It warns them also against the carnal attraction of a woman's words, such as the Wife's. It challenges us to make the best (a virtue of necessity) of both a debilitating delight of an appetite for butterflies and an edifying slide toward the fox's maw. The tale, like the laxatives never found by Chauntecleer, has the power to purge. In brief, the Priest challenges his audience to read pilgrimage.[46] The Wife's tale quest culminates in sexual bliss, the Pardoner's in death; the quest of Thopas pits aery spirituality against elephantine materialism, while the struggle of Chauntecleer retrieves pilgrimage from the fill of the appetite to redirect it in a collaboration of thought and word toward a feast of reason and faith.[47] The Priest's tale is a menu of mediation for a harmonious service of natural and spiritual love. In the pleasure of engaging oneself in the tale, few can resist sitting in Harry Bailly's judgment seat to award the festival prize to the Priest. Harry's final words to the Priest indicate, perhaps, his own tentative choice: "I blessed be thy breche and every stoon! . . . Now, sire, faire falle yow for youre tale!" (7, 3448–60). No one so well as the Priest fills word and time on the road to Canterbury with so fine a menu of solace and sentence and thereby so well reflects the spirit of pilgrimage itself.

# 8

## Ends of the Chain: Parson and Prologue

He who knows not the sweetness proceeds badly toward it.
—*Il Convivio*

That which is marred at birth shall mend,
  Nor water out of bitter well make clean,
All evil thing returneth at the end
  Or elseway walketh in our blood unseen.

—Chaucer/Kipling

PREVIOUS CHAPTERS HAVE TRACED A NUMBER OF EMANATIONS OF THE chain of love in Chaucer's poetry, but the *Canterbury Tales* and the pilgrimage which is its plot frame also figure the chain. Beginning and end of the book, and the *tertium quid* of the story of pilgrimage and its tales which lie between, imitate the ends of the chain of being and the uncertain and commutative order of elements between. Like the first word spoken to a woman desired and the first written word of love-tidings, the beginning of pilgrimage, whose first steps are a move away from the dis-ease of sin, reflects God's creation. Pilgrimage is a thrust forward on a highway of love which joins the substantial world of the flesh with the essential world of the spirit. The earthy Miller pipes Chaucer's pilgrim group out of town (1, 566), so that first *paas* of pilgrimage coincides with a musical note played on an instrument regularly associated with sexual love. Three or four days later, at a "thropes ende" within sight of their goal, Harry turns his office over to the Parson (10, 19), who converts the ordinance for entertainment into instruction on soliciting the divine love they seek.

The first tale is begun by the Watering of Saint Thomas, and the last is performed before the walls of Canterbury, where the Parson knits up of the feast to "make an ende" (10, 47).[1] The record of the pilgrimage starts earlier in narrative space but later in recollected time when Chaucer describes the assembly at the Tabard. Before the start of this "fiction"

138

there is a "non-fictional" invocation to spring which is a vertical backdrop to the pilgrimage event.[2] The *whan* which opens the General Prologue celebration of spring is not loaded with the abrupt entry and weight of meaning that "Almighty," the first word of "An ABC" and "Perle," the initial word of the Middle English *Pearl* carry, but it establishes a considerable syntactic tension. *Whan* and *Amen,* the last word of Chaucer's benediction in the leave-taking of the author are the *termini* of the book, though neither is part of the story of the pilgrimage or of a tale contained within it.[3] In effect, there are at least three marked beginnings to the *Tales:* the "invocation" to spring, the story of the assembly of pilgrims at the Tabard, and the Knight's tale; and at least two formal closings: the Parson's tale and the author's leave-taking, although some have argued that the Manciple's tale, the last poem in the collection, marks the closure of the "tales."[4]

In the *ars praedicandi* of Chaucer's day, envelope structures are common, and several of Chaucer's tales have more than one start and stop. The Clerk's tale has an "Envoy" added to its story; the Pardoner ends his tale, only to announce that he has forgotten something, which turns out to be not part of the tale but part of the sermon which contains it (6, 919), though it is probable that his "forgetting" is a rehearsed part of his usual performance. The Canon's Yeoman has trouble finding the beginning of his tale as well as the location of the tale itself in the jumble of his memory (8, 898, 971–72, 1012, 1019). Chaucer calls his General Prologue a "tale," (1, 36), though it is the tale about the occasion for telling tales.

No matter how hard it is to chart the steps from one terminus of the book to another, there is formal opening and closure to its text. The opening eighteen lines of the General Prologue, a *reverdie* which I read as an invocation to spring, describe the perpetual and cyclical stretch of the life of the created world, while the prologue to the final tale contains the Parson's characterization of the goal of pilgrimage as man's eternal spiritual residence. As Paul aptly puts it in 1 Corinthians 15: 42–44: *Seminatur in corruptione, surget in incorruptione. Seminatur in innobilitate, surgit in gloria; seminatur in infirmitate, surget in virtute; seminatur corpus animale, surget corpus spirituale* [Man is sown in corruption, but raised pure. He is sown in imperfection, but raised in glory; he is sown in infirmity, but raised in virtue; he is sown a natural body, but raised spiritual]. The purpose of pilgrimage is to rehearse exactly this spring of the spirit. Appropriately, the sun's ascent in Aries with its attendant fertility and power propels the body's vector toward Canterbury, while the sun's descent in Libra, when the Parson begins his tale, figures spiritual judgment.[5] What reaches between these poles are story links in the chain of love.

*Incepisse aliquid iam pars est quantula facti* [to have begun something is already a part, however small, of completing it] is a popular saying attributed to Heiric of Auxerre, and even if the pilgrimage and its tale-telling are left unfinished, spiritual credit is gained in the effort made. After all, man cannot fully earn grace, but only work toward it with hope of God's free granting. The pilgrims' road runs eastward, toward the direction of beginnings and rebirths. It ran westward in the spring of 1381 for the rebellious peasants of Kent in their march of civil revolt against social chains of rank and privilege. Pilgrimage and revolt are secular acts whose lateral motions reflect ascent and descent, respectively, along the cosmic bond of love, as well as up and down the story scale of solace and sentence.

The first tale is told, we are led to assume, on the morning following the gathering of the pilgrims at the Tabard during the evening of 16 April, according to a date the reporter puts into the Host's calculations of time, and the last tale is situated at four in the afternoon on 16 April, according to the calculations given by the pilgrim-reporter himself.[6] In the mundane temporal calculations of the *viage,* then, the pilgrimage, like so many dreams, seems to occupy no time at all. After the Parson's tale concludes, early in the evening of the 16th, let's say, it is time for the pilgrims to gather at the Tabard, ready to begin their pilgrimage.

The last tale is invited "as we were entryng at a thropes ende" (10, 12), an axial moment of motion, and since the "ende" is a border or margin, the "entering," like the quest of the Pardoner's rioters, is across a limen which divides worlds. In this case, the end of the town separates the world of game and fable from the world of earnest and sentence. The throp is not identified as Canterbury itself, though it logically should be; but it *could be* Southwark or any other town on the route.[7] The town is any geographical place about to be transmuted by the power of word into what the Parson calls "Jerusalem celestial" (10, 51). Canterbury differs from Southwark appreciably in the facility of its transformation in man's mind from visible to invisible city. It is eminently appropriate that the pilgrims arrive at the border of the town, for life itself goes right to the edge. To pass through the gate would turn the proceedings into a symbolic passage into death, and would erase the necessary typological tension between pilgrimage and the passage of the soul.

It is also appropriate to the structural imagery of pilgrimage that large Harry of Southwark, an imposing worldly form, should surrender his secular governance in sight of Canterbury, a sign of the more imposing though invisible form of God,

> Now lakketh us no tales mo than oon.
> Fulfilled is my sentence and my decree,

> I trowe that we han herd of ech degree;
> Almoost fulfilled is al myn ordinaunce.
>
> (10, 16–19)

The language is eschatological, and the inference in *almoost* is that the first word of the Parson is the last moment of Harry's ordinance.

The Parson's knitting up a great matter is the last unit in the concatenation of tales, and is a *tertium quid* between the jesting seasonal entertainment along the road and the earnest spiritual feast at its end. The Parson explains the appropriateness of his closure of game: "Sith that Crist is sovereyn, and the preest meene and mediatour bitixe Crist and the synnere, and the synnere is the laste by wey of resoun, / thanne sholde nat the synnere sitte as heigh as his confessour, but knele biforn hym or at his feet" (10, 990–91). Where the General Prologue had ordered word in the service of deed, the Parson closes with a moral treatise on penitence which exposes the confessional word as mediator between contrition in thought and satisfaction in deed. The General Prologue opens *in limine* and moves to a fictive *hic et nunc;* the Parson moves from the here-and-now to *in aeternum.* Harry had served the season of Ceasar, and now the Parson serves the feast of God. In keeping with the process between one and the other, Harry's last words combine the imagery of Nature's spring to life with imagery of spiritual rebirth: "Beth fructuous, and that in litel space, / And to do wel God sende you his grace!" (10, 73–74)[8].

Feast and fruit images are significant links between the beginning and the ending of Chaucer's book, and in keeping with that imagery the Parson announces his treatise as a Tree of Penitence whose roots are man's heart, whose branches are his words and whose fruit are his deeds (10, 112–27): *cordis, oris,* and *operis.*[9] The fruit of penance is the harmony of heart, tongue, and hand (10, 1076), and the Parson explains Christ's name, Nazarene, to mean "florysshynge . . . for in the flour is hope of fruyt in tyme comynge" (10, 288). Confession, then, mediates man's desire for spiritual fruit.

One thing that the Parson's tale accomplishes in this respect is the rehabilitation of word as reflector of thought and informer of deed. Just before him, the Manciple had concluded his tale of the crow who lost his tongue with the advice: "Be noon auctor newe / Of tidynges . . . Kepe wel thy tonge" (9, 359–61). This is the Manciple's despairing denial of the efficacy of language to communicate with profit the simplest of truths. "Cokkow! cokkow! cokkow!" (9, 243) has uttered the crow, echoing Chauntecleer's "cok! cok!." The Manciple characterizes language as an agent of death and destruction, before the Parson steps forward with good tidings to infuse his audience with hope, just as the virtue of spring rains infuses the parched earth with life.

This is not to say that the Parson's word needs no ear of reason or eye of insight to mediate its truth. To begin with, consider his announced text from Jeremiah 6, 16: "Standeth upon the weyes, and seeth and axeth of olde paths (that is to seyn of olde sentences) which is the good wey, / and walketh in that wey, and ye shal fynde refresshynge for youre soules, etc" (10, 77–78).[10] The context of the passage is Jeremiah's reproach to the Jews for both having abandoned God's law and refused to repent; but, the Parson's "etc." hides the continuation which at least some of his audience would be expected to know: "We will not go . . . we will not hear. . . ." "Therefore [said Jeremiah] I will bring evil over this people, into the fruit of their thoughts who will not listen to my words and who have rejected my law."[11] The Parson's "etc." implies, then, the same choice for his fellow pilgrims between attending to his lesson or remaining obdurately attached to things of the world. The choice is between moving upward or plunging downward on the chain of love.

Over two-thirds of the Parson's tale is concerned with the language of confession which mediates between the contrition of thought and the satisfaction of deed, and therefore between invisible thought and measurable deed. *Satisfaction* means, literally, achievement of the mean, *satis;* and so confession, like the mediation of Grisilde for Walter's peace, mediates an *otium* of perfection. The long section on the Seven Deadly Sins elaborates *what* to confess: "Synne is in every word and every dede, and al that men coveiten, agayn the lawe of Jhesu Crist; and this is for to synne in herte, in mouth, and in ded, by thy fyve wittes, that been sighte, herynge, smellynge, tastynge or savourynge, and feelynge" (10, 959). The attraction to sin pulls one away from virtue, and the force of sin erodes the tensile strength of the bond of love.

Until the Parson makes an issue of it, sin is only an occasional thematic issue in the pilgrims' storylines. Sin can be found figured somehow in every tale, but the tellers make much more of the public and social than of the private and moral consequences of human acts. The Parson sets himself to balance worldly with eternal accounts, to show others that the road to Canterbury which the Canon's alchemy can pave with gold is indeed a golden path to salvation, and the tales told along its way are dim shadows of the confession necessary to penitence.

The Parson does not overtly refute the peripatetic diversion of the tale-telling contest. After all, he agrees to and participates in it despite his distaste for the Host's language. His knitting up, then, is not a denying of the game but a conjoining of it with the earnest of an eschatological design.[12] It is appropriate to the occasion, then, that the Parson should speak the language of love, that is, the love that lifts man toward God. Chaucer's portrait of him in the General Prologue confirms the example:

He was to synful men nat despitous,
Ne of his speche daungerous ne digne,
But in his techynge discreet and benygne.
To drawen folk to hevene by fairnesse,
By good ensample, this was his bisynesse.

(10, 516–20)

The Parson, then, reflects something of the popular image of Becket, offering a sanitizing wash to the infectious mouths of the pilgrims after much eating, drinking, and telling on the way.[13] In short, with the things of God, the Parson authenticates the things of Caesar.

In speaking of the power of language to heal the infection of sin, he declares: "The amyable tonge is the tree of lyf . . . and soothly, a desclavee tonge sleeth the spirites of hym that repreveth and eek of hym that is repreved" (10, 629).[14] The bellows of pride which heat the devil's furnace are wicked words (10, 555), but Christ's word is the true alembic (10, 1046). The *corage* which in the General Prologue combines natural and spiritual incitement is explained by the Parson as steadfastness of heart, mouth, and deed against spiritual sloth (10, 737). Sin is the breaching of the bond between thought, word, and deed "by delit in thynkynge, by reccelnesse in spekynge, and by wikked synful werkynge" (10, 111). The recklessness of speech which some of the tales as well as many of the exchanges between pilgrims exemplify is the language which serves modes of behavior rather than modes of truth such as the language of love that Alceste would have Chaucer speak in the *Legend*. From the Parson's perspective, much of the language uttered on the way is *flatus vocis*, sound without real referent. This is most obvious in the late performances of the Canon's Yeoman and the Manciple, both of whom expound a kind of nominalistic *aporia* concerning the semantic referentiality of language.

The Parson's remedy for dalliance is "axe and have" (10, 705), the interrogative key to grace. Sins of the tongue such as vain words, japes, and vanities are all redressable by confession. Where homicide destroys the flesh, the waste word kills spirit (10, 565ff.), but the word restored to meaning is the spirit restored to health. Speech is to the soul as clothes are to the body, says the Parson, as if he were commenting upon Grisilde's smock or the Wife's dress, for it is a sign of the heart (10, 412). He plays neither summoner to spiritual trial nor pardoner of sins, but would teach the conversion of sin to virtue, so that neither he nor the pilgrims should have to sing the new French song, as the Manciple and Apollo's crow might well, *Jay perdu tout mon temps et mon labour* (10, 47).[15]

The Parson's moment marks only the end of *one* pilgrimage in a life-long cycle of pilgrimages along what Augustine calls the King's Highway of the Church (*De civ. Dei* 10, 10, 32), and there is no reason to assume that the Parson considers pilgrimage differently. Afterwards, the pilgrims will return to their secular occupations, the seasons will run their course again, and another spring will prick desires for pilgrimage. Returning from pilgrimage is turning back into the sinful world. After celebration of the Eucharist, the move away from the shrine is a dispersal rather than a reunion. Each pilgrim goes his own way, for although there is an authorized route *to* the shrine, the choice of routes *from* it is free.[16]

The book does not conclude with the Parson's tale, but with Chaucer's own leave-taking, which looks back to all his works to ask forgiveness for those worldly writings he revokes in his *retracciouns*. What Chaucer is saying "literally" is that he *recalls* his works in his *retracings* of them. Both terms pertain to confession where the word must recall the deed which is to be absolved. Chaucer himself is responding to the Parson's essential message.[17] *Retracciouns* are retracings of words to find the redeeming intent behind them. Saints' lives and the *Boece de Consolatione* whose language express poetic intent clearly need no retracing. Retracing is erasure by speaking out or writing over a deed. It is the use of word to purify.

Leave-taking is both repetition and recollection, as I have said, and both function to close the gap between story and its potential meaning. Confessional and penitential repetition is not only a religious practice, but a strategy of linking two states of being of which sin and grace are but one example. Like pilgrimage, leave-taking renounces neither this world nor its book, but it celebrates the time and space man has to work for the restoration of his bond of love with God. Chaucer takes his leave in conformity with the Parson's suggestion that the Canterbury road must be retraced again and again until, under the sure guidance of the Virgin Mary and her Son, it is freshly paved as Christ's highway home.

The end of the proceedings not only follows the beginning, but brings us back to it.[18] The disembodied voice which opens the General Prologue asserts as a universal reality the perfection of presence which the Parson labors to expose at the end of the voyage.[19] The omniscient perspective of these lines locates all Christians, then England, and finally Canterbury. It draws a line of sight from common and universal things to punctual and local processes, from complex to simple instances; and, in doing so, it conjoins the immediate attractions of flesh with the timeless attractions of spirit:

> Whan that Aprill with his shoures soote
> The droghte of March hath perced to the roote,
> And bathed every veyne in swich licour
> Of which vertu engendred is the flour;

Whan Zephirus eek with his sweete breeth
Inspired hath in every holt and heeth
The tendre croppes, and the yonge sonne
Hath in the Ram his half cours yronne,
And smale foules maken melodye,
That slepen al the nyght with open ye
(So priketh hem nature in hir corages),
Thanne longen folk to goon on pilgrimages,
And palmeres for to seken straunge strondes,
To ferne halwes, kowthe in sondry londes;
And specially from every shires ende
Of Engelond to Caunterbury they wende,
The hooly blisful martir for to seke,
That hem hath holpen whan that they were seeke.
    Bifil that in that seson on a day. . . .

(1, 1–19)

I display these familiar lines here to show how they illustrate the chain of love as a dynamic connection between spirit and nature, and between all natural things. In an omniscient voice which is distinct from the "naïve" narrator of the pilgrimage, they expose the Platonic triad of sky, earth, and the intermediary spirit of life's seed in the falling rain and inspiring wind. Here is a seasonal succession in one solar cycle from dormant to flowering earth. The reanimation of life reenacts God's beginning of things and is a model for man's own reanimation of conjoined natural and spiritual longings.

The taut syllogistic movement from "whan" to "whan" to "thanne" connects nature with spirit.[20] The line of sight in the first eight lines binds the four elements in a concatenative vernal venture in which the sky is joined to the parched earth by an impregnating *licour*.[21] The eye is led upward again from the flowers engendered by rain to the breath of Zephirus which inspires the earth with crops,[22] and then to the sun moving into its seasonal station in the sky. The infusion of the four elements into life forms in springtime is a repetition of the original ordinance of nature in its primal perfection. The final seven lines of the passage draw attention from the fulfillment of the created design of plants and animals to man's urge to revivify his spirit. Even the vocabulary of pilgrimage conjoins physics with metaphysics. The verb *longen* has a sense of "to desire over a length of time," and the rhyme link of *corages* with *pilgrimages* joins natural with spiritual incitement, the *seson* with the *feeste* (*Tr.* 1, 168). The things of this world have priority, but not preeminence, over the things of the next.

All this is held taut by the anaphoric "whan" which initiates and sustains the sequence (something akin to the "whilom" of the opening tales).

"Whan" is the creative source, a pointing toward God's *logokinesis*. God is the conjuncture of all things, and springtime is an attraction of all living things toward refortifying their proper natural bond with him. The Parson recalls this harmonious union when he says: "God, and resoun, and sensualitee, and the body of man been so ordeyned that everich of thise foure thynges sholde have lordshipe over the othere" (10, 261). There is more example than allegory here, for Chaucer is not occupied with inventing *visibilia* to represent ideas, but with coordinating physics with metaphysics.[23] His Invocation offers a phenomenological example of the abstract design which Theseus claims the body's eye can verify.

Once past this passage, the author narrows his scan to one season, one day, and one person, "redy to wenden" on pilgrimage.[24] The middle of the chain of love is also figured by the road connecting Southwark with Canterbury. This is but a stretch of Watling Street, which in English lore is an earthly reflection of the heavenly *via lactea* (*HF,* 936–39).[25] The shrine at Canterbury joins man with the City of Love, which is Rome, and with the Worldly Paradise which is Jerusalem, a figure of the City of God.[26] Just as the revitalized earth is mediant between man and God, the animal *corage* for reproducing kind mediates the *devout corage* for pilgrimage, a moving upward toward God along the path from Philosophy's hem to her crown. The pilgrimage to Canterbury joins thanks to Becket for past intercessions with expectations of his future help. For the pilgrims, the road is a way of physical, social, and spiritual revitalization, and Chaucer's poetry is one vehicle for getting there.

The portraits of the pilgrims which occupy the greater part of the General Prologue reflect God's plenty without trying to imitate its diversity; and yet the poet claims that he pauses in his narrative while he has "tyme and space" (1, 35), as if the universe of his text has voids that need filling. There are first and last instances in the portraits as well. Chaucer begins with the Knight (1, 42) and ends with the Pardoner, all within a "clause" (1, 715–19). The portraits range from under ten lines (the Cook) to over sixty (the Friar), and some pilgrims are mentioned but not described. The forms of the portraits are elastic, expandable as long as there is time and space. Like Zeno's paradox of Achilles and the tortoise, while the event recorded has temporal and spatial bounds, its pace is infinitely divisible into smaller units.

Knight and Pardoner are first and last in the row of portraits. The former exemplifies a secular rank of mastery which defends both clergy and commons (as the cover representation on the hardcover *Riverside Chaucer* illustrates). The latter is a servant in ecclesiastical office who practices for his own rather than for a common good. It is obvious that moral and professional judgments are bound to be incompatible in certain cases, just as outer array is often out of harmony with the observation

of character and recounted experience. The digression which encloses
the portraits contains itself a digression on the language of poetry. At
first sight the digression seems out of place because it identifies a concern
with recording a tale-telling pact which has not yet been agreed to by
the pilgrims assembled in the Tabard:

> For this ye knowen al so wel as I:
> Whoso shal telle a tale after a man,
> He moot reherce as ny as evere he kan
> Everich a word, if it be in his charge,
> Al speke he never so rudeliche and large,
> Or ellis he moot telle his tale untrewe,
> Or feyne thyng, or fynde wordes newe.
> He may nat spare, althogh he were his brother;
> He moot as well seye o word as another.
> Crist spak hymself ful brode in hooly writ,
> And wel ye woot no vileynye is it.
> Eek Plato seith, whose kan hym rede,
> The wordes moote be cosyn to the dede.
>
> (1, 730–42)

This passage has been so heavily glossed that I need make only a few
brief observations.

The obvious argument of the passage concerns the referential fidelity
of word to fact, something like Dante's wish that *dal fatto il dir non sia
diversa,* "the fact does not differ from the word" (*Inf.* 32, 12). Some
readers react to the passage as if it were a narrative credo, "something
of a touchstone in his rehearsing of other people's words."[27] Man's words,
however, even in the most extreme conceptions of philosophical realism,
are not facts, though God's Word is everything. In *Cons.* 5, pr. 4, 62–66,
Philosophy explains that a sign may show what a thing is, but it does not
effect what it signifies.

While the aphorism "words must be cousins to deeds" seems to support
a language of factual representation of things, its history illustrates a
basic duplicity in the semantics of referentiality.[28] Language can recall
what has happened, invent what might have happened, and prophesy what
will happen. Chaucer borrows the saying from his own *Boece* (3, pr.
12, 205–7) where Philosophy replies to her pupil's complaint that her
exposition of God is interlaced and labyrinthine in its circuit of reasoning
rather than clarified by "resouns takyn fro withouten." "Thow hast lernyd
by the sentence of Plato," she says, "that nedes the wordis moot be cosynes
to the thynges of whiche thei speken." Chaucer borrows the phrase here
from Jean de Meun's rendering of the same passage in the *Roman,*
15188–92, where Sallust is cited as its source. Livy and Pliny the Younger

repeat it, and Chaucer would have known it directly from Chalcidius's translation of Plato's *Timaeus*. Sallust uses it to express the historian's concern with depicting the reality of an event, but Plato and his commentators use it to illustrate the task of inventing a language to produce a "likely account" of an event not seen, such as the creation of the world. Like God's Word, such a language speaks a reality into being. On another level of understanding, the Manciple appeals to the aphorism to excuse his plain description of fornication (9, 207–8).

Both senses of the saying are complicated, however, by the word *cousin*. Chalcidius and Boethius have *cognatos*. *Cousin,* which is not etymologically related, has the pejorative sense in Chaucer's day that it has in Shakespeare's and ours. The French *cousiner* means "to make a cuckold of," and *cousin* is glossed "cocu" (Chaucer's "cukkow") in the fifteenth-century *Cent nouvelles nouvelles*. Though not cited in the *OED* from so early a time, the word may well have carried the later recorded sense of "to take advantage of someone by assuming a blood-relationship."[29] Words, then, can dupe deeds and misrepresent them as well as reveal them.[30]

Other shards of meaning are chipped off the apparently solid sense of the apology for reportorial style by its appeal to the authority of Christ's speaking "ful brode." While "rude and large" words are called for in presenting the rude and loose speech of the Miller, for example, Christ's "broad" speech is, rather, parabolic figuring of truth. If Chaucer intends to speak broadly in the manner of Christ, we must be on guard to do better than the apostles to read him. Finally, the explanation that a reliable reporter "may nat spare, althogh he were his brother" implies the function of language to expose and shame others.

One way that Chaucer cozens us while claiming verisimilitude of style is the repetition of the expression "hir wordes" (728 and 729). The language of both the frame narrative and the speech of the pilgrims is verse, though one is permitted to doubt that the rhythmic cadence of most of his speakers is iambic pentameter. Chaucer's verse is "cousin" to common speech, one could say, anticipating Wordsworth's and Coleridge's claim for the speech of common men in their Preface to *Lyrical Ballads*. If we are not unsettled by the Parson's claim that he cannot "rum, ram, ruf" by letter while he is doing it (10, 43) or puzzled by the Man of Law speaking in verse while announcing that he will speak in prose it is because Chaucer has so inured us to the look and sound of his verse line that we do not call into question its particularity as "poetry." Many feel that something is askew when the Man of Law's goes on to tell his tale in rime royal, but in a world of commutative orders and values, anything can change places with another. Chaucer's digression is not so much an apology to his audience for rude language, then, as it is a warning that the realities which language shapes are beyond the control of its users. The word is not only cousin to the deed it describes but father to the deed it informs.

The tale of the gathering of pilgrims at the Tabard on a particular day and their departure toward Canterbury the next morning is an exercise in adapting word to the deed. It is clear from the beginning that a horizontal vector of narrative—a serial report of happenings in chronological sequence—is neither realistically possible or poetically profitable for Chaucer. To begin with, the opening invocation to spring is his investment of a referential value for that movement, and the plenitude of portraits gives descriptive weight to what is moved. The pause to consider the function of language engages the reader in an interpretive complicity in the verbal fiction of fact, as well as in the verbal fact of fiction.

After that arrest of time and motion, the narrative recalls in four lines the sufficiency of food and drink served at the Tabard before pausing once more to describe the Host (1, 751–57). It is Harry's posture, or mien, which strikes the reporter's eye, and the largesse of his figure fits the large role he offers to play for the pilgrimage. Then the narrative resumes with Host and pilgrims doing things backwards, for common assent is made to a promise of sport and comfort that Harry has not yet even proposed.

The call for tales of "best sentence and moost solaas" (1, 798) contains a challenge for language to both instruct and delight. The combination of tasks is conventional. Chaucer might have known of Horace's *dulce et utile* (*Ars poetica* 333–34) and would have been familiar with the homilest's *delectatio et utilitas.* Jean de Meun aims for *profiz et delectation* (*RR,* 15211), and in the *Parliament of Fowls,* line 15, Chaucer reveals his taste in reading "what for lust and what for lore." Gower announces in the Prologue to his *Confessio Amantis,* 17–19, that he will write a book between the two, "somewhat of lust, somewhat of lore." It is easy to equate solace and sentence with chaff and fruit, with game and earnest and with lie and veracity, but the problem for both the poet and his audience is to *not* know the difference. The pleasure in the letter of a text should not be distinct from the pleasure of its spirit. All is, after all, written for our doctrine. In *Contra mendacium, PL* 40, 517ff., Augustine sees the peril of insisting on too-rigid distinctions. While a lie does not admit of a good intention, *tropi non sunt mendacia, metaphora, antiphrasis* [tropes are not lies, nor metaphors, nor antiphrasis]. Scripture is full of figures and even lies such as David's pretended insanity. In the Epilogue to *Il decamerone,* Boccaccio explains that, if his tales read foul, unseemliness is to be attributed to the mind of the reader and not to his text.

Harry sets himself to judge sentence and solace, and to guide and provide for the pilgrims. Like Chauntecleer with his hens, he gathers his wards into a flock to begin the pilgrimage. Harry is the pilgrims' dynamic mediator of word, way, and sustenance. He is a shadow of Theseus's First Mover bringing diverse mankind along a path of love towards a sign of its source. Chaucer's recollection of the event rehearses that gathering of diverse material into one book, reharmonizing the earnest and game that man's fall from God set asunder. If he usurps Harry's role as reporter (1, 814), it is not to better record the event, but to recall and record in a way which makes something of his own sense out of it.

# Epilogue: Memory and Design

Sir Thopas (The Canterbury Pilgrims) says (to Chaucer)
  Namoor—
  Thy drasty ryming is not
  worth a toord
—and Chaucer seemed to think so too for he stopped
       and went on in prose.
                    —William Carlos Williams

Exit the mental moonlight, exit lex,
Rex and principium.
                    —Wallace Stevens

THE *CANTERBURY TALES* OPENS WITH AN EMANATION OF GOD'S CREATIVE breath, continues with examples of tales and events of profit and waste of word along the pilgrimage way, and concludes with a redressing of word in the service of God's creative design. The book begins with Mother Earth being filled with spirit and ends with thanks to Christ and his blissful mother. The flowchart of the progress between these two poles has the U-shaped curve of spiritual history.[1] This shape is emminently suitable to a work which imitates God's providential design. Like that design, the beginning and end are firm and stable, but the middle has all the semblance of the world's disorder. The middle in the space of the chain of love is the realm of nature. The middle in the temporal concatenation of God's salvific design is fallen man's spiritual progress. Nature's fall is visible in the changing of substantial forms, and man's falling away from God is perceptible in the lack of accord between his thoughts, words, and deeds. The shape and structure of the *Canterbury Tales* imitates the triune form figured by Theseus's chain of love.

Like the chain's middle reach between invisible perfection and visible corruption, the whole of Chaucer's book has indeterminate shape. Its size and the size of the individual tales lack limiting definition. The scheme which Harry calls for neither controls order nor dominates the content and expanse of the stories called for. As current critical disputes over "Chaucer's own order" suggest, the tales in the great middle of the book

151

are *commutative,* or endlessly shiftable. Many, like the Monk's tragedies and the tale of Thopas, shift in size, prosodic pattern, and genre.[2] In other words, the middle of the narrative is infinitely variable, and if readers sense an incompleteness or unfinished shape in Chaucer's book, it is because its form imitates nature's, whose essential design ordained by the Creator is beyond human comprehension.

Put another way, man's life is divisible into three times, or tenses, while God's perfection is outside time. Man's fall from the specific and perfect time—or timelessness—of Eden is a fall into tense where future is death, past is memory, and present is man's struggle to understand the bond between them. The past is remembered as a record of man's spiritual fault, and the shifts of man's memory, if not the fact of it, are marks of his ontological imperfection.[3] Man's tri-form temporality reflects the tri-form universe, which is in Boethian terms a falling off from Oneness of God.

Chaucer draws particular attention in all his major poems to the struggle of art to put a structure to memory, and the struggle of memory to inform art with a sense of concatenation of event and impression. The poetic voice of the recorder of the Canterbury tales struggles to remember and order an experience which happened sometime in the past, and finally in his most personal moment at the close of his book where he submits his art to God's mediation, he confesses to unnamed works "if they were in my remembrance." Surely Chaucer means by this surprising admission of forgetfulness that memory is fallible and that any record of it is an imperfect guide to fact and meaning.[4] On the other hand, what one has forgotten one cannot confess, and so memory is a fallible agent of the penitential process. Admitting memory's imperfection in the Boethian dialectic implicitly contrasts man's art with God's timeless spontaneity. It is a negative way of acknowledging the perfection of God's memory-less being.[5] All those "lapses" of credibility and completeness attributed to Chaucer by readers of the *Tales* are qualities of an art whose purpose is to represent the ontological blur between what *is* and what is known of the world.

Philosophically speaking, the poet's art, whether Chaucer's or William Carlos Williams', works upon a store of matter in wait for form. It does not reproduce, but *translates* images stored in the mind, just as Sir Thopas translates a dream image of an elusive elf queen into a real object of quest. Artistic memory conjoins old with new, past with present meanings, and other places and voices with this place and a new voice.[6] One voice of remembering claims to recall or forget things which have happened, and another admits its reshaping, or misshaping of them.[7] The former is historical and imitative, and the latter is creative and original.[8] It is idle labor to try to fathom the collaboration of the two in the *Tales,* for there is no way to sift out the fruit of impersonation from the chaff of representation.

In this respect, the poet is created by and exists only within his own text, where there is no speaking voice in control of material, only a text's discourse.[9] So the Knight describes the temple murals as if *he* as well as the characters of the story were seeing them fresh (1, 1995–2028), and the Wife of Bath is mentioned by a character *within* a tale told by one of her companions on the road.[10] Verisimilitude in the recollection of performance would necessarily reproduce such slips: "Whoso shal telle a tale after a man . . . / He may nat spare, althogh he were his brother." Chaucer disdains what critics today scorn as the "imitative fallacy." His poetic account of the tale-telling is in constant collaboration with the pilgrims' own agony with their texts.[11]

Were Chaucer recording his own uncertain remembrance of the order of tales, or imitating the commutative structure of nature, he would not set a transitive order for the pilgrims' tales. It is possible that he never intended one, though his intentions are beyond consultation.[12] The lack of a common manuscript order is a historical fact which seems to have had little critical incidence on interpretation of tale or reading of design.[13] Intentionally or no, Chaucer's narrative strategy in the *Tales* imitates the confusion of creation between its *termini* of space and time and the unachieved possibilities of purgatory. The thematic and structural organization of the *Tales* imitates the *confusione* that Dante recognizes as the unavoidable condition of man on a quest which begins with a yearning to know, and then passes by a way of wonder before arriving at a just admiration of the ungraspable.[14] Confusion is the way toward God's clarity. It is the way of Chaucer's Canterbury pilgrims who cannot make order out of what they "han seyn with ye" and "herd seyd".[15] Where Dante's *Commedia* records a sure role of mediators in guiding the poet up a scale of vision and love from hell and Medusa, through purgatory and Matelda, to heaven and Beatrice, we are guided by Harry through a nebulous cloud of narrative signifiers which defy conjunction with coordinate meaning.[16]

There is no uncertainty of design in the beginning and end of the book, but the middle which mediates between them is all uncertain. The reader is trumped and frustrated repeatedly by Chaucer's stylistic feints. His art cozens whatever meanings we come to his text prepared to discover. He breaks the rules of literary convention which his audience is prepared to follow with him. We are aware that violations of rules are purposeful, but we are unsure of Chaucer's purpose. *Troilus,* with its swift switch at the end from an exposition of a rich and complex secular experience to a brief glimpse of spiritual authority gives us a sense that the truth of God, no matter how absolute and enduring it be, has the immeasurably small textual dimensions of a nap compared to the vast fabric our memory and art make of life's experiences. We feel the heaviness of worldly things easily, but conceive hardly the lightness of things spiritual. The truth of God is a cipher beside the long shelves of volumes dedicated to its search. There are meanings everywhere in Chaucer's book and in our world, but no one shape of order can contain all of them.

The problem is epistemological and universal. What is unstable along the perceptible reaches of the Chain of Love is ungraspable as a design of human life. Signs stray from meanings. What can we make of the significance in the Miller's tale of the hole in Nicholas's door, just big enough to let a cat pass to and fro (1, 3440–43), or of the magic which lifts that door unobserved back onto its hinges (1, 3471–99)? Are we to solve the riddle of the equal division of Mabely's pan between the hell-bound summoner and the touring devil (3, 1629)? What are we to make of Hector's letter to Troilus concerning if "a man was worthi to ben ded" (*Tr*, 2, 1698–1701), or of the "maid child" in the company of the merchant's wife as she makes her love bargain with the monk of the Shipman's tale (7, 95–97)? Before these signs we are put in the position of the Pardoner's rioters, challenged to weigh the gold on their path for its power of purchase of bread and wine as well as for its purchase of truth. Like them, we are apt to read wrong, if we dare read at all. What is an artist like Chaucer to select out of his experience to make meaning of if he is unsure of meanings himself?

If the floating middle world of the *Tales* between the Prologue celebration of spring and the final explicit impersonates the confused, uncertain, and conditional life of man between its inception and terminus, like Harry's calculation of time it is not without a speculative notion of organization. Each witness can construct his own design,[17] and even absence of design can be understood, like a musical *cadenza,* as a plastic container for countless forms.[18] We are not sure whether we must make sense of the pilgrimage process in order to make sense of the tales, or sense of the tales to make sense of the pilgrimage.

Perhaps it does not matter, for if a pilgrim's eye strays from the strait path in its imaginative engagement on the array of tale or teller, his foot still carries him closer to a goal that is his intent. The art of recollection need not fit with the narrative structure of a succession of events on the road. Even if the tales are a "local color" digression in a tourist guide for wayward pilgims, they serve the goal of pilgrimage. Pilgrimage and tales partake of the same force of propulsion, but how close to each other their trajectories are is not evident. Each activity invites measure against models set up by the reporter. The authority of Saint Thomas as mediator for the English folk validates pilgrimage just as spring fulfillment validates man's yearning for refreshment. The tales, however, stray from the Host's authoritative design for sentence and solace, fail the spirit of storial competition, and ignore their pilgrimage context. In any order of the fragments one wishes to follow, one can see a succession of redirected narrative drifting away from order in a continuing imitation of Theseus's successive repairs of amputated schemes and the Miller's refusal to obey orders.[19]

Chaucer's own tale of Thopas, it seems to me, can be read as a reflection of the whole book, no matter where in the middle of the pilgrimage journey it is performed. The archetypal quest to rescue an imprisoned queen has, of course its paradigmatic source in the legend of Troy, but although readers have wondered why Chaucer does not seem to draw from the the familiar stories of Chrétien de Troyes,[20] the story of Thopas is a recongizable reflection of Chrétien's *Chevalier de la Charrette,* where Lancelot's voyage to rescue Guenevere from Meleagaunt, son of the king of Gorre, is first blocked by the theft of his horse, and then frustrated by the queen's disarming attitude toward her rescuer. Lancelot is lured from the direct path to his goal by deeds and words he cannot read.

Thopas's quest is replete with such lures, the most striking of which is the style of the teller of his story. The persona who recalls it even attributes to Harry Bailly an uncharacteristic slip into rime-royal to invite it, as if the Host had fallen under the spell of the Prioress's prosody. The tale trots along in at least six distinct metrical gaits. Its diction is a curious mix of courtly formula and lewd idiom. *"Par ma fay . . .* Thy mawe shal I percen" (7, 820–23) is a typical example. Tautological sequences like "chaast and no lecchour" (7, 745) illustrate wonderfully the telling difference of two ways of saying [almost] the same thing. The quest itself is just as confused. As God holds the thought of creation eternally in his mind before it is realized by his word, Thopas holds an idea in his mind for an immeasurable instant before he sets out to realize it. While God exists in the perfection of his stable *otium,* Thopas, who claims to have dreamed all night, falls asleep in the middle of the day, when sleep is sloth and dreams are noontime demons.

On his grail quest, told by Chrétien in his incompleted *Conte du Graal,* Lancelot falls asleep within sight of the object of his search, the grail itself. The incompleteness of the tale of Thopas and the incompleteness of the pilgrimage and of its book, reflect the incompleteness of the grail quest by those unable to read its road signs, while the completeness of the tale of Melibee, like the achieving of the grail by Lancelot's son Galahad, is a reflection of the completeness of God's design which one is liable to read as confusion. The tale of Thopas looks to the pilgrimage actors and their tales, while the tale of Melibee looks past this particular rehearsal of man's quest for grace to its end. Harry Bailly can only block what he hears as a misdirected narrative amble, and only praise what he reads as an example of domestic harmony; but his praise of the story of Melibee as a reflection of his own family is a negative lesson in hermeneutics for all the pilgrims.

The pilgrim Chaucer's two tales mediate nicely between the opening tale by the Knight and the knitting up by the Parson. Olifaunt's blocking of quest in the one and Prudence's redirecting of a quest for vengeance in the other reflect Saturn's amending of Theseus's governance in the Knight's tale and foreshadow the Parson's exposé of the virtues which counter the hindering of man's pursuit of grace by the seven deadly sins. Theseus rearms himself with Platonic wisdom in the service of political optimism, Thopas rearms himself with food and war-gear to win a spirit, Melibee arms himself with prudence, and the Parson arms his audience with spiritual armor. The plenitude of detail in the rhetorical figures of *divisio* and *occupatio* with which the Knight and Parson fill their tales is present in Chaucer's lingering over details of flora, food, armor, and tales of adventure. The "privy woon" of the elf queen is both heaven and hell (and one recalls the "privee stoon" of the alchemists [8, 1452] which mediates between dross and gold ). As the haunt of love, it is heaven; as the haunt of the three-headed Olifaunt, it is hell. The *gras* which is both grace and grass links spiritual, sexual, and natural love. Thopas's *goore* is a tabard, a smock, and an alb. The body of woman with which Theseus orders chaos into order, and which in the figure of the Virgin Mary is man's mediator in the penitential process, is but an aery form in Thopas's high fantasy.[21]

Where Thopas searched for a body to realize an idea, Melibee is led from attention to the wounded body of his daughter Sophie [wisdom] to an idea of forgiveness. She, like Christ, is the sacrificial mediator of man's redemptive process. Melibee himself figures the confusion of words which cannot restore love until instructed by Prudence, whose traditional virtue is an ability to accord past and present with the future, i.e. God's Providence. She is the power of confession which moves man toward grace. She is, in brief, the mediation Thopas would find in the body of the fairy queen, and her language is antithetical to dalliance but conducive to.Christian charity, or love.

Should the reader resist the notion that Chaucer plays more loose than fast with the Platonic humanistic idea of God's providential design, he need only remind himself that Chaucer delights in questioning belief and knowledge, and in mocking his own quest for knowledge. I believe that Chaucer prefers the Boethian model to various opposing Scholastic and Nominalist speculations, but he is too cautious to take the confident stance of the zealot and proselytizer. He knows that his art is a distant and riotous imitation of God's order. His *Canterbury Tales* is a book of the life of fallen man trying to understand where he is in order to know where he must go. So he writes himself on the way in hopes he is closing the gap with God instead of with the devil. His fictional pilgrimage route connects the secular array of the Tabard tavern with the spiritual sign of the shrine of Becket. The narrative entertainment on the way poses Knight and Parson at opposite ends of a spectrum of interests whose connecting bond is not so much a steady-state motion from punctual to timeless values as an errant groping for a right way. As man's memory is sharpest on first and last images of a significant event, the design of the whole is clearest in its opening and in its closing, but the value of the art, like the value of life, is in the middle. The middle is wits and words and all of man's knowledge of things seen and heard.

Finally, the structure and style of *The Canterbury Tales* is a testing of memory and meaning. It is an exposition of man's incapacity to love, that is, to read whole or true the *invisibilia* behind things which give them meaning. Man cannot see the "real thing." Chaucer's poetry challenges assurance of discernible sense in any ontological system, particularly religion, philosophy, and society. It does so by subverting the dominant trends of thought and expression of his day. His poetry is no ventriloquist's dummy parroting another's thought; it is, rather, a questioning of the bond between his time and his art, for Chaucer tests the capacity and power of language to represent and test thought, as well as to express its truth.[22] This is, essentially, Chaucer's negative poetics. While Chaucer places himself as an artist in an intellectual gap between reason and faith, percept and concept, the pilgrimage he describes to figure his interrogation of language is itself a gap between rules of one system and rules of another. Pilgrimage is a *tertium quid* between worlds. It figures chance, disarray and, indeterminacy. Thopas's quest road, traversed without knowing what lies ahead of him, is, in Pauline terms, the gap between being and becoming. Chaucer's fictional struggle, and struggle with fiction, as one trying to report an event in which his consciousness plays a part, aligns the task of writing with the search for grace.

In effect, Chaucer writing his text is Chaucer writing himself out of it, and his reader risks finding himself trapped in his place, forced to look for an art of escape. Chaucer's poetry is a trespass, a transgression of boundaries between thought and word, between sight and insight, and between the hand's flight with pen across a paper's space and the soul's flight across the cosmos. *The Canterbury Tales* is a motion past the easy confidences in Platonic ideologies and Christian dogma toward an ironic and comic agony of doubt and wonder and fun.

# Notes

## Prologue: A Tale of Two Cities

The text is *The Riverside Chaucer,* ed. Larry D. Benson, 3d edition, (Boston: Houghton Mifflin, 1987). All susequent quotations from Chaucer's works are from this text, with fragment and line numbers in parentheses.

1. See the vision of Jerusalem in *Apocalypsis* 21: 18: *Et erat structura muri eius ex lapide: ipsa vero civitas aurum mundum simile vitro mundo* (The wall was built of diamond and the city of pure gold like polished glass).

2. So Boethius's *De Consolatione* 4, m. 1, 23–46:

> Huc te si reducem referat uia,
> Quam nunc requiris immemor:
> "Haec," dices, "memini, patria est mihi,
> Hinc ortus, hic sistam gradum."

Chaucer's translation is: "And yif thi wey ledeth the ayein so that thou be brought thider, thanne wiltow sey now that his is the contre that thou requerist, of whiche thow ne haddest no mynde—'but now it remembreth me wel, here was I born, her wol I fastne my degree, here wol I duelle,'" Unless otherwise noted I rely on Chaucer's *Boece* for the Latin of *De Consolatione* throughout.

3. In *De Consolatione,* a source for the Monk's account, Lady Philosophy impugns with authority man's shallow view of beauty: "The shynynge of thi forme (*that is to seyn, the beute of thi body*), how swiftly passynge is it, and how transitorie! . . . For so as Aristotle telleth, that if that men hadde eyghen of a beeste that highte lynx, so that the lokynge of folk myghte percen thurw the thynges that withstoden it, who lokide thanne in the entrayles of the body of Alcibiades, that was ful fair in the superfice withoute, it shulde seme ryght foul. And forthi yif thow semest fair, thy nature ne maketh nat that, but the deceyvaunce of the feblesse of the eighen that loken" (*Boece* 3, pr. 8, 35–49).

4. In the *Roman de la rose,* 6119–201, the story of Nero is introduced by a passage in which Fortune is described in splendid array until it falls away and she sees her real self. In spite, she turns her powers against worldly order.

5. Linda Georgianna, "'Love So Dearly Bought': The Terms of Redemption in *The Canterbury Tales,*" *SAC* 12 (1990): 87, argues that redemption "informs the treatment of pilgrimage and penance as twin frames for narrative—to elicit not scorn but hope."

6. Anne Middleton, "The Idea of Public Poetry in the Reign of Richard II," *Speculum* 53 (1978): 102, explains that for the public, the poetic enterprise is the middle way between truth and the audience's need for it. Chaucer's style, she points out (95) is "medium" between ernest and game. Charles Muscatine, *Chaucer and the French Tradition* (Berkeley: University of California Press, 1957), 136, locates Chaucer's style "somewhere" between comic and tragic.

7. The image is used by King Edwin's unnamed advisor in his argument for conversion to Christianity, according to Bede's *Ecclesiastical History,* II, 13. Insistence upon the tension in Chaucer's style between competing and opposite attractions is common. For

representative views, Lee W. Patterson, "The 'Parson's Tale' and the Quitting of the 'Canterbury Tales,'" *Traditio* 34 (1978): 379, claims that Chaucer's basic structure is binary. Alfred David, *The Strumpet Muse: Art and Morals in Chaucer's Poetry* (Bloomington: University of Indiana Press, 1976), argues that Chaucer's poetry tries to reconcile authority to the experience of his own age. Peter Elbow, *Oppositions in Chaucer* (Middletown, CT.: Wesleyan University Press, 1975), 13–14, argues that opposition is Chaucer's dialectical pattern, but that the endings of *Troilus* and the *Tales* undo opposition (131ff.). Derek Brewer, "Class Distinction in Chaucer," *Speculum* 43 (1968): 290–305, points to Chaucer's binary social conceptions, which oppose the gentle and the churlish, the free and the bonded, etc. William Ryding, *Studies in Medieval Narrative* (The Hague: Mouton, 1971), 25–27, asserts that binarism is the basic narrative structure of all medieval poetry. On the other hand, Claude Lévi-Strauss, *Structural Anthropology* (New York: Basic Books, 1963), 154, argues that dyads are nothing but disguised triads: two poles and an axis of a different nature, and D. W. Robertson, Jr., *A Preface to Chaucer* (Princeton: Princeton University Press, 1963), 51, reminds us that "the medieval world was innocent of our profound concern for tension."

8. The Monk's own language contributes to this tension between values. *Array* designates the naked appearance of one's body, but elsewhere more often refers to the clothing which hides it. *Tolde* means "valued" (cf. a "telling" remark), and draws attention to the paucity of Nero's respect for his mother as well as to the penury of his words. Just before the Monk tells his tale, Harry brags that he is "perilous with knyf in honde" 7, 1919).

9. Chaucer has earned the title of philosopher. Eustache Deschamps and Thomas Hoccleve compare him to Aristotle, and Thomas Usk calls him "the noble philosophical poete in English." To Hoccleve, he is the Aristotle of his time. To Caxton, Dunbar, Skelton, and Douglas, Chaucer is model of learning. Chaucer himself lists under the epithet "philosopher," physicians, alchemists, astrologers, and magicians, and he who "kan suffre it as a philosophre" is for Chaucer someone indifferent to the slings and arrows of the world (8, 490), and who, like Socrates, wears the same countenance in good or bad circumstances (*Roman de la rose*, 5842–50). Modern critics are less confident in the status of Chaucer's philosophy. Robert Burlin, *Chaucerian Fiction* (Princeton: Princeton University Press, 1977), 150, observes: "The totality of the fictive experience is the philosophic substance, and its conceptual explicitness is mere accident." John M. Hill, *Chaucerian Belief: The Poetics of Reverence and Delight* (New Haven: Yale University Press, 1991), 16, says that Chaucer is "vestigially Neoplatonic" (if only through the accident of his sources), and that the metaphysical context for gathering the tales is a "vaguely" Neoplatonic search for truths that can be tested through the matter of the tales. Hill, 20, stresses the "feeling" that affects perceptions and understanding of human experience.

# Chapter 1. Chaucer's Chain of Love in the European Tradition

1. Homer's chain is *seiron*, the etymological ancestor of Latin *serere* "to tress, interlace," French *serrure* "lock" and English *sark* woven shirt." The combined natural and artificial connotations of the term are reflected in Old English *seorðan* "to copulate," and in the noun *searo* "artifice, magic." The chain image has been traced through English literature by Arthur O. Lovejoy, *The Great Chain of Being* (Cambridge: Harvard University Press, 1936), who describes the hierarchy implied a "unilinear gradation in continuity" (69). See also Emil Wolff, *Die goldene Kette; Die Aurea Catena Homeri in der englischen Literatur von Chaucer bis Wordsworth* (Hamburg: Hanischer Gildenverlag, 1947). Ernst Robert Curtius, *European Literature in the Latin Middle Ages*, trans. Williard R. Fisk

(New York: Pantheon, Bollingen Series 36, 1953), 101–27, discusses the image in relation to the figure of *Natura*. The eighteenth-century philosopher George Berkeley, in *Siris: A Chain of Philosophical Reflections,* describes the chain as one whose extreme links are incorporeal and whose center alone is capable of motion.

2. *Platonis Timaeus, interprete Chalcidio,* ed. Ioh. Wrobel (Frankfurt: Minerva, 1903). I quote the original Latin when I assume that Chaucer might have had it before him. Winthrop Wetherbee, "Philosophy, Cosmology, and the Twelfth-century Renaissance," *A History of Twelfth-Century Western Philosophy,* ed. Peter Dronke (Cambridge: Cambridge University Press, 1988), 21–53, reviews the effect of this passage on the philosophy of science and on literary imagery. Nothing rivals, however, the elegance of Giordano Bruno's late sixteenth-century essay on the chain of love, "De vinculo et quodammode in genere," *De Magia: De vinculis in genere,* ed. Albano Biondi (Pordenone: Biblioteca dell'immagine, 1987), which adapts the *Timaeus* to Renaissance philosophy.

3. *Omnia continuis successionibus se sequantur degenerantia per ordinem ad imum meandi:inuenietur pressius intuenti a summo deo usque ad ultimam rerum faecem una mutuis se uinculis religans et nusquam interrupta conexio. Et haec est Homeri catena aurea, quam pendere de caelo in terras deum iussisse commemorat.* The text is *Macrobius Opera,* ed. Franz Eyssenhardt (Leipzig: Teubner, 1893), and the translation is by William Harris Stahl, *Macrobius: Commentary of the Dream of Scipio* (New York: Columbia University Press, 1952). Arthur O. Lovejoy, *The Great Chain,* 63n., remarks that "this, of course, was not 'Homer's golden chain'" but Macrobius had access to Plato's readings of Homer's chain. Of the same passage, Francis M. Cornford, *Plato's Theory of Knowledge* (New York: Bobbs-Merrill, 1957), 38, argues that "Socrates, in the vein of sophistic interpretations of the poets, misuses the passage where Zeus challenges the gods. . . . Homer means nothing else by the golden chain than the sun." In the Book of Job, 26:7, Bildad praises God thus: "Qui extendi aquilonem super vacuum, / Et appendit terram super nihilum" ["He spread the North above the void, and posed the earth on nothingness"]. In *The Travels of Sir John Mandeville,* chapter 20, this is garbled into *"qui suspendi terram ex nihilo"* ["He hung the earth from nothing"].

4. *The Discarded Image* (Cambridge: Cambridge University Press, 1964), 43. *Martianus Capella, De nuptiis,* ed. Adolf Dick (Stuttgart, 1978), 8, 589, identifies the perfection of the cosmic triad in the harmony of Fates, Graces, and the rule of heaven and earth.

5. With his eye on other aspects of Plato's works, Paul G. Ruggiers, "Platonic Forms in Chaucer," *ChauR* 17 (1983): 367, identifies the four Platonic topics in Chaucer's writings as eating and drinking, sexuality and love, play and seriousness, and the making of art.

6. Cited by Brian Stock, *Myth and Science in the Twelfth Century: A Study of Bernard Silvester* (Princeton: Princeton University Press, 1972), 259–60n. Stock notes the influence of Asclepius's discussion of the chain between heaven and earth which binds all nature (153–56).

7. All quotations and translations from the *Commedia* are from Charles S. Singleton, *The Divine Comedy,* 6 vols. (Princeton: Princeton University Press, 1970–75); and for *Convivio* the edition of G. Busnelli and G. Vandelli (Florence: Felice le Monnier, 1968).

8. All quotations from the *Roman* are from the edition of Daniel Poirion (Paris: Garnier Flammarion, 1974), and for Lydgate's *Troy Book,* the edition of Henry Bergen, EETS ES 97, 103, 106, 126 (London, 1906–33).

9. *Harley 2724, F. 131r.* Peter Godman has provided me with the translation in a personal communication.

10. Stanza 4b. A recent edition with full discussion is offered by Peter Godman, "Literary Classicism and Latin Erotic Poetry of the Twelfth Century and the Renaissance,"

*Latin Poetry and the Classical Tradition,* ed. Peter Godman and Oswyn Murray (Oxford: Clarendon Press, 1990), 163–69.

11. So John Scotus Erigena, cited by Peter Dronke, *The Medieval Poet and his World* (Rome: edizione de storia letturatura, 1984), 461.

12. Pierre Courcelle, *La Consolation de Philosphie dans la tradition littéraire* (Paris: Etudes augustiniennes, 1967), documents the popularity of the image of an intermediary *nexus* in medieval art: chain, pillar, ladder, etc. In the Anglo-Saxon *Exeter Book* Riddle 55, Christ is a ladder "which lifts us to the skies." Mircea Eliade, "The Yearning for Paradise in Primitive Tradition," in *The Making of Myth,* ed. Richard M. Ohmann (New York: G. P. Putnam, 1962), 84–98, reviews the *axis mundi* images which connect heaven with earth.

13. *Hali Meiðhad,* ed. Bella Millett (London: EETS OS 284), 23.

14. Dronke, *The Medieval Poet,* 449, citing Apuleius.

15. "Lanquan li jorn," 36–37. The edition is James J. Wilhelm, *Medieval Song* (New York: E. P. Dutton, 1971), 388–90. The first two lines in each of the first seven stanzas describe the complicity of God with earthly love. P. G. Walsh, *Love Lyrics from the Carmina Burana* (Chapel Hill: University of North Carolina Press, 1993), 190, finds *amor de lonh* the "counterpart of Christian amicitia."

16. See Jan Ziolkowski, *Alan of Lille's Grammar of Sex* (Cambridge, MA.: Medieval Academy of America, 1985), 1–6.

17. *Mater est materia* [mother is matter] is a medieval commonplace derived from Isidor of Seville's *Etymologiae.*

18. Cited by Joan M. Ferrante, *The Image of Women in Medieval Literature from the Twelfth Century to Dante* (New York: Columbia University Press, 1975), 157.

19. Stock, *Myth and Science,* 87–97 and 259–60. In *Timaeus,* 35a, *noys* is mediant between the indivisible world of ideas and the divisible form and matter of creation.

20. Stock, *Myth and Science,* 44–45.

21. *Altior en caelo rimor secreta tonantis / Et tamen inferior terris tetra tartara cerno.* The text is from *Through a Glass Darkly: Aldhelm's Riddles in the British Library MS Royal.12. C. xxiii,* ed. Nancy Porter Stork (Toronto: PIMS, 1990), 232.

22. Bernard Silvester, *Cosmographia,* ed. Peter Dronke (Leiden: Brill, 1978).

23. A. J. Minnis and A. B. Scott, eds., *Medieval Literary Theory and Criticism c. 110–c. 1375.* The Commentary Tradition (Oxford: Clarendon Press, 1988), 134. The etymology is fanciful, of course, for *dema,* and not *demas,* is "chain."

24. *Natura formatrix* is God's moneyer, minting according to his design. This agency is the topic of the *Timaeus* 31c–32c, explained in Chalcidius's *Commentary,* 1, 21–25, as the union of a creative idea, *intelligibilis,* with time, *temporis,* bound together by an ordinance called *aevum.* D. W. Robertson, Jr., *A Preface to Chaucer* (Princeton: Princeton University Press, 1963), 114–17, reviews Augustine on the principle of beauty as governing creation and the proccesses of nature. Beauty is both a positive and negative bond, an inspiration to piety and a snare to the senses.

25. For Trevet's commentary on this meter, see A. J. Minnis, *Chaucer and Pagan Antiquity* (Cambridge: Derek Brewer, 1982), 145.

26. R. W. Southern, *Robert Grosseteste* (Oxford: Clarendon Press, 1986), 216–17.

27. Citing Grosseteste, Eugene Vance, "*Pearl:* Love and the Poetics of Participation," in *Poetics: Theory and Practice in Medieval Literature,* ed. Piero Boitani and Anna Torti (Suffolk: Boydell and Brewer, 1991), 143, says that "the *lumen* which shines from (or through) the Forms of things is therefore adequate to the *lux* that is their source." For Grosseteste, *lumen* is God in us, and *lux* is we in Him. See also Richard Sorabji, *Matter, Space, and Motion* (Ithaca: Cornell University Press, 1988), 107–10. For Bernard Silvester on light, see Stock, 141 ff.

28. Cited by William Gass, *The World Within the Word* (New York: Alfred A. Knopf, 1979), 309. Though Nicholas lived after Chaucer, the conic design has origins at least as early as the dress of Boethius's Philosophy.

29. John Herman Randall, *Aristotle* (New York: Columbia University Press, 1960), 35 and 112–14.

30. James Weisheipl, O. P., *Nature and Motion in the Middle Ages,* ed. William E. Carroll (Washington, D. C.: Catholic University of America Press, 1985), 5.

31. *Paradiso* 33, 92. In *Vita Nuova,* 25, Dante elaborates on this relation. Both Dante and Chaucer may have known Pope Innocent's *De Miseria,* which incorporates the classical terms into Christian doctrine. See Robert E. Lewis, ed., *Innocent III, De miseria condicionis humane* (Athens: University of Georgia Press, 1978), 5–17.

32. Cited by Stock, 112. Stock's discussion of twelfth-century conceptions of creation could well fit in place of this entire chapter. Curtius, 544–46, notes the conceit of the craftsman in Sapientia 11, 21, and discusses its influence on the distribution of the image in medieval literature.

33. *De Planctu Naturae,* trans. James J. Sheridan (Toronto: PIMS, 1980).

34. Chaucer would have found the conceit in the opening lines of Geoffrey of Vinsauf's *Poetria Nova.*

35. Minnis and Scott, *Medieval Literary Theory,* p. 158.

36. The standard discussion of the principle of plentitude remains Walter Clyde Curry's *Chaucer and the Mediaeval Sciences,* 2d ed. (New York: Barnes and Noble, 1960), 155ff. John H. Fisher, *John Gower* (London: Methuen, 1965), 161, explains that the principle of plenitude is maintained by natural law, or the impulse to procreate (Chaucer's law of kind). A modern equivalent of the principle is steady-state physics.

37. *The Enchaféd Flood* (New York: Random House, 1967), 46.

38. Cited by Etienne Gilson, *History of Christian Philosophy in the Middle Ages* (London: Sheed and Ward, 1955), 11. C. S. Lewis, *The Discarded Image,* 1–5, discusses the continuity through the Middle Ages of the Classical traditions concerning the invisible occupants of space.

39. The text is *Metamorphoses,* vol. 1, ed. Frank Justus Miller (London: Heinemann, 1951).

40. The translation is from *Augustine,* ed. William Benton, Great Books of the Western World, vol. 18 (Chicago: Encyclopaedia Britannica, 1952).

41. *John Gower, The Complete Works,* ed. G. Macaulay, vol. 2 (Oxford: Clarendon Press, 1901).

42. Martin Stevens and Kathleen Falvey, "Substance, Accident, and Transformation: A Reading of the *Pardoner's Tale,*" *ChauR* 17 (1983): 154, suggest that transformations in the tale result only in nothingness. Very much to the philosophical point is Shakespeare's "A king may go a progress through the guts of a beggar" (*Hamlet* 4, 3, 30–31).

43. In *De civ.* 2.1, Augustine speaks of the *via pietatis, ab humilitate ad superna* [the way of devotion which rises from the low to the sublime].

44. Siegfried Wenzel, *The Sin of Sloth* (Chapel Hill: University of North Carolina Press, 1967), 39–40 and 43–45.

45. In *Purgatorio* 1, 46, Cato refers to the *leggi d'abisso,* which prevents movement upward from hell to purgatory. There is no paradox here, for God did not create hell anymore than he created sin.

46. Jacques LeGoff, *The Medieval Imagination* (Chicago: University of Chicago Press, 1988), 66–77, and *La Naissance du purgatoire* (Paris: Gallimard, 1981), traces the development of the idea of purgatory. See also Alan E. Bernstein, "Esoteric Theology: William of Auvergne on the fires of Hell and Purgatory," *Speculum* 57 (1982): 509–31.

47. For a survey of the poetizing philosophers such as Bernard, Alain, John of Salisbury.

Hildebert of Lavardin, etc., see R. McKeon, "Poetry and Philosophy in the Twelfth Century," *MP* 43 (1946): 217–34.

48. John Donne describes love's bond as a turning compass in "A Valediction Forbidding Mourning," and Milton describes Christ as the agent of God's conceptual compass:

> He took the golden Compass, prepar'd
> In God's eternal store, to circumscribe
> This Universe, and all created things.
> One foot he centered, and the other turn'd
> Round through the vast profundity obscure.
>
> *(PL 7, 225–29)*

William Blake has a vivid illustration of God's compass measuring of the world's circumference in his engraving "The Ancient of Days," the frontispiece to *Europe.*

49. *The Complete Plays of Christopher Marlowe,* ed. Irving Ribner (New York: Odyssey Press, 1963). In chapter 20 of the Harley MS of *The Travels of Sir John Mandeville,* the firmament moves like a wheel on an axle tree between the Pole Star and the Antarctic.

50. The enduring appeal of the image is exemplified by T. S. Eliot's borrowing from *Faustus* of the axle tree in the "Burnt Norton" section of the *Four Quartets.*

51. Cited by Minnis and Scott, *Medieval Literary Theory,* 328–31.

52. Wilhelm, *Medieval Song,* 393.

53. Cited by Mary Carruthers. *The Book of Memory* (Cambridge: Cambridge University Press, 1990), 5–6. George Steiner, *After Babel* (London; Oxford University Press, 1975), 6, notes that in Hebrew mystical tradition, a syllabic sequence is a metaphysical bond. If one breaks *Elohim* [God] for example, into hidden subject *im* and hidden object *eloh,* the bond is broken, for "only in His name do we discern the promise of ultimate unity." *Elohim* is a plural noun, however, and perhaps is better rendered as God's agents.

54. Cited by Gilson, *History of Christian Philosophy,* 119.

55. The Parson explains later that all affliction "is sent by the rightwys sonde of God" (10, 625).

56. Penn R. Szittya, *The Antifraternal Tradition in Medieval Literature* (Princeton: Princeton University Press, 1986), 246, remarks that the fire that the Antichrist shoots down from heaven in medieval iconography parodies God's descent in the Gift of Tongues.

57. "Words are not a mere vehicle," says William Wordsworth in a letter to William Rowan Hamilton, 23 December 1829, "but they are powers either to kill or animate." R. Howard Bloch, "New Philology and Old French," *Speculum* 65 (1990): 58, observes that "one always betrays, or even kills, something whenever one sings, boasts, or even talks about it." Launfal's magical lady forbids him to speak of her at the risk of losing his love.

58. Cited by D. W. Robertson, Jr., *A Preface to Chaucer,* 115–17.

59. *De Arithmetica,* cited by David S. Chamberlain, "Philosophy and Music in the *Consolatio* of Boethius," *Speculum* 45 (1970): 86–89.

60. . . . *nam ideo in hac uita omnis anima musicis sonis capitur, ut non soli, qui sunt habitu cultiores, uerum uniuersae quoque barbarae nationes cantus, quibus uel ad ardorem uirtutis animentur, uel ad mollitiem uoluptatis resoluantur, exerceant, quia in corpus defert memorian musicae, cuius in caelo fuit conscia.*

61. *The Works of Robert Henryson,* ed. Denton Fox (Oxford: Clarendon Press, 1981).

62. Patrick J. Gallacher, *Love, the Word, and Mercury* (Albuquerque: University of New Mexico Press, 1975), 21–25, outlines the figure of Mercury with particular reference to Gower's *Confessio Amantis.* Chaucer knew of Mercury's mediating role from Martianus Capella's *De nuptiis Philologiae et Mercurii,* where Mercury's voyage to earth and Philology's to heaven figure the bond of love in creation. See Joan Ferrante, *Woman as Image,* 50–54.

63. The text is *Claudii Claudiani Carmina,* ed. J. Koch (Leipzig: Teubner, 1893).

64. Thomas Aquinas defines the mean as the point between two extremes which joins or reconciles them (*Summa* Q. 44, art. 2). Judson Boyce Allen, *The Ethical Poetics of the Later Middle Ages: A Decorum of Convenient Distinction* (Toronto: University of Toronto Press, 1982), 217, cites Averroës's explanation that a *medium* has the best features of both extremes, but gives nothing of its own virtues to either.

65. The etymological root of *foyson* is Latin *fundare* [to pour]; see Modern English *foundry.* According to Paul A. Olson, *The Canterbury Tales and the Good Society* (Princeton: Princeton University Press, 1987), 12, Chaucer restricts his use of the term to God's gifts.

66. "Dame Alice and the Nobility of Pleasure," *Viator* 13 (1982): 275–93.

67. Jill Mann, "Satisfaction and Payment in Middle English Literature," *SAC* 5 (1983): 17–48, surveys Chaucer's use of *sad, enough,* and *suffisaunce.* I am reminded of Dante's "Donna ch'avete intelletto d'amore," in which the poet remarks that an ideal love is "in forma quale convene a donna aver, non for misura" [in a form proper for a woman, not out of measure].

68. Elaine Tuttle Hansen, "The Powers of Silence: The Case of the Clerk's Griselda," *Women and Power in the Middle Ages,* ed. Mary Erler and Maryanne Kowalski (Athens: University of Georgia Press, 1988), 84, argues that Grisilde's surrender to Walter's will is the means by which she defeats his purpose to expose her as an ordinary woman.

69. Cf. Shakespeare's Sonnet 15: "When I consider every things that grows / Holds in perfection but a little moment."

70. For *kind* as *genitalia,* see *MED* definition 14a, and the *OED* definitions 6b and 6c. Saint Hildegard of Bingen, *Liber divinorum operum (MS 1942, F. 27v,* Biblioteca giovernativa Lucca), inscribes the human body within a circle whose center is its genitals. According to chapter 10 of the Harley MS *Mandeville's Travels,* the midpoint of the world is where Joseph of Arimathea laid down Christ from the cross.

71.

> Concreato fu ordine e construtto
> a le sustanza; e quelle furon cima
> nel mondo in che puro atto fu produtto;
> pura potenza tenne la parte ima;
> nel mezzo stringa potenza con atto
> tal vime, che già no so divima.

*(Par.* 29, 31–36)

72. The text is V. L. Dedeck-Héry, "Boethius' 'De consolatione' by Jean de Meun," *Mediaeval Studies* 14 (1952): 165–275. Peter Dronke, *Fabula: Explorations into the Uses of Myth in Medieval Platonism* (Leiden: Brill, 1984), 85, offers something quite different: "You connect the triple-natured to the centre of the universe the soul that moves all things." Dronke, perhaps taking his lead from Alfred the Great's translation of Boethius, III, m. 9, associates this "triple-natured" with the World Egg. Threefold worlds are common in mythic systems. The Buddhist *tribhuvana* comprises *bhu* [earth], *swar* [sky] and *bhuvas* [air] between them. Nordic myth has Asgard (home of the gods), Midgard (home of man), and Utgard (home of giants and elves).

73. See the *Commentary* on Marianus Capella's *De Nuptiis* in *Cambridge Lib, MS mm,* 1, 18 (ca. 1200–29), brought to my attention by Christopher Baswell of Barnard College. Similar wheels are depicted in plates 3, 4, and 5 between pages 78 and 79 of Stock's *Myth and Science.*

74. Michael J. B. Allen, *The Platonism of Marcilio Ficino* (Berkeley: University of California Press, 1981).

75. See James A. Coulter, *The Literary Microcosm: Theories of Interpretation of the Later Neo-Platonists* (Leiden: Brill, 1976), 39–40.

76. Morton Bloomfield, *The Seven Deadly Sins* (East Lansing: Michigan State University Press, 1952), 16–17. In pagan Norse myth, Odin's valkyries carry the battlefield slain to Valhalla.

77. *PL,* 75, 509.

78. Cited by J. A. W. Bennett and G. V. Smithers, *Early Middle English Verse and Prose* (Oxford: Clarendon Press, 1966).

79. *Porphyrium 1, PL* 64, 71a–b, cited by Brian Stock, *The Implications of Literacy* (Princeton: Princeton University Press, 1983), 386–87.

80. Cited by Gilson, *History of Christian Philosophy,* 103–6.

81. Gordon Leff, "Wyclif and the Augustinian Tradition, with Special Reference to his *De Trinitate,*" *MH* 7 (1970): 29–39.

82. *Etymologiae* 11, 1, sec. 13 (*PL* 57, 399).

83. *Piers Plowman: The B Version,* ed. George Kane and E. Talbot Donaldson (London: Athlone, 1988).

84. *Sir Gawain and the Green Knight,* ed. J. R. R. Tolkien and E. V. Gordon; 2d ed., ed. Norman Davis (Oxford: Clarendon Press, 1968).

85. Cited by Minnis and Scott, *Medieval Literary Theory,* 329.

86. This scale was not universally agreed upon in Chaucer's day. Mystics such as Julian of Norwich conceived of a transcendental touch, sight, and feeling as a trinity in the phenomenological as well as spiritual world. In *Revelations of Divine Love,* ed. Frances Beer (Heidelberg: Carl Winter, 1978), the shorter version from *BL Add. MS* 37790, XXIII (76), she speaks of a triple chain of "schewynge": " . . . that es to seye be the bodely sight, and be worde formed in myn vnderstandynge, & by gastely syght." In I (40), she exposes the three physical sensations which draw her to God: the wound of contrition, the wound of compassion, and the wound of willful longing.

## Chapter 2. Love's Progressions and Successions

1. "Vertical" and "horizontal" are conventional terms. Derek Brewer, *Chaucer: The Poet as Storyteller* (Cambridge: Derek Brewer, 1984), 67–68, recalls Auerbach's use of "vertical" for background legend and "horizontal" for the foreground history of sequence and metonymy. Robert M. Jordan, *Chaucer and the Shape of Creation* (Cambridge, Mass.: Harvard University Press, 1967), 100–107, identifies Chaucer's narrative presence with "verticality" and his story with "horizontality." John Drury, "Luke," *The Literary Guide to the Bible,* ed. Robert Alter and Frank Kermode (Cambridge: Harvard University Press, 1987), 422, identifies parable and prophecy as vertical occupations of a discourse whose horizontal deployment is narrative. See also E. Meletinskij, "Scandinavian Mythology as a System," *Journal of Symbolic Anthropology* 2 (1973): 4–6; and Vladimir Nabokov, *Lectures on Literature,* ed. Fredson Bowers (New York: Harcourt Brace, 1988), 3–4. In Saussurean linguistics, "vertical" identifes diachronicity and "horizontal" synchronicity.

2. Paul Ricoeur, "Narrative Time," in *On Narrrative,* ed. W. J. T. Mitchell (Chicago: University of Chicago Press, 1981), 166–67, cites Heidegger's "within time" as chronological linearity.

3. "To see in order to understand" would be appropriate to Scholastic empiricism, but compare May's specious chastizing of Januarie: "He that mysconceyveth, he mysdemeth" (4, 2410).

4. Lee Patterson, *Chaucer and the Subject of History* (Madison: University of Wisconsin Press, 1991), 203, remarks that "the 'First Movere' speech is thus an explanation of

how closure is possible within the historical world, an explanation that inevitably and appropriately invokes a transhistorical authority."

5. Ricoeur, "Narrative Time," 166–67. Patterson, 86, notes that the Augustinian view of time as a divine design conflicts with the instability of history.

6. *Non praevidentia sed providentia potius dicitur, quod porro ab rebus infimis constituta quasi ab excelso rerum cacumine cuncta prospiciat* (*Cons.* 5, pr. 6, 69–72). In retracing this argument to find a way to save Criseyde from being surrendered to the Greeks, Troilus makes the tragic mistake of confusing the two, and so concludes to his despair that foresight ordains his inevitable loss (*Troilus* 4, 961–66).

7. *"Saturnus apocatasticus,"* id est dispositur et destructor fatorum, explains the anonymous hagiographer of *In Sancto Sebastiano, Vatican 1469, 83r* (Biblioteca apostalica Vaticana lat.). Dante identifies Saturn with Christ in *Purgatorio* 6, 118–19. Kronos the god became associated with *chronos* "time" sometime after Hesiod's day. The Romans then associated him with Saturn, their god of grain and sowing.

8. See Richard C. Dales, "Discussions of the Eternity of the World during the First Half of the Twelfth Century," *Speculum* 57 (1982): 495–508, and "Robert Grosseteste's Place in Medieval Discussions of the World," *Speculum* 61 (1986): 544–63. Edward Grant, *Planets, Stars, and Orbs: The Medieval Cosmos, 1200–1687* (Cambridge: Cambridge University Press, 1994), chapters 4–9, appeared too late to be considered fairly here.

9. Gabriel Josipivici, *The Book of God* (New Haven and London: Yale University Press, 1988), 67, notes that there is not a beginning to creation, only an activity. There is nothing before or behind it, only its own time.

10. Cited by Gordon Leff, *The Dissolution of the Medieval Outlook* (New York: New York University Press, 1976), 101.

11. A. J. Minnis and A. B. Scott, *Medieval Literary Theory,* 336–38. Grisilde herself turns the maximic tables on both her husband and the teller of her tale by claiming that those nurtured in poverty have a virtue of forebearance that the well-bred lack. In her reply to Walter's trying demand to know what she thinks of his new wife, she says:

> . . . She is fostred in hire nourissynge
> Moore tendrely, and, to my supposynge,
> She koude nat adversitee endure
> As koude a povre fostred creature."

(4, 1040–43)

This "error" of judgment is noted by the Parson, who reproves those who look for excuses, including "gentilesse of his auncestres" (10, 585) for not shriving oneself.

12. See Virgil, *Eclogue* IX, 51: *Omnia fert aetas moeris* [Time carries all things away, even our wit].

13. *A Brief History of Time* (New York: Bantam, 1988), 147. See also Osmund Lewry, *On Time and Imagination* (London: Oxford University Press, 1987), xviii.

14. Jill Mann, "Chaucer and Destiny in *Troilus and Criseyde* and the Knight's Tale," *The Cambridge Chaucer Companion,* ed. Piero Boitani and Jill Mann (Cambridge: Cambridge University Press, 1986), 84–85, considers that Criseyde's sliding courage refers to "readily observable mutation in worldly affairs." E. D. Blodgett, "Chaucer's Pryvetee and the Oppositon to Time," *Speculum* 51 (1976): 477–93, understands "sliding" as a time-bound concept; and Peggy A. Knapp, "The Nature of Nature: Criseyde's 'Slydyng Corage,'" *ChauR* 13 (1978): 133–34, observes that Criseyde slides as nature slides.

15. John E. Murdoch, *"Subtilitatis Anglicanae* in Fourteenth-Century Paris: John of Mirecourt and Peter Coffins," *Machaut's World: Science and Art in the Fourteenth Century,* ed. Madeleine Pelner Cosman and Bruce Chandler (New York: New York Academy of Sciences, 1978), 59. V. A. Kolve, *The Play Called Corpus Christi* (Stanford,

CA: Stanford University Press, 1966), 102, cites the medieval conception of time as a period within which man must work to earn his place in heaven.

16. Aurea prima sata est, quae vindice nullo, / sponte sua, sine lege fidem rectumque colebat (*Metam.* I, 89–90) [Gold was the first age, when there was no law and no compelling, and one kept faith and did right].

17. Lee Patterson, *The Subject of History,* 203, would agree when he equates Jupiter to Boethian roundness to conclude that Theseus's world has no place for *this* Jupiter.

18. Romans 7: 7–10. For a terse and lucid summary of the ages of law, see D. W. Robertson, Jr., *The Literature of Medieval England* (New York: McGraw-Hill, 1970), 3–4.

19. *Tempus preteritum presens* . . . etc., *Prologus,* insertion between lines 93–94. The translation is Macaulay's note to his edition of the *Works* (Oxford: Clarendon, 1901).

20. According to the Liddel-Scott *Greek-English Dictionary,* it is "measure, proportion," and in relation to time, "opportune occasion." Frank Kermode, *The Sense of an Ending* (London: Oxford University Press, 1967), 47 defines *kairos* as a "point in time filled with significance, charged with a meaning derived from its relation to the end." It is an instant within chronos, or duration. W. H. Auden's poem, "Kairos and Logos" (1940?), depicts Christian martyrs inviting death as their *kairos.*

21. *The Human Condition* (Chicago: University of Chicago Press, 1958).

22. Jerome Mandel, *Geoffrey Chaucer: Building the Fragments of the "Canterbury Tales"* (Rutherford, NJ: Fairleigh Dickinson Press, 1992), 69, says that the Old Man reveals the duration of life which is in God's governance.

23. Then, "By the shadwe he took his wit," notes the narrator (2,10), another way of saying *nox nocti indicate scientam.* J. D. North, *Chaucer's Universe* (London: Oxford University Press, 1988), 124–25, chides Chaucer for using the wrong calendar tables for his calculations, but the calculations are Harry's and not the narrator's. Patricia J. Eberle's note to the passage in *The Riverside Chaucer* confirms the error, but assumes that "it is unlikely that many of Chaucer's listeners noticed it."

24. Note the Squire's remark that excess of detail is "los of tyme" (5, 74).

25. Chaucer's *House of Fame* is about a quest for tidings of love. See Gabriel's message to Zacharias in Luke 1: 19: *"Missus sum loqui ad te."*

26. Mandel, *Geoffrey Chaucer,* 32.

27. For a discussion of "sadness," see Jill Mann, "Satisfaction and Payment in Middle English Literature," *Studies in the Age of Chaucer* 5 (1983): 17–48. Grisilde is characterized by various voices as "sad stidefast" (564), "sad and kynde" 602), "ferme and stable" (663), "with sad visage" (693), "sad for everemo" (754), "meke and stable" (931); and it is her "stedfastenesse" that Walter finally acknowledges as having proved (1050, 1056).

28. See Colossians 4, 5: *In sapientia ambulare ad eos, qui foris sunt: tempus redimentes.*

29. Chrétien de Troyes's story of Philomene, "et de la hupe," in the *Ovide moralisé,* has her weaving the story of her rape on a *cortine.* The Wife is herself a weaver, and the hag's *curtyn* hangs between the knight and the light which reveals a beauty which is the grace he achieves in an adventure beginning with a rape. J. Hillis Miller, "Arachne's Broken Woof," *Georgia Review* 31 (1977): 36–48, points out that a woman's weaving is the sexual inversion of male penetration, a way of restoring what has been marred in time.

30. Northrop Frye, "History and Myth in the Bible," in *The Literature of Fact,* ed. Angus Fletcher (New York: Columbia University Press, 1976), 9–10, uses these terms to distinguish world history from spiritual history. The graph of the soul's fall into flesh and rise out of it at death contrasts with the graph of the passage of man's body which rises through time to strength before falling into dust.

31. The concluding "Lenvoy de Chaucer," which I assume is sung by the Clerk to neatly balance the authority of Petrarch at the beginning of his performance, "kills" Grisilde in its first line, as if to cancel her and the tale.

32. See Revelations 10: 6: *Quia tempus non erat amplius.*

33. Pamela King, in a paper, "Urban Devotion and its Subversions: Reception of the York Cycle," delivered at the second Esse Conference in Bordeaux, 7 September 1993, points out that in the tradition of charitable works of Chaucer's day (see Matthew 25: 31–46), men provide the poor with food, drink, and clothing, while women provide them with books of instruction.

34. Ricoeur, "Narrative Time," 174, paraphrases Heidegger to the effect that story combines what is chronological (horizontal and episodic) with what is nonchronological (vertical and configurative), so that retelling takes the place of telling, and recollection reverses the arrow of time.

35. Ricoeur, 178.

## Chapter 3. Frayed Bonds of Sight and Word: *The Legend of Good Women*

1. Unless otherwise noted, quotations are from the F-text of the Prologue.

2. Brian Stock, *Myth and Science,* 73n., cites Manilius's claim that the poet possesses the special capacity to reveal the physical and astronomical wonders of the world. Shakespeare's Theseus, echoing somewhat the wisdom of the hero of the Knight's tale, says it well:

> As imagination bodies forth
> The form of things unknown, the poet's pen
> Turns them to shapes.
>
> (*MND* 5, 1, 12–16)

3. Dante, in *Paradiso* 30, 70–81, compares the immediate grasp of angelic intelligence with the labyrinthine confusion through which man must pass to understand meaning in things.

4. Chaucer's use of rhymes to signal disparity and incongruity is well known. Eugene Vance, "Mervelous Signs," 309, points out the binary tensions in *Troilus* produced by rhymes like Criseyde/dede, Eleyne/peyne and Troye/joye.

5. Chaucer's *visible* and *invisible* at the close of *Troilus* (5, 1866–67) is the authority for my use of the terms. Augustine's *De Civ. Dei* 11, 4, may have been in the poet's mind: *Visibilium omnium maximus mundus est, inuisibilium omnium maximus Deus est. Sed mundum esse conspicimus, Deum esses credimus* [Of all visible things the world is the greatest. Of all invisible things God is the greatest. The world is to be seen, God to be believed]. Augustine adds that man must trust those who have seen what he has not seen himself, and trust especially those who have seen things in their incorporeal light. The friar of the Summoner's tale claims that his order can see more of spiritual things than "burel folk" (3, 1872). D. W. Robertson, Jr., *The Literature of Medieval England,* 4, explains that the blindfold over Synagogue's eyes on the portal of the Cathedral in Strasbourg is an indication of her inability to see the spiritual realities beneath the surfaces of things visible and tangible. Jean de Meun has Nature explain the optics of figure and form in the *Roman de la rose,* 16855–71.

6. Cited by Minnis and Scott, *Medieval Literary Theory,* 328–31.

7. Patrick J. Gallacher, "The Conversion of Tragic Vision," 615, notes: "The hierarchy of vision in the poem must be paralleled by the appropriate hierarchy of emotions through which shame, intensified . . . by love, becomes magnaminity."

8. Seeing participates in what is seen. Virtuous looking, as Dante's of Beatrice reveals (*Par.* 30, 76–78, and 31, 64–65) is accompanied by a shame of being seen.

9. *Malory: Works,* ed. Eugène Vinaver (London: Oxford University Press, 1971), book 13, 7, p. 521.

10. *Soliloquae* 2, 10. Shakespeare's Cressida laments that "minds sway'd by eyes are full of turpitude" *(TC* 5, 2, 112). The dreamer in *Pearl* is told not to believe what he sees "wyth yghe" (301–2).

11. Jason is a stock figure of inconstancy. John Gower, in *Vox Clamanti* 6, 1323, and in *Confessio Amantis* 8, 2563–65, refers to his causeless infidelity.

12. The *OED* cites Chaucer for the philosophical sense of form: "The essential principle of a thing; that which makes anything (matter) a determinant species or kind of being: the essential creative quality."

13. *The Golden Book of Marriage,* cited by Jerome in *Adversus Jovinian.* See the extract in *The Canterbury Tales: Nine Tales and the General Prologue,* ed. V. A. Kolve and Glending Olson (New York: W. W. Norton, 1989), 327.

14. Preserving the daisy in a book anticipates the practice of pressing flowers between leaves of a book to preserve them.

15. In *Troilus* 2, 904–5, the narrator addresses the sun as "dayes honour and the hevenes yë," and Lydgate calls Apollo "daies eye" *(Troy Book* 2, 5592).

16. For cupid's arrows, see *Roman de la rose,* 5245. I assume from the explanation of Cupid's two arrows by the third Vatican Mythographer, cited by Erwin Panofsky, *Studies in Iconology* (Oxford: Oxford University Press, 1939), 105, that when he had them, Cupid's eyes had beam-darts comparable to the beam of light that carries God's love in the form of the Holy Spirit down from heaven into Mary's bedchamber. Cupid's eye is carnal, however, and each of his five arrows—*quinque linea amoris*—incites one of the five senses: sight, hearing, touching, kissing, and coitus, or *factum.* For Chaucer's Parson, these are the five fingers of the devil's left hand *(CT* 10, 852ff). The lance Venus wields is *aurea telum* (dart of gold). For illustrations of Eros and Venus shooting arrows of love, see Charles Dahlberg's *The Romance of the Rose* (Princeton: Princeton University Press, 1971), plates 14 and 60; and Robert V. Fleming, *The Roman de la Rose* (Princeton: Princeton University Press, 1969), plate 41.

17. Marcia L. Colish, *The Mirror of Language* (Lincoln: University of Nebraska Press, 1983), 3, in her trace of the epistemological heritage of Chaucer from Augustine to Dante makes the disarmingly simple but very important point that in Chaucer's age "language is a cognitive intermediary between the knower and the object of knowledge," that is, between man and God.

18. Ivan Ilich and Barry Sanders, *The Alphabetization of the Popular Mind* (San Francisco, CA: North Point Press, 1988), 134–38, discuss the process by which books replaced the ear as witness in the fourteenth century. Though they cite Chaucer's style as evidence of the imposition of literacy on human activity, Chaucer's characters swear on natural items like heads and hearts, rather than upon Scripture, a practice the Parson reproves (10, 589). A notable and ironic exception is the "Britoun book" upon which the lying pagan knight takes his oath in the Man of Law's tale *(CT* 2, 666).

19. Apuleius's *Metamorphosis,* which Chaucer knew, has Cupid loving Psyche who, in return, is deprived of the capacity to see her. Chaucer would have appreciated the etymological sense in Alceste's name which accords with the "day's eye": *alki* [strength, radiance].

20. There is an intricate and significant link here between the dreamed poet's unnamed identity and the topic of the poem. The *explicit* in two of the thirteen extant manuscripts of *The Parliament of Fowls* names the poet in the Latin form *Galfridus.* This form is recorded earlier in the Household Accounts for 1357 of Elizabeth Burgh (Lionel's wife and Duchess of Ulster). This is the form for both Geoffrey of Monmouth and Geoffrey of Vinsauf, both of whom Chaucer cites in the form *Gaufred (HF* 3, 1470 and *CT* 7,

3347). The elements *-fred* and *-fridus* point to Old English *freo* and Old Norse *friðr*, both meaning "love." *Gal/wal* signifies "servant." So, the name *Geoffrey* signifies "servant of love," a sense appropriate to the description he gives himself at the outset of *Troilus:* "that God of Loves servantz serve" (1, 15). If the earlier Norman form is *Godefroy*, as it is for Geoffery of Boulogne, then the etymological roots might be *Gautar Freyr* (Frey of the Geats), and Frey is the Norse god of love. See my "Chaucer's Names," *NM* 95 (1994): 243–48.

21. For a contrary example in the *Tales*, Januarie reads virtue in the body of his young bride with an eye of reasonless lust (4, 1599–1604).

22. V. A. Kolve, "From Cleopatra to Alceste: An Iconographic Study of the *Legend of Good Women*," in *Signs and Symbols in Chaucer's Poetry*, ed. John P. Hermann and John J. Burke, Jr. (University, AL: University of Alabama Press, 1981), 17, reads the poem as a move from identifying Alceste to reading the meaning of her story. The god of love's stern eye on the kneeling poet reminds me of Philosophy's instructive eye in the *Consolation*, which knows the poet right away: "Art nat thou he . . . that whilom, norissched with my melk and fostred with myne metes, were escaped and comyn to corage of a parfit man?" (1, pr. 2, 4–7). One recalls the medieval tradition of Christ nourishing the bride of the Canticles with the milk of his breasts. See Caroline Walker Bynum, "' . . . And Woman His Humanity': Female Imagery in the Religious Writing of the Later Middle Ages," *Gender and Religion: On the Complexity of Symbols*, ed. Caroline Walker Bynum, Steven Harrell, and Paula Richman (Boston: Beacon Press, 1986), 264.

23. In *Troilus* 1, 16, Chaucer admits an *unliklynesse* for love, and in the *Parliament of Fowls*, 8–11, he admits to not being a lover though he knows of love through books. Pertinent to the *Legend* are Chaucer's words in "Lenvoy de Chaucer a Scogan," 29–32:

> I dred of thy unhap,
> Lest for thy gilt the wreche of Love precede
> On alle hem that ben hoor and rounde of shap,
> That ben so lykely folk in love to spede.

24. Cited by Larry D. Benson, *Morte Darthur* (Cambridge: Harvard University Press, 1976), 157.

25. Malory judges Guenevere, despite her tragic adultery, "a trewe lover, and therfor had a good ende" (*Morte Darthur* 8, 25). Foolish fidelity is contrary to Andreas's Rule 17 of *De amore: Novus amor veterem compellit abire* [New love forces the old to disappear]. Chaucer's Miller says it better: "Alwey the nye slye / Maketh the ferre leeve to be looth" (*CT* 1, 3392–93).

26. *De Consolatione* 3, pr. 10 (1–22 in Chaucer's *Boece*). The Man of Law remarks that God's Providence "ful derk is / To mannes wit" (*CT* 2, 481–82). Expressions of doubt and uncertainty are figures of *aporia*, whose French form *aporie* designates "hardship." *Ekphrasis*, or a plain assertion, is its opposite. Augustine, *De doctrina* 1,6. 6 notes that one cannot say God is unspeakable, because saying it cannot be spoken.

27. Of course, it stands to reason that writing of imperfection involves writing imperfectly. V. A. Kolve, "Cleopatra," 178, notes that a quest for a truer poetry begins or ends virtually all of Chaucer's poetry.

28. In the G-text, the confusion is avoided by having Alceste's attendants sing the balade as they dance about the daisy (199–227).

29. Piero Boitani, "Old books brought to life in dreams: the *Book of the Duchess, the House of Fame, the Parliament of Fowls*," in *The Cambridge Chaucer Companion*, traces the process by which books diffused and blended in dreams are given new life in poems. On the ending of the Prologue, Rita Copeland, *Rhetoric, Hermeneutics, and Translation in the Middle Ages* (Cambridge: Cambridge University Press, 1991), 197, makes the

NOTES TO CHAPTER 3

observation that while the F-text ending sends the poet off to rehearse old authors, the G-text reveals him following the command of Love to start with Cleopatra.

30. Anelida is thirled by remembrance of Arcite's falsity (*Anel.* 201), whereas Grisilde's ability to remain steadfast derives from her ability to forget adversity (*CT* 4, 923–24). Philosophy advises Boethius to forget things and events but to remember himself (*Cons* 1, pr. 2). Pandarus advises Troilus of the harm of remembering even bliss:

> The worst kynde of infortune is this,
> A man to han been in prosperitee,
> And it remembren whan it passed is.
>
> (*Tr.* 3, 1625–28)

In his *Confessions,* 11, 26, Augustine says that memory apprehends the presence of the past, sight the presence of the present, and expectation the presence of things to come. There is a failure of coordination of the three in the *Legend.*

31. So Anelida suffers a hell on earth (*Anel.* 166–67). Donald W. Rowe, *Through Nature to Eternity: Chaucer's "Legend of Good Women"* (Lincoln: University of Nebraska Press, 1988). 17, sees the heaven-hell opposition as a frame for the poem. Lisa J. Kiser, *Telling Classical Tales: Chaucer and the "Legend of Good Women"* (Ithaca: Cornell University Press, 1983), 95–131, surveys the infernal imagery in the poem. The "truth" in love that should be rewarded is, first, fidelity to word, but it includes compassion, gentleness, courtesy, good cheer, and concern for one's good name. In his *ABC,* line 56, hell is "stink eterne," and stink, says Chaucer's Parson, is the *factum* of fornication (*CT* 10, 862).

32. The continuation of the story in the sources has Demophon return late to find Phyllis already transformed into an almond tree.

33. In Ovid's continuation, Ariadne is rescued from the island by Dionysos, to whom she bears Thoas, future father of Hypsipyle.

34. Elaine Tuttle Hansen, "The Powers of Silence," 238, accuses the women of the *Legend* of putting the "love of a man above all other responsibilities, even life itself." La Vieille, in the *Roman de la rose,* 13173–274, refers to the stories of Dido, Phyllis, and Medea as examples of the folly of loving only one man. In Ovid's *Heroides* 2, Phyllis is an example of foolish love, while Medea exemplifies unchaste love (see Minnis and Scott, *Medieval Literary Theory,* 21–22).

35. A good name is the "authorized" public fiction of things seen and heard of someone. *Shame* is the fear of having one's name exposed. Shame in sin, as Chaucer's Parson points out, is necessary in the penitential process (*CT* 134–40). The irony of Lucrece's fate, as R. Howard Bloch argues in "Chaucer's Maiden's Head: 'The Physician's Tale' and the Poetics of Virginity," *Representations* 28 (1989): 124, is that Collatinus, in the game of praise of wives, displays rather than describes his. There is complicity in rape of eye, heart, and mouth. The eye sees, the heart wills, and the mouth speaks it. From one perspective, then, Chaucer the poet, in speaking the shame of rape, commits rape.

36. Ovid makes the fault of sight even more decisive by describing Tereus's imagination dwelling on what he has not yet seen of Philomela's body. One recalls Andreas de Capellanus defining love in his *De Amore* 1, 1, as an inordinate contemplation of the *form* of the opposite sex.

37. Robert Worth Frank, *Chaucer and "The Legend of Good Women,"* (Cambridge: Harvard University Press, 1972), 133, sees in the poem an attack upon courtly codes without offering an alternative. *The Legend,* he argues, is an escape from idealized love.

38. Philomene and Cleopatra are not on the Man of Law's list of Chaucer's topics (*CT* 2, 63–185).

39. *Ovide Moralisé,* ed. C. de Boer (Vaduz: Hans R. Wohlend, 1984), vol. 4., 2217–3684.

40. Lucrece, facing rape, "no word she spak . . . / What shal she seyn?" (1796–97), but then, "she axeth grace and seyth al that she can" (1804).

41. Chrétien's moral to the tale identifies Pandion as *diex, rois d'immortalité,* Progne as *l'âme* in his image, Tereus *cors* in pursuit of "Philomene, qui signifie / Amour decevable et faillie." In Ovid's account, Procne wished to avenge herself by cutting out Tereus's tongue, eyes, and penis. *Philomela* means "love of song," though *melos* also designates a bodily member. Chrétien might have found his version of the name, meaning "wellloved," in Alain de Lisle's *De Planctu,* or both may have found the form elsewhere. Boccaccio has a Filomene as one of the storytellers in *Il decamerone.*

42. The previous tales prepare this constriction of trust. The tales of Cleopatra and Thisbe close with remarks on the rarity of men true in love, those of Dido and Medea with reproaches to false men, and the tale of Lucrece with a warning against brittle trust of even the truest. Richard Firth Green, "Chaucer's Victimized Women," *SAC* 10 (1988): 3–21, argues that the *Legend* is Chaucer's attack on Ovid's and Jean de Meun's "cavalier" attitudes towards fidelity to sworn word. Sheila Delany, *The Naked Text: Chaucer's Legend of Good Women* (Berkeley: University of California Press, 1994), a study which has come into my hands too late for use in this chapter, shows the incompatibility of Dante's redemptive possibilities of human love with Chaucer's sensibility on an ideological level (231).

43. Patterson, *the Subject,* 238, remarks that Chaucer in this work takes his "revenge upon authority."

44. In *Troilus,* Chaucer turns from his initial task to "don gladnesse / To any lovere, and his cause availle" (1, 19–20) to persuade his audience, finally, to forsake worldly love "and loveth [Christ] . . . / For he nyl falsen no wight" (5, 1842–45).Vance, "Mervelous Signals," 334–35, refers to the shift of perspective at the end of *Troilus* as a denying of the language of history and lust, to find Love and the Word inextricably bound in the presence of Christ.

45. Eugene Vance, "Mervelous Signals," 317, recalls the conventional triadic division of communication of the time. Angels know each other's thoughts without speech, by force of spirit. Animals know others through their own nature. Man must communicate with his fellows with the sound of speech. Philomene rises above the necessity of sound.

46. At the beginning of the sixth book of *Metamorphoses,* Ovid tells the story of Arachne's weaving contest with Minerva which she wins with her illustrations of gods' assaults upon mortal women—bonds of love between two worlds, if you will. In anger, Minerva transforms Arachne into a spider, but leaves her with her weaving skill. The spider's web, then, is an enduring image of the art which spans the worlds.

47. See Hillis Miller, "Ariachne's Broken Woof," *Georgia Review* 31 (1977): 36–48.

48. Nancy K. Miller, "Arachnologies: The Woman, the Text, and the Critic," *The Poetics of Gender,* ed. Nancy K. Miller (New York: Columbia University Press, 1986), 282, cites the feminist argument that Philomela makes weaving an art of resistance to males.

49. Particularly in V. A. Kolve's *Chaucer and the Imagery of Narrative,* which shows the extent to which Chaucer links his text to pictures familiar to his audience. In *De magistro,* 2, 5 (*Patrologia Latina* 32, 1194–95), Augustine insists that words are meaningless without the hearer's knowledge of the things they designate. Aristotle's *Ethics,* 1, 3, has "Everyone judges well what is known to him."

50. C. David Benson, *Chaucer's Drama of Style* (Chapel Hill: University of North Carolina Press, 1986), 42, argues that Chaucer's style proves the text, not its "truth."

# Chapter 4. Word-Chains of Love: *The Parliament, Troilus* and the *Knight's Tale*

1. P. G. Walsh, ed., *Andreas Capellanus on Love* (London: Duckworth, 1982).

2. Cited by Winthrop Wetherbee, *Platonism and Poetry in the Twelfth Century,* 100.

3. Aristotle, *De sensu et sensibili,* 437b, denies the theory attributed to Empedocles and Plato that the eye gives off light. The eye's proper element, he argues, is water. One suspects that Chaucer knows and draws upon both positions without taking sides. In philosophical matters, Chaucer is remarkably eclectic.

4. Jacqueline Cerquiglini, "Le clerc et le louche: Sociology of an Esthetic," *Poetics Today* 5 (1984): 479–91, speaks of the structural marginality of sight. The *borgne,* or one-eyed, is a defective poet as well as defected lover. Appropriately, in modern French, *hôtel borgne* is a house of ill repute.

5. D. W. Robertson, Jr., "The Wife of Bath and Midas," *SAC* 6 (1984): 1–20, discusses the Wife's infirmity in these terms

6. Jan Ziolkowski, *Alan of Lille's Grammar of Sex,* 43–44.

7. Cited by R. Howard Bloch, "Chaucer's Maiden's Head," 116.

8. John Bayley, *The Characters of Love* (London: Constable, 1960), 55, emphasizes the almost exclusive verbal character of courtly love: "Its tendency to humanize is its natural mode of expression, a way of feeling that merges into a method of describing the feeling." In other words, the effort and time put into verbalizing the feeling restrains the natural physical act. Bayley goes on to distinguish between spiritless rhetoric by the book, exemplified in the *Tales* by the Squire, and vigorous and natural use of the same rhetoric, exemplified by the Franklin.

9. In the *gradus amoris* of Scripture, Adam exemplifies the mind, Eve, the heart, and Satan the genitals. In Chaucer's day, *kind* meant "semen" and "genitals," as well as "nature." It is remarkable that English seems to be the last of the Germanic languages to borrow the latinate *nature* to complement, and then replace, the native *cynd.* According to the *MED,* the earliest English use of the noun and its adjectival forms dates from the end of the thirteenth century in the *Kentish Sermons.*

10. This puzzles me, but it is obviously no simple oversight on the part of Chaucer who uses the terms *may, mayde,* and *mayden* sparingly. Troilus addresses Criseyde as "may" in his letter to her in the Greek camp (5, 1412), but this may be just one more example of the language of courtly service which does not fit its recipient. Antigone's "goodlieste mayde" foreshadows the last line of the poem where Chaucer solicits Christ's defence "for love of mayde and mother thyn benigne." The Virgin Mary can sing such a love, but she is not of "gret estat in al the town of Troy." Chaucer's Antigone, who is first met reading the story of the Seige of Thebes, carries the name of the Theban sister of Orestes (Horaste?) who witnesses a breach of honor to the dead. Her song is balanced at the end of Chaucer's story with Cassandra's recollection of the Theban lineage in a reading of Criseyde's breach of fidelity. Perhaps Chaucer's audience would recognize Cassandra herself as the "goodliest mayde."

11. For a recent view of Chaucer's strategic "contradictory poses" in shaping his text, see Richard Waswo, "The Narrator of *Troilus and Criseyde*," *ELH* 50 (1983): 1–25.

12. Marvin Mudrick, "Tall Stories and Short Hairs," *The Hudson Review:* 38 (1985) 133–39, in reviewing V. A. Kolve's *Chaucer and the Imagery of Narrative,* says that the sting of the lash makes a bitter joke of the notion of free will. Eugene Vance, "Mervelous Signals," 321 and 329, draws attention to the image of the horse as a sexual referent throughout *Troilus.*

13. Romans 5: 13–14: *Usque ad legem enim peccatum erat inmundo; peccatum autem non imputabatur, cum lex non esset. Sed regnavit mors ab Adam usque ad Moysen* [Before there was law there was sin, but no one could be accused of sin, since there was no law, but death reigned from the time of Adam to Moses]

14. *The Literature of Medieval England,* 3–4.

15. The two Venuses is a medieval commonplace whose source is probably *Cons.* 2,

m. 8. The commentaries of Trevet, Hugh of Saint Victor, and Remigius of Auxerre, among others, elaborate on the distinction. See D. W. Robertson, Jr., *A Preface,* 124–26.

16. The current editorial practice of capitalizing "God" and "Love" selectively to distinguish between Christian and pagan deities has no authority in the manuscripts and slants interpretation. Skeat is least guilty in his 1913 Oxford edition, but it is a mystery to me why he capitalizes *God* at the end of the Knight's tale, and has the Nun's Priest's tale close with *god.* In general, Skeat follows the manuscript's unmarked form. Silent altering removes a significant artistic ambiguity between Love the god and love the natural force.

17. Stephen A. Barney, "Troilus Bound," *Speculum* 47 (1972): 454, notes this triadic Venus as "goddess, planet and natural principle" and aligns her with Troilus's "holy bond of thynges" (3, 1261).

18. This is not a case of love at first sight. Troy is not so populous a town that Troilus and Criseyde should not know one another. Indeed, Troilus knows at once *who* she is. He falls in love the moment her eyes meet his, the moment when seeing and being seen coincide.

19. Adam's naming of the animals in Genesis 2: 20 is ordained by God, and is a model of the referential match of word and thing.

20. *Love* and *law* are dialectical homophones in some northern dialects of English in Chaucer's day. So lovedays (from Norse *lov* "Law") are days set aside for amicable settlement of disputes, a practice derived from the regular scheduling of "quarter-courts" at Nordic "things." In the medieval Christian scheme, there are three loves: love as vainglory, love of worldly glory, and love of celestial glory. In general, Pandarus is guilty of the first by mediating the second, Troilus exemplifies the second in pursuing the third, and the poet, at the end of his story, preaches the third.

21. Barney, "Troilus Bound," 454, notes that Troilus's bondage to cosmic love is a paired alternative to the bondage to animal, or sexual, love.

22. Arcite in the Knight's tale, in soliciting Mars' help for the ensuing fight, makes a similar indelicate allusion to Mars' being caught by Vulcan in bed with Venus (1, 1389–90).

23. Davis Taylor, "The Terms of Love: A Study of Troilus's Style," *Speculum* 51 (1976): 69–90, sees Troilus harmonizing conceptions of cosmic with human love here and emphasizing the links between gods and mortals in the myths he cites. Evan Carton, "Complicity and Responsibility in Pandarus' Bed and Chaucer's Art," *PMLA* 94 (1979): 56, in admitting that "Troilus begins to pray nervously to every god he can think of," argues that Pandarus's language is in control of the situation and of Troilus. A more sympathetic view of Troilus is Robert P. apRoberts, "The Central Episode in Chaucer's *Troilus,*" *PMLA* 77 (1962): p. 384, who argues that the hero's weakness under the onset of love is meritorious, for it impresses upon us the power of love and the sincerity of his passion.

24. Compare Dante, *Purgatorio* 27, 95–96: ". . . *Citerea / che di foco d'amor par sempre ardente*" [Citherea, who seems always burning with the fire of love].

25. Monica McAlpine, *The Genre of Troilus and Criseyde*" (Ithaca: Cornell University Press, 1978), 157–58, argues that Troilus's "Benigne Love" speech here is evidence of Troilus's arrival at a "most just estimate of himself and of his beloved," and shows that he "gives up the fantasy of a goddess for the reality of a woman. He is at the point when he can transcend his self-deceiving fantasies and his conception of himself as a servant." I am reminded of Troilus's view when he has more rational control of what he is doing. For example, when he writes his first letter to Criseyde, under Pandarus's theatrical direction, he laughs as he proclaims himself of "litel worth" (2, 1078).

26. Making the most of being trapped, Criseyde's words make a sufficiency of Troilus's excessive dalliance. In effect, she mediates the thought or intent behind his words.

27. apRoberts, "The Central Episode," 282, notes that Criseyde is experienced in love but as fearful of her honor as a virgin. After the love is consummated, Criseyde takes a wife's stance toward her lover, swearing upon Juno, the goddess of marriage, to be true to Troilus (4, 1538).

28. Apollo, who with Poseidon built the walls of Troy but never received pay, is associated with the fate of the city in war. It is at his shrine that Calkas calculates the Greek victory (1, 64–77).

29. Bayley, *The Characters of Love,* 66, takes another stance toward this language, arguing that, although Troilus is not perspicacious, he is well-informed, and it is the conventions of courtly love that allow him to talk about love "with real point." He admits that the courtly code is all of a piece, and that one point of failure lets the air out of the whole thing (81–82). Vance, "Mervelous Signals," 332–33, and Alexandra Hennessey Olsen, "In Defence of Diomede: 'Moral Gower' and *Troilus and Criseyde,*" In *Geardagum* 7 (1988): 1–12, argue for Diomede's superiority over Troilus in the use of words in loving.

30. Donald W. Rowe, *O Love, O Charité! Contraries Harmonized in Chaucer's* Troilus (Edwardsville: Illinois University Press, 1976), 151, sees Troilus spinning in cupidity as the universe is spun by God. While God's word makes a universe of matter, the union of Troilus and Criseyde generates chaos. D. S. Brewer, *"Troilus and Criseyde,"* in *The Middle Ages,* ed. W. F. Bolton (London, 1970), 228, notices the narrator's own "calculated hint of excess" when he comments for himself, "Why nad I swich oon with my soule ybought" (3, 1319), and to the accompanying challenge to the reader "t'encresse or maken dymynucioun / Of my langage" (3, 1335–36). The same challenge extends to Criseyde.

31. The break in the anaphoral pattern in the first strophe by *halt* underscores that word's amphibological possibility of an adjective, "lame," as well as a verb," holds."

32. Vance, "Mervelous Signals," 298, cites *De Vulgari Eloquentia* 2, 4, where Dante describes the subjects of tragedy as love, public safety, and virtue. In *Troilus,* the three are interlaced issues.

33. Barney, "Troilus Bound," 450. At the same time, Norman Eliason, *The Language of Chaucer's Poetry* (Copenhagen: Rosenkilde and Bagger, 1972), takes a more sceptical view of Chaucer's achievement, calling the Knight's tale "a stately and stuffy prelude to the program which is to follow," adding that its trifling plot denies philosophical issues (110).

34. Augustine, *Soliloquium* 2, has *legem non habet necessitas* (necessity has no law). Boethius, *Cons.* 3, m. 12, 52–55, explains Orpheus's backward look by *quis legem det amantibus? Maior lex amor est sibi* (But what is he that may yeven a lawe to loverys? Love is a grettere lawe and a strengere to hymself thanne any lawe that men mai yyven). Virgil's *Eclogue* 2, 68, has *Quis enim modus adsit amori?* (What law does love admit?) See also *Legend of Good Women,* 1186–87 and *Troilus* 4, 618. The old saying continues. Malory has Arthur, Lancelot, and Palomides pronounce versions of it (*Morte Darthur,* book 10, chapters 71 and 86; book 18, chapter 20). James Joyce uses it in *Exiles:* "No law made by man is sacred before the impulse of passion." John Hurt Fisher, *John Gower,* 222–24, explains that the Knight's tale reflects a current conception that *lex gentium* was established to mediate between *lex naturalis,* or law of kind, and *lex civilis,* the marriage contract.

35. Ovid has a variation of the saying in *Remedia amoris, 749: Non habet unde suum paupertas pascat amorem* (love and poverty do not take nourishment together). The popular Italian variation is "l'arte e al morte non van bene insieme" [art and death do not go well together].

36. *De Gestis Rerum Anglorum,* trans. Joseph Stephenson (Dyfed, 1989), 3, 235.

37. The Franklin repeats the maxim (5, 764–67) to assert that love cannot exist if either man or wife claim mastery over the other. The Cook has a version of the proverb

which alters the terms: "Revel and trouthe, as in a lowe degree. / They ben ful wrothe al day, as men may see." (1, 4397–98). Chaucer's Knight's particular version of the saying is quoted by John Clarke two and one-half centuries later in *Paroemiologica Anglo-Latina* (1639): "Love and lordship like no fellowship." This is translated from a Latin text I have not seen by H. L. Mencken, *A New Dictionary of Quotations* (New York: Alfred A. Knopf, 1942), 710.

38. See Ovid's *Metamorphoses* 5, 357–58. The oak he burns is the same tree that he cites later as a figure of the life of man (*CT* 1, 3017–20).

39. John of Salisbury, *Polycraticus* 4, 8, ed. Murray F. Markland (New York: Frederick Ungar, 1979), characterizes a good prince as one who mediates for justice and mercy. John Norton-Smith, *Geoffrey Chaucer* (London: Routledge & Kegan Paul, 1974), 234, cites Cicero's *Res publica* to the effect that an ideal ruler exercises public reason for moderation or the principle of harmony which orders the different elements in a state (236).

40. The same formula in the mouth of the love-wounded falcon of the Squire's tale is glossed to "take well" what one cannot change (5, 593). Criseyde uses the same proverb in her argument to Troilus that, since she must go to the Greeks, they should make the best of it (*Tr.* 4, 1586–87). Joseph Westlund, "The Knight's Tale as an Impetus for Pilgrimage," *PQ* 43 (1964): 534, notes that the concept of a "virtue of necessity" does not match Lady Philosophy's teaching to the effect that there is no "bad" in God's providence to adjust to (*Cons.* 4, pr. 6, 178ff.). The tale subverts efforts for order, he argues, and so the need for a Christian virtue of pilgrimage is the implicit meaning of the Knight's fiction (537). George Steiner, *After Babel* (London: Oxford University Press, 1975), 148–52 discusses the implications of *unfulfilled necessity* to prophecy and futurity. "To make a virtue of necessity" is, in effect, to combine future with present in the manner in which Christ's presence does.

41. It is impossible for me to scan here the wealth of criticism of Theseus's First Mover speech, but the following references are representative. Judith Ferster, *Chaucer on Interpretation* (Cambridge: Cambridge University Press, 1985), 23, offers three ways to read it: as an echo of universal order, as a fiction concocted to secure his people against despair and his rule against revolt, and as a leap of faith. Thomas A. Van, "Theseus and the 'Right Way' of the *Knight's Tale*," *SLI* 4 (1971): 100, reads it as a "regimen for the prudent public man," a right way which is the achievement of a rational nature unabetted by revelation. Kurt Olsson, "*Securitas* and Chaucer's Knight," *SAC* 9 (1987): 152, says that the consolation within the speech gives to the Knight who relates it a godlike pose of security for the pilgrims. Jörg O. Fichte, "Man's Free Will and the Poet's Choice: The Creation of Artistic Order in Chaucer's *Knight's Tale*," *Anglia* 93 (1975): 335, sums up the speech as an affirmation of man's capacity to create order if he uses right judgment. Representative scorners include David Aers, *Chaucer* (Brighton: Harvester, 1986), 30, who says that "Theseus transforms the *Consolation of Philosophy* into a *Consolation of Political Authority* . . . [which] actually aims to persuade us that whatever is, is right." Terry Jones, *Chaucer's Knight* (London: Weidenfield and Nicolson, 1980), 203, empha-sizes Theseus's misuse of Boethian thought, saying that "Theseus reduces Boethius's argument to a tyrant's demand for passive submission." He denounces the substitution of Jupiter for the bond of love. Jerome Mandel, *Geoffrey Chaucer: Building the Fragments of the Canterbury Tales* (Rutherford, NJ: Farleigh Dickinson University Press, 1992), 137–40, reviews criticism of Theseus's philosophical thought.

42. Dale Underwood, "The First of the *Canterbury Tales*," *ELH* 26 (1959): 465, challenges Theseus's understanding of the implications of the image of the chain's descent. Kathleen Ann Blake, "Order and the Noble Life in Chaucer's *Knight's Tale*," *MLQ* 34 (1973): 17, argues that Theseus is deluded in believing in a "chain" order, for the gods above are capricious, and any order that exists derives from their "capricious impulses

of will." D. Brooks and Alastair Fowler, "The Meaning of Chaucer's *Knight's Tale*," *MAE* 39 (1970): 141, say that Theseus does not understand mutability and fails to comprehend his father's advice. A. J. Minnis, *Chaucer and Pagan Antiquity* (Cambridge: D. S. Brewer, 1982), 128, sees Theseus as a Jupiter figure who fails to see the link between the First Mover and a loving God who can intervene in the determined scheme of things. C. David Benson, on the other hand, "The *Knight's Tale* as History," *ChauR* 3 (1968): 107–23, sees in Theseus's Boethian consolation a foreshadowing of a Christianity that Chaucer's Christian audience would recognize. Payne, *The Key of Remembrance,* 257–58, sees Theseus's speech as a parody of Boethius which subverts order.

43. Jean Seznec, *The Survival of the Pagan Gods* (New York: Harper, 1961), 99n, cites Rufus Mutianus: *Quum Jovem nomino, Christum intellige* [When I say Jupiter, understand me to say Christ].

44. The standard patristic mythographic reading of the birth of Venus from the testicles of Saturn cast into the sea by his son Jupiter is the loss of primal justice in the world, *carencia justitiae originalis.*

45. Minnis and Scott, *Medieval Literary Theory,* 162, cite Ralph of Longchamp's description of Saturn the Almighty's four sons: Jupiter, the father of the gods, Juno, who rules nature, Neptune, who rules the sea, or flux, and Pluto, who rules numbers or cities. The Jupiter of the Second Nun's tale is the false god whose idol Almachius commands the Christians to worship (8, 364). Jean Seznec, *The Survival of the Pagan Gods,* 156–57, reproduces an illustration from a mid-thirteenth-century astrological manuscript which groups together Saturn, Jupiter, Venus, and Mars. Of course, Saturn as Time resolves all things, but rarely pleases all parties in doing so.

46. In his edition of the *Tales,* A. C. Baugh glossses *welle* as "will" rather than "well," or "source." Jill Mann, "Chance and Destiny in *Troilus and Criseyde* and the *Knight's Tale,*" *The Cambridge Chaucer Companion,* 89, notes that Theseus confuses the powers of the gods with those of the planets. Charles Muscatine, *Chaucer and the French Tradition,* 190, explains that Saturn alone has the power to mediate between powers of love and forces of war. Brooks and Fowler, "The Meaning of Chaucer's *Knight's Tale*," 129–30, point to Theseus's poor grasp of the power of time.

47. Saturn is the planet furthest from the earth and closest, in a design of concentric circles, to the *Primum Mobile.* It would stand to reason, then, that Divine mediation should descend toward man through the orbit of Saturn, whose place in the sky, of course, can indeed be seen and understood by eye.

48. Creation is marked in the Vulgate, item by item, with the phrase *factum est,* and Christ's last words are *consummatum est* (John 19: 30). Curious it is that two legal terms for sexual coupling are scriptural terms describing creation and death.

49. Troilus rejects a public good for his private interests (1, 477–83), and his guarded privacy is Troy's inner canker, tantamount to Simon's treason in the *Iliad.* His early departure from the public fesitivites at Sarpedon's house for a private allegorizing of Criseyde's empty house (5, 540–53) is a sad example of amatory displacement. D. W. Robertson, Jr., "The Concept of Courtly Love," in *The Meaning of Courtly Love,* ed. F. X. Newman (Binghampton, NY; CMRS, 1968), 1–18, argues that civic ceremonies are ignored in the poem in favor of love. Instead of worshipping Pallas (wisdom), Troilus, Pandarus, and Criseyde tempt Cupid.

50. *Versus de Patribus Regibus,* ed. Peter Godman, *Alcuin, the Bishops, Kings and Saints of York* (Oxford: Clarendon Press, 1982). In the Trinity of the Orthodox Church, the Holy Spirit, or *Hagia Sophia,* is *logos.*

51. R. Allen Shoaf, "Dante's *Commedia* and Chaucer's Theory of Mediation," 102.

52. Augustine, *De Doctrina* 2, 36, points out that it is not words but the perversity of their users that is to blame for the sins they incite.

53. Jerome Mandel, "Courtly Love in the *Canterbury Tales*," *ChauR* 19 (1985): 286, argues that there is no real courtly love in the tale simply because, as Emily's tacit subjection to Theseus's rule demonstrates, "the woman's desire is never considered." But, courtly love needs no woman's speech, only obeisance to the desires the lover is able to articulate of what she *would* speak.

54. The Black Knight of the *Book of the Duchess,* though he loves nobly, cannot detach his love from White's person to secure it to an *idea* of love after she dies. His succeeding waste is not hate, but despair. Troilus, like Orpheus, looks backward through time to a love lost, and we see him last, even in death, looking downward to the little spot of earth. Troilus does not earn heaven with his jealousy and vengeance. He merits, rather, a pagan purgatory for his misdirected devotion. The text has him carried to *holughnesse* (hollowness) which echoes "holiness," but the majority of manuscripts locate him in the seventh, rather than the eighth sphere (Boccaccio has *ottava*). Counting outward from Earth, seven designates the sphere of Saturn, whereas Dante arrives at the sphere of the fixed stars for his final view of things. The realm of chaos lies between the seventh and eighth spheres, and Saturn-Chronos is Troilus's foe. Macrobius's *Commentary* and Lucan's *Pharsalia* count spheres inward toward the earth, which would place Troilus in the sphere of the moon, the wandering planet, which seems appropriate to one bound to purgatorial whirling. From a strictly Christian point of view, Troilus's salvation is possible despite error, for God is free to grant it. What would argue against his salvation would be his lack of *trying* to redeem himself. Man cannot hope for salvation without using his time on earth working for it.

## Chapter 5. Economies of Word as Bonds of Love: Dorigen and Grisilde

1. *Chiertee* is Modern English "charity," but in the mouths of the Wife of Bath and the Shipman, for example, the term qualifies sexual and social affections.

2. Morton Bloomfield, "*The Franklin's Tale,* A Story of Unanswered Questions," *Acts of Interpretation: Essays in Honor of E. Talbot Donaldson,* ed. Mary J. Carruthers and Elizabeth Kirk (Norman, OK: Pilgrim Books, 1982), 189. Of course, every "Why was I ever born?" is an implicit questioning of providence, excusable only as cliche jesting. The questioning of God's good in the birth of Tereus at the opening of the tale of Philomela in the *Legend* is comparable. Gertrude M. White, "The Franklin's Tale: Chaucer or the Critics," *PMLA* 89 (1974): 457, mitigates Dorigen's words on the grounds that "she addresses the Almighty respectfully but almost as an equal." The second-person singluar pronoun is not exceptional in pious praise and supplications to God, though here it raises some doubt as to the respect Dorigen shows.

3. W. Bryant Bachman, Jr., "'To Maken Illusion': The Philosophy of Magic and the Magic of Philosophy in the Franklin's Tale," *ChauR* 12 (1977): 55–67, discusses the Boethian implications of Dorigen's complaint and the rocks. *Timaeus* 28b–29a discusses the immutable perfection of nature's form, but adds that any copy of it must be made with imperfect materials. No *created* pattern is, then, perfect, but the invisible and perfect model behind it can be read in the corporeal and imperfect copy.

4. Man's lordship in marriage was a fundamental law of nature in the world of romance. See John V. Fleming, *The Roman de la Rose,* 150–52.

5. Russell A. Peck, "Sovereignty and the Two Worlds of the Franklin's Tale," *ChauR* 1 (1967): 264–65, argues that Dorigen's view of the rocks is as illusory as her conception of marriage. The confusion is not in nature, he argues, but in herself.

6. See 1, 1568, 2243, 3281, et passim.

7. Gertrude M. White, "The Franklin's Tale," 457, says that Dorigen's vow is moti-

vated by a principle of truth to Arveragus. By promising the impossible, she demonstrates her fidelity to her husband.

8. Andreas, *De Amore* 2, 7, I, records a case of a woman who ordered a lover not to serve her, but the Countess of Champagne overruled her treatment as too harsh.

9. See J. Laplanche and J. B. Pontalis, *The Language of Psycho-Analysis* (London: Hogarth Press, 1983), 92, and Jacques Lacan, *Ecrits* (Paris: Seuil, 1966), 522, who defines *tranfert* as "lien intersubjectif." The concept would not seem novel to Chaucer whose Manciple says: "He is his thral to whom that hath sayd / A tale of which he is now yvele apayd" (9, 367–68).

10. Curiously, the Latin form of Orleans is *Aurelianus,* so the squire's name identifies him with something of the spirit of the magician's place.

11. Chaucer's Franklin may have Augustine's *De civ. Dei* 8, 19, in mind in his remarks about the magical arts, in which "the fruits of one field are said to be transferred to another." Augustine identifies much of what is called *magic* with the demons of the air which mediate between the gods and men (8, 18).

12. This point has been made in chapter 3, but see the *OED* definitions 1, 3 and 10. See Modern English *witness.* I would not accuse Aurelius of a deceitful pun on *rokkes* "rooks," but it would be a neat ploy.

13. Gertrude M. White, "The Franklin's Tale," 461, defends Dorigen on the grounds that her "truth" does not depend upon verification: "Why Dorigen did not go to see with her own eyes that the rocks had actually disappeared, instead of taking Aurelius' word, [has] little to do with the life of the poem," that is, in regard to truth. The life of the poem, it seems to me, is in the tension between word and sight.

14. Patterson, *The Subject of History,* 196–97 questions whether Arveragus's love of "trouthe" comprises his honor. Leonard Michael Koff, *Chaucer and the Art of Storytelling* (Berkeley: University of California Press, 1988), 193, links Dorigen's sworn word to her husband's conceptual world: "Dorigen's word guarantees his conceptual world. *Her not committing adultery* would constitute his self betrayal." Anglo-Saxon jurisprudence of the day held that any contract which contradicts an earlier contract is nul and void unless the earlier contract is abrogated by *both* concerned parties.

15. Caroline Walker Byrnum, "'And Woman His Humanity,'" 262–64, discusses the late medieval commonplace of Christ's femaleness. Christian iconography of the thirteenth and fourteenth century shows him with female breasts, and the spear wound in his side as he suffers crucifixion is often detailed to resemble a vagina.

16. Hildebert, *Sermones de Sancto, PL* 171, 609.

17. Georges Duby, *The Knight, the Lady, and the Priest* (New York: Pantheon, 1983), 28 and 225.

18. Mircea Eliade, *The Sacred and the Profane* (New York: Harcourt, Brace and World, 1959), 141–42, notes from the anthropologist's perspective that "generation and childbirth are microcosmic versions of a paradigmatic act performed by the earth; every human mother only imitates and repeats this primordial act of the appearance of life in the womb of the earth."

19. Peter Godman, "Literary Classicism and Latin Erotic Poetry," 149–82, discusses descriptions of woman's body in Christian Latin poetry, particularly in the works of Peter of Blois.

20. Ironically, Chaucer himself was brought up on charges of rape and complicity to rape just before he was knighted for the shire of Kent. On 1 May 1380 he was released by Cecily Chaumpaigne *tam de raptu meo, tam de alia re vel causa* (both of my rape and of conspiracy with another in the matter). The coincidence of her name with Saint Cecilia and the date of acquitment with the festival of love is remarkable. Recently, Christopher Cannon, "Raptus in the Chaumpaigne Release and a Newly Discovered

Document Concerning the Life of Geoffrey Chaucer," *Speculum* 68 (1993): 89, shows that the charge *de rapto* was subsequently changed to *de feloniis transgressionibus,* probably due to Chaucer's influence in court.

21. The extent to which the figure of the Wife of Bath, like the Whore of Babylon, is a counter to the Virgin Mary is suggested in many ways. For one, the Wife's comparison of her own love to wild fire that consumes everything (3, 374–75), recalls the conventional praise of the Virgin as Moses' bush unburnt (7, 467–68). Rodney Delasanta, "Alison and the Saved Harlots: A Cozening of our Expectations," *ChauR* 12 (1978): 218–35, characterizes the Wife as a parody of Mary Magdalena, the paradigm of redeemed sexuality.

22. One would expect the elevating music associated with Saint Cecilia to oppose the debilitating song of the sirens, but Chaucer's Cecile in the Second Nun's tale is not associated with music. Some stories of Cecilia associate her with music by her practice of opposing the pagan rites of marriage which included playing the phallic flute.

23. *De Perfectione Monachorum, PL* 145.

24. See Peter Dronke, *Medieval Latin and the Rise of the European Love Lyric,* vol. 2, 454, 459:

> Cum rapit in peius / nos ardor et inpetus eius,
> Virtus, maigestas, / gradus altus honoris, honestas
> Miliciam veneris / et castra secuntur amoris.
>
> (*Anon.*)

[When its heat and force take us into a worse state, virtue, dignity, reputation, and honor enlist in Venus's service and Amor's wars.]

25. This is Chaucer's qualification of the term in his balade "Womanly Noblesse": steadfast governance, gentleness, and so forth, but particularly a mediating *ordynaunce.*

26. Chaucer moves subtly from his sources to suggest distinctions. The Clerk's "tempte" at line 452 is matched by the French *experimenter et essaier* and Petrarch's *experiendi altius.* At line 735, the French is *approuver* and the Latin *severitate experiendi;* at 786 *essaier et tenter* and *redemptaret.* Elaine Tuttle Hansen, "The Powers of Silence," 232, argues that Grisilde's silence and submission are threats to Walter's rule, if not to his sense of his own good. He tests her to have her fall from virtue and reveal herself to be like any other woman. The Monk's tale of Cenobia traces the transformation of a good *woman* into a fettered *wife:* "And she that bar the ceptre ful of floures / Shal bere a distaf, hire cost for to quyte" (7, 2373–74).

27. It is curious that the Clerk adds the detail that the girl is taken off when she has been at the breast only a short time, but the son is taken away after he has been weaned (4, 450, 617–18). The Latin text suggests sufficient suckling for the daughter: *ablactata esset infantula,* but the French does not mention the detail at all.

28. *Beauty* and *bounty* are etymological doublets. The former, as Augustine argues in *Confessions* 7, 23, is the visible sign of the invisible good of the latter. The beauty of a thing signals its goodness and truth in medieval esthetics, D. W. Robertson, Jr., points out in *A Preface,* 114ff. Russell A. Peck, "Number as Cosmic Language," *Essays in the Numerical Criticism of Medieval Literature,* ed. Caroline D. Eckhardt (Lewisburg, PA: Bucknell University Press, 1980), 30ff, discusses beauty as *numerosa* and notes that delight mediates between the apprehension of a thing and understanding of its beauty.

29. Patrick J. Gallacher, "The Conversion of Tragic Vision in Dante's *Comedy,*" *Romanic* 80 (1989): 609–10, cites Thomas Aquinas's *Summa* 2. 3. 144, 1, 4, where shame is discussed as a mean between shameless and excessive shame, or *inordinata stupor.* Shame is associated with the wonder and bewilderment that leads to appreciation of the

providential order of things. In this context one recalls the Monk's Nero who shamed his mother's body by slitting open her womb, but he felt no shame for having done so.

30. Peggy A. Knapp, "Deconstructing *The Canterbury Tales:* Pro," *SAC* Proceedings 2 (1987): 79–80, points out that the smock is read by Janicula as his daughter's youth and innocence. Grisilde's smock reminds me of Christ's wound, his sacred bleeding heart as a privileged place of refuge in devotional lyrics of Chaucer's day and later, and collected under the rubric "Five Wounds of Christ." Douglas Gray, "The Five Wounds of Our Lord," *N & Q* 208 (1963): 82–89, discusses many of these.

31. *PL*, 40, 373. Grisilde very much resembles Marcia Catoun, the model of womanly fidelity mentioned in the *Legend*, F 252. Marcia was divorced from her husband Marcus against her will, but returned to care for him later. Matthew of Vendôme tells her story in *Ars Versificatoria*, 1, 57. See Marie Hamilton, "Chaucer's 'Marcia Catoun,'" *MP* 30 (1933): 361–64. In the *Roman de la rose*, 6151–55, Reason describes Fortune as one who, when stripped of her finery, is worth nothing.

32. Compare the Prioress's praise of the Virgin Mary:

> By the mouth of children thy bountee
> Parfourned is, for on the brest soukynge
> Somtyme shewen they thyn heriynge.

$$(7, 457–59)$$

33. I find in the "Envoy" a subtle invitation to read the Wife of Bath's prologue and tale allegorically as well. Grisilde's figure of divine mediation flatters womanhood as a whole and is a "fair" reflection of the less seemly example of Alison's and her fictional hag's domestic mastery. Roger Ellis, *Patterns of Religious Narrative in the Canterbury Tales* (London: Croom Helm, 1986), 57, sees the "Envoy" as a denial of the womanly perfection which Grisilde's steadfastness exemplifies.

34. If the "Envoy" is Chaucer's, then it is added by the "reporter" of the tales, nicely balancing with an English authority at the performance's end the Italian authority at Petrarch at its beginning. Secondly, whereas Grisilde does not die in the tale, she is "killed" in the opening line of the "Envoy." *The Riverside Chaucer* notes to the "Envoy" associate the diction with the Wife's language (3, 248–70), and cite a source in Ami's advice in the *Roman de la rose*, 8597–8600, on how to win a wife. More to the point is La Vieille's lengthy advice to women on how to deceive men by making their less attractive natural features look fair by the artifice of clothing (13265–344).

35. Pertinent to the Wife's *amblere* and her ambling preamble of a tale is Boccaccio's "Day Six, Tale One" in the middle of the *Il decamerone*. Filomene tells of Madonna Oretta who is bored by the repetitions and recapitulations in a knight's tale. Finally, made ill by his style, she stops him with the complaint, *vostro cavallo ha troppo duro trotto* [Your horse has an excessively hard trot].

## Chapter 6. Aping God's Chain of Love: The First "Fragment"

1. *Testes* does not appear in the Benson glossary to *The Riverside Chaucer* edition but is glossed at the bottom of the page "Cupels, crucibles." The OED has no such definition for the term. The priest's *veyne* recalls inevitably the "veyne of swich licour" in which virtue is engendred, that is, a channel of love.

2. Chauncey Wood, "Chaucer's Use of Signs in his Portrait of the Prioress," *Signs and Symbols in Chaucer's Poetry,* ed. John P. Herman and John J. Burke, Jr. (University,: University of Alabama Press, 1981), 97–99, argues that the public display of beads without any description of their use suggests that they are worn for esthetic appeal rather than used as a spiritual tool. As such, the brooch is a possible sign of shallow understanding.

John Finlayson, "Chaucer's Prioress and *Amor Vincit Omnia*," *SN* 60 (1968): 171–74, would have the inscription point to her own "suppressed sexual instincts."

3. E. Randolph Daniel, "The Double Procession of the Holy Spirit in Joachim of Fiore's Understanding of History," *Speculum* 55 (1980): 477; and Peter Dronke, *Fabula: Explorations into the Uses of Myth in Medieval Platonism* (Leiden: Brill, 1974), 146ff.

4. For a discussion of this lyric, see Winthrop Wetherbee, *Platonism and Poetry in the Twelfth Century* (Princeton: Princeton University Press, 1972), 99–100.

5. C. V. Langlois, *La Connaissance de la nature et du monde* (Paris: Hachettte, 1911), 293. For discussion of the World Egg in medieval texts, see Peter Dronke, *Fabula,* pp. 79ff. According to *Orphic Fragments,* 60, 61, 70 and 89, Eurynome, Goddess of Things, laid the World Egg.

6. Compare William Blake's *Milton,* 2, plate 34:

> Around this Polypus Los continual builds the mundane shell.
> Four Universes round the Universe of Los remain Chaotic,
> Four intersecting Globes and the Egg form'd World of Los
> In midst; stretching from Zenith to Nadir, in midst of Chaos.

The yolk of Blake's egg is the World Eye.

7. Daniel, "The Double Procession," 476–77.

8. Recently Paule Mertene-Fonck, "Life and Fiction in the *Canterbury Tales:* A New Perspective," *Poetics: Theory and Practice in Medieval English Literature,* ed. Boitani and Torti, 105–9, argues that the "A" identifies the Aiglantine of the French poem *Hueline et Aiglantine.*

9. Donald R. Howard, *Writers and Pilgrims* (Berkeley: University of California Press, 1980), 89, calls the Prioress's "A," like the patience of Griselde, an "ideal fiction" in that it figures a number of meanings without being burdened by local and topical "realism."

10. For two critical responses to the Miller's attack on the Boethian model, see Morton Bloomfield, "The Miller's Tale—An UnBoethian Interpretation," *Medieval Literature: Essays in Honor of Francis Lee Utley,* ed. Jerome Mandel and Bruce A. Rosenberg (New Brunswick, NJ: Rutgers University Press, 1970), 205–11, and Patrick J. Gallacher, "Perception and Reality in the *Miller's Tale,*" *ChauR* 18 (1983): 38–48. Bloomfield shows how the tale makes a nothingness, or an essential disorder out of the desire for mastery and control, while Gallacher shows how the failures of perception in the tale contribute to a triumph of the real over the imaginary.

11. Beryl Rowland, "The Play of the Miller's Tale," *ChauR* 5 (1970): 140–46, reads the tale as a parody of medieval stage productions of the Fall, the Flood, and the Annunciation.

12. John Stevens, "*Angelus ad virginem:* The History of a Medieval Song," *Medieval Studies for J. A. W. Bennett,* ed. P. L. Heyworth (Oxford: Clarendon Press, 1981), 297–328.

13. Patrick J. Gallacher, *Love, the Word, and Mercury,* 26ff., discusses the medieval view of Annunciation as a bond reflecting the Word made flesh at the moment of creation.

14. Matthew 24, 43 et passim. I am reminded, as well, of Ecclesiastes 2: 14, "The fool walketh in darkness," and of the "treasures of darkness, and the hidden riches of secret places" of Isaiah 45: 3. Absolon's is, rather, the treasure of practical experience.

15. Both the Wife of Bath and the Parson recall the proverb which likens a fair woman who is unchaste to a gold ring in a sow's nose (3, 784–85 and 10, 155). In the *Summa,* Suppl. 3, Q. 96, Art. 2, Obj. 3, Thomas Aquinas associates a gold ring with the aureole of grace. In many mythologies a ring is a sign and fetish of sexuality.

16. *Piers Plowman,* C Text, *Passus* 8, 65.

17. The tubs recall the legends of Nicholas's namesake, Nicholas of Myra, who was venerated for having restored three children from their deaths in brine tubs. Other versions of the legend have him saving three daughters from becoming prostitutes by throwing

gold purses through a window to provide their father with sufficient dowries. His reputed stilling of the sea made Saint Nicholas the patron saint of mariners. Nicholas is also the patron saint of scholars and thieves, identities which fit the Miller's Nicholas.

18. Cited by D. W. Robertson, Jr., *A Preface to Chaucer,* 374.

19. Significantly, the name Oswald derives from Old English *os* [God] and *weald* [power].

20. If, as Larry D. Benson's glossary of names in *The Riverside Chaucer* indicates, Malyn is a form of the name Malkyn, Chaucer would have known the French form *maligne*—"one who takes pleasure in evil" and Latin *malignus,* which has the added meaning "sterile." According to the MED, the common English "Molly" and "Moll" derive from *Malyn.* Chaucer's grandfather was Robert Malyn. For a discussion of Chaucer's use of his own and his family names see my article "Chaucer's Names," *NM* 95 (1994): 243–48.

21. A quick scan of the *MED* entries for *bisemare* reveals the opprobrium the word carries. It is a favorite homiletic quality of Jews, false priests, and so forth. Definition 3, "Degraded condition," cites *Cursor Mundi* 22029, where the Antichrist is full of bisemare.

22. A. C. Baugh and John H. Fisher, in their editions of the *Tales,* gloss *ympes* as "shoots" and "offshoots," respectively. *The Riverside Chaucer* offers no gloss at all. Since the Host goes on to say that wives assay religious folk because they are better in making love, it seems that by *ymp* he includes the sense "graft." Borel men make wretched grafting partners and so produce with their wives small fruit.

23. The rapist-knight of the Wife's tale, forced to hold to his marriage offer to the old hag, cries: "Allas! that any of my nacioun / Sholde evere so foule disparaged be!" (3, 1068–69). It is the voice of an invisible force in the Man of Law's tale who accuses the false knight of having "desclaundred, giltelees, / The doghter of hooly chirche" (2, 674–75).

24. There is an interesting play of words here. The word *love,* as in *love-dayes* (1, 258), means "law" (from Norse *lov*). So does the word *lay* (1, 1001). This word, which derives from OE *lagu* (that which is laid down) is homophonous with *lay* "song, poem." Compare Old French *lei/lai* [law/poem].

25. "God's soul" and "Christ's soul" are expressions found nowhere else in the *Canterbury Tales* outside the Miller's and Reeve's tales. "God's soul" sounds strange in the mouth of a clerk, since God *is* rather than *contains* soul.

26. See Isaiah 49: 19:

> Quia deserta tua, et solitudines tuae,
> Et terra ruinae tuae,
> Nunc augusta erunt prae habitatoribus.

[For your desolate places and your ruins will now be too small for all your inhabitants]

27. The Parson later cites the Book of Job: "In the lond of myese and of derknesse ... ther is noon ordre or ordinaunce but grisly drede that evere shal laste" (10,177).

28. John Gower, in the *Miroir de l'omme,* 27229ff., describes the Peasants' Revolt as a rebellion of the senses against the head.

29. Charles A. Owen, Jr., "The Design of the *Canterbury Tales,*" in *Companion to Chaucer Studies,* ed. Beryl Rowland (London: Oxford University Press, 1968), 192–97, traces a unity in the fragment, not only in the various rivalries between lovers, but in the progression of change of place from town to country to city.

30. Few readers are insensitive to the lowering of issues from tale to tale in this group. Donald Howard, *The Idea of the Canterbury Tales* (Berkeley: University of California Press, 1976), 237–47, calls it a degeneration from ideals to realities. E. D. Blodgett, "Chaucerian *Pryvetee* and the Opposition to Time," *Speculum* 51 (1976): 492, refers to it as a movement against the ideals of pilgrimage by illustrations of the fall of flesh away

from spirit. Jerome Mandel, *Geoffrey Chaucer* (Rutherford, NJ: Fairleigh Dickinson University Press, 1992), 132–33, notes a progressive deterioration in the first fragment from simplicity to multiplicity, mirroring Theseus's chain image.

31. *A Connecticut Yankee in King Arthur's Court* (Berkeley: University of California Press, 1979), chapter 1 (56).

## Chapter 7. Quests and Parodies of Quests for the Chain of Love

1. Robert R. Edwards, "Narration and Doctrine in the Merchant's Tale," *Speculum* 66 (1991): 363–65, explains Proserpine's and May's words as means of righting a fallen word. Like Alceste, each defends a mortal who has offended higher powers.

2. David Chamberlain, "The Music of the Spheres and the *Parliament of Fowls*," *ChauR* 5 (1970): 49, cites Macrobius to the effect that "learned men . . . win heaven by imitating the music of the spheres." In the *Commentary* 2, 3, 7, Macrobius says that "Every soul in this world is allured by musical sounds, so that not only those who are more refined in their habits, but all the barbarous peoples as well, have adopted songs by which they are inflamed with courage or wooed to pleasure; for the soul carries with it into the body a memory of the music which it knew in the sky." Leo Spitzer, *Classical and Christian Ideas of World Harmony* (Baltimore: Johns Hopkins Press, 1963), 51–54, notes that according to old Christian tradition, Jews have no heart because it is law and not nature which mediates between man and God in their religion. *Musica mundana* is incorporate in nature, music and nature are bound emanations of God's creative design, and so Jews are enemies of music (30–31).

3. See Aristotle, *Metrologica* 2, 6 (378c) where vapours of elements are considered their purist forms.

4. In the English translation of the *Chirurgie of Guy of Chauliac, licour* is the physician's term for the life-giving sperm of men and women (sic). Boccaccio calls it *l'umido radicale* (*Il decamerone,* day 9, tale 10). In Thomas Norton's *Ordinal of Alchemy,* 2185–96, *licour* is not only sperm, but the element which joins other elements, purifies, and nourishes the Philosopher's Stone, and "licours to oure stone be chief nutricioun" (2192). See P. B. Taylor, "The Alchemy of Spring in Chaucer's *General Prologue,*" *ChauR* 17 (1982): 1–4.

5. Gower's *Confessio Amantis* 4, 1–439, compares lovers with drunkards, for both act in unstable ways contrary to their proper natures.

6. Britton J. Harwood, "Language and the Real: Chaucer's Manciple," *ChauR* 6 (1972): 268–79, sees in the "intoxicating" language of Phebus's crow a reflection of the intoxicating wine the Manciple gives to the Cook.

7. The Pardoner's exposition of the channel between gluttonous womb and privy throat (6, 522–540) is a grotesque perversion of the channel of love between God and the Virgin Mary.

8. Georges Duby, *The Knight, the Lady, and the Priest,* 224–25, remarks that, in the violent amorous pursuit of knights in thirteenth-century France, women who were supposed to possess magical powers were particular targets: "When they imagined themselves winning, by violent and dangerous means, these enticing, elusive, dominating fays, they must have felt they were conquering their anxieties and returning to the warm bosom of their earliest infancy." The Wife says nothing of the fairy status of the virgin, but the hag who "redresses" the ill is a magical being.

9. In Chaucer's time the king's chancellor had extraordinary powers to temper equity with grace—*juxta aequum et bonum*—that is to mitigate sentence, although chancery court was not formally established until the middle of the fifteenth century. The chancel-

lor's judgment depended upon nature and conscience. See Alan Harding, *The Law Courts of Medieval England* (London: George Allen & Unwin, 1973), 98–103.

10. Compare Orfeo's Heurodis who falls asleep in an "orchard-side" and is spirited away by an otherworldly king. *Sir Orfeo,* ed. A. J. Bliss (Oxford: Clarendon Press, 1966), line 66.

11. On the literal level of the tale, the hag performs as Theseus does to contain a wild sexual urge within the order of marriage, except that there is no expressed motive on her part for doing so. In effect, she is engaging the knight in an amorous combat whose weapons are words. The knight's physical and verbal powers are no match for her language, and she succeeds in converting his will to her desire. She rapes with words. Susan Crane, "Alison's Incapacity and Poetic Stability in the Wife of Bath's Tale," *PMLA* 101 (1987): 24, applies the term "erotic combat" to this encounter.

12. The popular theology alluded to here is grotesque. God does not represent himself in unseemly shapes, but the devil can take on a beautiful aspect. The woman who can, like Spenser's Duessa in the *Faerie Queene,* take on either fair or foul appearance is, most likely, really foul.

13. Michael D. Cherniss, "The Clerk's Tale and Envoy, the Wife of Bath's Purgatory and the Merchant's Tale," *ChauR* 6 (1972): 242–45, says that the message of the Clerk's "Envoy" is that wives who ignore Grisilde's model will end up being purgatories for their husbands. A purgatory on earth however, has a reasonable chance of serving an ascent to paradise.

14. Curtius, *European Literature,* 103, discusses the trope of the old woman becoming young as a figure of Holy Church. Rejuvenation of Church by the virtue of her bridegroom would be an attractive form of allegory for the Wife's tale, but Church does not invite the bridegroom into her embrace. The knight's "conversion" has certain parallel's with Walter's by Grisilde, but Grisilde converts by submission, whereas the hag converts by domination.

15. In contrast, the Man of Law's Constance does not "earn" her grace other than by accepting God's *sonde* in whatever form it manifests itself.

16. See 1 Corinthians 15: 53–54: "When this perishable nature has put on imperishability, and when this mortal nature has put on immortality, then the words of Scripture will come true: Death is swallowed up in victory" (*Absorpta est mors in victoria*).

17. The Wife speaks of virginity as gold (3, 100), and Chauntecleer in the Nun's Priest's tale reads gold in dreams as a token of death (7, 3021). Augustine, *De civ. Dei* 12, 8, says that the substance of gold does not contain the defect of greed which is attached to it by man's will.

18. The Pardoner's tale is read often in tandem with the Physician's tale which precedes it in the *Ellesmere MS* order. Gerhard Joseph, "The Gifts of Nature, Fortune and Grace in the *Physician's, Pardoner's* and *Parson's Tales,*" *ChauR* 9 (1975): 237–45, points out how the Pardoner's revelation of his own nature, unredeemed by fortune, counters the Physican's theme of grace's triumph over nature's harms. Michael R. Haines, "Fortune, Nature and Grace in Fragment C," *ChauR* 10 (1976): 220–35, shows how the Pardoner abuses all three.

19. H. Marshal Leicester, Jr., "'Synne Horrible': The Pardoner's Exegesis of his Tale, and Chaucer's," *Acts of Interpretation,* ed. Carruthers and Kirk, 45, compares the rioters and the Old Man with the pilgrims and the Pardoner, who is able to assoil them along the way, with the pardon which carries God's grace.

20. The third teller after the Wife and Pardoner to offer of revelation of self as preface to tale is the Canon's Yeoman whose tale makes of the craft of alchemy a reflection of pilgrimage. His tale is not of a quest-journey, but of a labor for a secret knowledge. Like the Pardoner, the Yeoman displays his body to authenticate his grimy occupation. The

self-revelations, or confessions, which introduce the Wife's and Pardoner's quest tales, figure the penitential confessional of pilgrimage.

21. *De mendacio, PL,* 40, 487–518.

22. The image of the hare elsewhere in the *Tales* combines sexual with religious values. Hunting for the hare is all the Monk's lust (1, 191–92), and among the features of the Pardoner which signal his suspect sexuality are eyes that glare like a hare's (1, 684). The Friar's tale associates the Summoner's harlotry with the fact that he is crazy as a hare (3, 1327–28). In the Shipman's tale, the lecherous monk John ridicules married men for sleeping long in their leporine *fourmes* because of their sexual weariness (7, 104).

23. The *MED* defines *elf* as a "supernatural being having powers for good and evil, a spirit, fairy, goblin, incubus, succubus, or the like," and it cites the *Medulla* gloss: "*satirus; an helfe.*" The force of the term in a northern pagan context is evident in the Old Icelandic *Njál's saga,* chapter 25, when the hero Skarpheðin Njálsson uses the epithet *rauðálf* [red elf] to sexually debase his enemy. The term seems to have something of the sexual implications of contemporary English "fairy."

24. Northrop Frye, *The Secular Scripture* (Cambridge: Harvard University Press, 1976), 24, explains the romance genre as "designed mainly to encourage irregular or excessive sexual activity."

25. Criseyde worries about people "that dremen thynges whiche that nevere were" (*Tr.* 3, 585), and Chauntecleer tells Pertelote of the fate of the man who dismissed the portents of dreams by declaring that "men dreme of thyng that nevere was ne shal" (7, 3094). In matters of love, Diomede tells Criseyde that "many a wight / Hath loved thyng he nevere saigh his lyve" (*Tr* 5, 164–65), but perhaps this means that many love at first sight. Of course, God is the proper invisible goal of love. Saint Paul charges Timothy to undertake the quest of teaching the Word with piety, justice and love, "irreproachably and without fault until our Lord Jesus Christ appears. That appearance God will bring to pass in his own good time. . . . He alone possesses immortality, dwelling in irreproachable light. No man has ever seen or can ever see him" (1 Tim. 6: 14–16). The climax of the *Commedia* is Dante's sight of the Divine Form of Love in His *etterna luce* (*Par.* 33, 83). Guillaume d'Aquitaine celebrates a love he has never seen in his third lay, "Ferai un vers":

> M'amigu 'ai ieu, no sai qui s'es,
> qu'anc non la vi, si m'ajut fes
> . . . Anc non la vi et am la fort.

[I have a woman, I know not who she is, for I've never seen her, I swear. . . . I've never seen her, but I love her very much.] The text is Goldin, *Lyrics of the Troubadours,* 26.

26. *Stone* looks like an alliterative "fill" here, but it inevitably suggests something of its sexual meaning, particularly next to the verb *prick.* The Pardoner's *coillons* come easily to mind (6, 952)

27. Many have commented on the name of Chaucer's hero. E. S. Kooper, "Inverted Images in Chaucer's *Tale of Sir Thopas,*" *SN* 56 (1984): 148, notes that the topaz is a bright jewel, a hollow mirror, and an emblem of chastitiy. She reviews its symbolic sense from Isidore to Alanus as perverted nature, reflecting Augustine's reference in *Sermo in Natale* (154n.). On the other hand, in the "London Lapidary of King Philip," *Mediaeval English Lapidaires,* ed. Joan Evans and Mary S. Serjeantson (London: Oxford University Press, 1960), 19, the topaz betokens the nine orders of angels, and is called "the second life of the high hevenly kyngdome." Nonetheless, the pronunciation of his name cannot be taken for granted. The initial sound represented by the digraph *th* is pronounced regularly as a dental *t* by my peers, but the same people pronounce Theseus with an initial unvoiced apico alveolar *th* as in *thick.* Helge Kökeritz, *A Guide to Chaucer's*

*Prounnunciation* (Toronto, 1962), and Norman Davis in *The Riverside Chaucer* are silent on initial *th* in names, though it is clear that Chaucer seems to prefer continental pronunciation of names. Of the twenty-three names beginning with *th* in Chaucer's works, three appear in two forms: Tharbe/Tarbe, Thesbee/Tisbe, and Thessalee/Tessalie, and six have an initial *th*, where the classical sources have *t:* Thelophus (Telephus), Thymalao (Timolaus), Thymeo (Timaeus), Thoas (Toas), Thobie (Tobias) and Thesiphone (Tisiphone). All assume that Thomas is pronounced as it is today. What this scan suggests is that Chaucer is free to use *th* in the continental fashion as a soft *t* sound, or as a variable sound. If variably, then *Thopas* can be sounded as *though-pass.*

28. Alan T. Gaylord, "The Moment of *Sir Thopas:* Towards a New Look at Chaucer's Loving Ways," *ChauR* 16 (1982): 311–29, makes this point another way by pointing to the affective style of the tale as a hiding of person, and that the tale's meaning is reduced to illustrating vanity. Style becomes its own subject.

29. See Chaucer's translation of *De consolatione* 3, m. 8, 1–6: "Alas! Whiche folie and whiche ignorance mysledeth wandrynge wrecchis from the path of verry good! Certes ye ne seke no gold in grene trees, ne ye gadere nat precyous stones in the vynes, ne ye ne hiden nat yowre gynnes in hey mountaignes."

30. Chaucer would have known Olivier's Olifant, the horn with which he signals the Saracen attack in *La chanson de Roland.* The horn is an item curiously absent from Thopas's hunting gear.

31. Considering that the tale of Thopas follows directly the Prioress's tale of the Jews' murder of a young boy, the curious detail of Jewish armor work seems pointed (7, 864–65). The notes to *The Riverside Chaucer* suggest that there is little factual evidence of Jewish armorers at the time, and that the attribution is not a literary convention. The reputation of Jewish workmanship in Chaucer's day, on the other hand, in contrast with the religious antipathy to Jews in the Prioress's tale and in official policy toward Jewish residence in England, was perhaps considerable. In the context of Thopas's arming to defend or rescue the elf queen, St. Paul's *arma lucis* (Rom. 13, 12), *arma iustitiae* (2 Cor. 6, 7) and *armaturam Dei* (Eph. 6, 11 and 13), are appropriate. The detail of Jewish collaboration in Thopas's quest is a subtle but sure counter to the Prioress's view of the Jews as enemies of the Virgin Mary.

32. As if to prove his point in the manner of its making, Chaucer forces different stress structures on the word *sentence* in lines 945 and 946 without altering the "sentence" of the word. Compare Augustine's explanation in *De doctrina* 2, 12–13, of the complementarity of different understandings and expressions of Scripture. One way of emending faulty interpretation, as Augustine demonstrates with a number of examples, is to change the style of its expression.

33. C. David Benson, "Their Telling Difference: Chaucer the Pilgrim and His Two Contrasting Tales," *ChauR* 18 (1983): 61–76, in an argument he repeats differently in his *Chaucer's Drama of Style,* perceives that the "real contest in the *Canterbury Tales* is between poems, not pilgrims" (61). Albertus Magnus, cited by Pierre Payer, "Prudence and the Principle of Natural Law: A Medieval Development," *Speculum* 54 (1979), 64, qualifies prudence as the virtue of *discretio,* a quality of *moderatio* which binds man to natural law. J. D. Burnley, *Chaucer's Language and the Philosopher's Tradition* (Cambridge: Cambridge University Press, 1979), 44ff. makes the same point with an emphasis on the place of prudence in the theology of salvation. In Classical tradition, Prudence has three eyes: past, present, and future. Thopas has an eye on the future as well.

34. Kooper, "Inverted Images," 147, describes the tale of Thopas as Chaucer's joke on his audience, but particularly on Harry, "by having their respective expectations reflect back on them invertedly," because they have expected something good from a poet, if not from the figure of the man to whom Harry draws attention.

35. I am reminded of the different versions in the Synoptic Gospels of Christ's last words: *Eli, Eli lama sabachthani* (Matthew 27: 46 and Mark 15: 34), *In manus tuas* (Luke 23: 46, and *Consummatum est* (John 19: 30). Thopas's last recorded words are a call for tales of "love-likynge" (7, 850).

36. Pilgrimage is a journey, as the Second Nun's Cecile implies, to that which is hidden in heaven ( 8, 316–18).

37. Cf. 2 Corinthians 6: 8: "God's grace can be received by honor and dishonor, by evil report and good report, as deceivers and yet true" (*ut seductores et veraces*). The shift of style from Thopas to Melibee anticipates the shift from the jest of the poetic tales to the prose earnest of the Parson.

38. Larry D. Benson, "The Order of the *Canterbury Tales*" *SAC* 3 (1981): 77–120, argues that the Ellesmere order, which has the tale of Sir Thopas follow the Pardoner's, which follows the Wife's, is Chaucer's final intention. Be it as it may, the order of the tales is not essential to my argument because any of the tales can be understood as a model for parodic imitation and comment, backwards or forwards. After all, the recorder of the tales, like God, knows what is ahead of any one of them.

39. Chauntecleer's and Pertelote's duet recalls the Pardoner's "Com hider, love, to me!" which the Summoner accompanies with a "stif burdoun" (1, 671–72). The cosmographic suggestion of the tale is obvious. A female trinity rules over all. The Widow has sufficiency in her moderate diet (7, 3837–38), and lives in patience (7, 3226). Her barnyard is described in plenitudinous terms. In other words, the Widow figures the goddess Natura.

40. Patrick J. Gallacher, "Food, Laxatives, and Catharsis in Chaucer's Nun's Priest's Tale," *Speculum* 51 (1976): 49–68, recalls the Platonic scale of nourishment and its connection with knowledge. The balance of the humors, he points out, accords with musical harmony, and so indigestion diminishes his power of song.

41. Harry had weighed the Monk's tale in the balance of worth with a butterfly (7, 2790). Proserpine estimates Pluto's words against women not worth a butterfly (4, 2304).

42. Lady Philosophy, in discussing the nature of good and evil (*Boece* 2, pr. 6, 82–103), explains that "contrarious thynges ben nat wont to ben ifelaschiped togydre. Nature refuseth that contrarious thynges ben ijoygned. . . . The nature of everythyng maketh his proprete, ne it is nat entremedlyd with the effectz of contrarious thynges."

43. The verbal and thematic echoes in the Priest's tale have been traced often in a variety of arguments. Most prominent are those which parody the Prioress and her tale. Where the Prioress takes on the role of a youth to tell of a seven-year-old martyr, the Priest recalls Saint Kenelm, martyred at seven, and notes that Pertelote is Chauntecleer's love since she was seven nights old. More significant for my argument are the pointed echoes of the quest tales. The Widow's diet of milk, brown bread, and bacon (7, 3844–45) contrasts with the Wife's vinolent sexuality characterized as barley bread (3, 144). Pertelote's cold counsel of woe (7, 3256) recalls the hag's verbal saving words. Chauntecleer, like the Wife of Bath, performs his sexuality more for delight than for the world to multiply (7, 3345). Where the Wife's knight rapes a virgin "maugree hir heed" (3, 887), Chauntecleer gives Colfox words to defy his pursuers, "maugree [hir] heed" (7, 3412).

44. The Priest pulls the same amphibological wool over his audience's ear when, after his long digression on free will, neccesity, and the peril of woman's counsel, he concludes in the spirit of Chauntecleer's Latin praise of Pertelote: "Thise been the cokkes wordes, and nat myne; / I kan noon harm of no womman divyne" (7, 3265–66). A neat deception since Chauntecleer has no time for verbal retrospection in this urgent instant, and it would be out of character for him to take the time. More to the point, the second line of the couplet has *kan* functioning both as a modal auxiliary, *"can"* [suppose any harm], and as a transitive verb *"know"* [any harm].

45. Editors exercise free will to distribute these words as they wish. Most editions

read: "Yet sholde I seyn, as wys God helpe me, / 'Turneth agayn, ye proude cherles alle!'" (7, 3408–9). If the oath "as wys God helpe me" is Chantecleer's, the reader is liable to read it as a sign that the cock has saved himself by petitioning God. On the other hand, the oath may just as well be part of the text dictated to the fox.

46. Saul Nathaniel Brody, "Truth and Fiction in the Nun's Priest's Tale," *ChauR* 14 (1979): 33–47, argues that the tale is purposely elusive and resists a simple reading. It is, he says, about the "very existence of moral possibilities." The Priest's challenge to read his tale both literally and figuratively reminds me of Augustine's *Contra mendacium* 13, 28, where he observes, in explaining Christ's rebuke of the Apostles for not understanding the old prophecies (Luke 24: 25–28), that the failure to read the figurative sense beneath the literal is tantamount to lying: *quasi mendacium sit omne quod fingitur, cum veraciter aliud ex alio significandi causa tam multa fingantur.* Roger Ellis, *Patterns of Religious Narrative in the Canterbury Tales* (London: Croom Helm, 1986), 297, draws attention to the centrality of the Pardoner's and Nun's Priest's tales in their reproducing the general form of the "great middle" of the tales, and in their unwillingness to impose single meaning on their stories.

47. Frank Kermode, "Secrets and Narrative Sequence," *CI* 7 (1980): 83–101, identifies the "secret potential" of narrative in its combined *clarity* in the presentation of a fable and *secrecy* of its progressive interpretation.

# Chapter 8. Ends of the Chain: Parson and Prologue

1. The text does not identify the "thropes ende" with the walls of Canterbury, but the Parson's gesture toward "Jerusalem celestial" (10, 51) suggests as much.

2. The first moment of text, however, is the book's first written words. "Here begynneth the Book of the Tales of Caunterbury" heads the *Hengwrt Manuscript* of the *Tales.* The *Ellesmere* has no heading at all. Only six extant manuscripts have headings in English, three of which, *Hengwrt, Harley 1758,* and *Fitzwilliam,* announce the tales, two of which, *Hatton* and *Selden,* announce the General Prologue, and *Harley 7333* which announces the prologue to the Knight's tale. *Christ Church* and *Egerton 2864* announce *gestis,* and *Landsdowne* has *prologus fabularum.* These comprise front matters, but there is no evidence that Chaucer himself thought of any title to encompass the collection, nor is it clear that Chaucer conceived of rubric titles for any of his works. Robert A. Pratt, "Chaucer's Title: The Tales of Caunterbury," *PQ* 54 (1975): 19–25, observes that the popular manuscript use of titles seems to derive from Lydgate. Chaucer refers to his poems by descriptive titles in his "Leave Taking."

3. "Whan" also opens the last tale told in rhyme. A more frequent opening phrase is "whilom," which appears in the opening lines of nine tales; forms of the verb "to be," and "to dwell" occur in nine opening lines, and forms of the verb "befall" in five. The Merchant's opening line contains three exordial markers: "Whilom ther was dwellynge. . . ." Nine tales are concluded by benedictions, while forms of either *ende* or *don* appear in eight final lines.

4. Most recently, Robert M. Jordan, *Chaucer's Poetics and the Modern Reader* (Berkeley: University of California Press, 1987), 168, argues for three endings, of which the Parson's is the second. Donald Howard, *The Idea of the Canterbury Tales,* 304–6, discusses the importance of the Manciple's tale as ending.

5. Rodney Delasanta, "The Theme of Judgment in *The Canterbury Tales,*" *MLQ* 31 (1970): 304–5, recalls Chaucer's descriptions of the Aries-Libra relationship in *Treatise on the Astrolabe,* and notices that Libra is figured on the tympanum of the cathedral at Canterbury as a judge in his robes.

6. See Siegfried Wenzel's notes to lines 2–11 of the Parson's prologue in *The Riverside Chaucer.*

7. Charles A. Owen, "The Transformation of a Frame Story: The Dynamics of Fiction," *Chaucer at Albany,* ed. Rossell Hope Robbins (New York: Burt Franklin, 1975), 144. Jesse Gellrich, *The Idea of the Book in the Middle Ages* (Ithaca: Cornell Univdrsity Press, 1985), 254, identifies the thrope's end as a trope's end.

8. I have given misleading line numbers and indications here, for although the manuscripts have these words as Harry's last, all editions I have consulted move them back to line 68. I cannot see a good reason for this, since the *he* of the edition's last line of the Parson's prologue—"And with that word he seyde in this manere"—are Harry's and not the Parson's. Helen Cooper makes the same point in the *Oxford Guide to Chaucer: The Canterbury Tales* (Oxford: Clarendon Press, 1989), 397, pointing out the relevance of the last word of the poetry—"grace"—to the last word of his prose tale—"synne."

9. These terms are from *Postquam (Harley 406,* 68v–93r) which Siegfried Wenzel, "The Sources for the 'Remedia' of the Parson's Tale," *Traditio* 27 (1971): 433–53, has shown to be a source of the Parson's exposition of the Seven Deadly Sins.

10. Ralph Baldwin, *The Unity of the Canterbury Tales,* 94, claims that the metaphor of the pilgrimage in the Jeremiah text is realized in *vita via.* Judson Boyce Allen, "The Old Way and the Parson's Way: An Ironic Reading of the Parson's Tale," *JMRS* 3 (1973): 259, argues that the text is both ironic and inappropriate.

11. *"Non ambulabimus . . . non audiemus. . . . Ecce ergo adducam mala super populam istum, fructum cogitationum eius, quia verb mea non audierunt, et legem meam proiecerunt"* (Jer. 6, 17–19).

12. Judson Boyce Allen, "The Old Way and the Parson's Way," 255–71, argues that the Parson's tale is a rejection of the whole enterprise and a demand that the pilgrims forget the banquet, mirth, and Canterbury.

13. Frank V. Cespedes, "Chaucer's Pardoner and Preaching," *ELH* 44 (1977): 1–18, characterizes the *Tales* as a a middle ground between the Pardoner's preaching methods which are evil but eloquent and the Parson's virtuous telling which is less effective. I suppose he means "less effective" to *us.*

14. *Lingua placibilis, lignum vitae: quae autem immoderata est, conteret spiritum* (Proverbs 15, 4).

15. E. Talbot Donaldson, *Speaking of Chaucer* (New York: W.W. Norton, 1970), 172, refutes the views of Tupper, Lawrence, and Baldwin that the Parson's expostion of sin implicates the pilgrims: "What Chaucer was good at is not the formulation of doctrines on sin but the revelation of the marvellous variety of life in a world which, however sinful, is the only world we've got, and one that can mingle much delight with its inevitable corruption."

16. J. A. Burrow, *Ricardian Poetry* (London: Routledge & Kegan Paul, 1971), 67, sees the "straightline" design suggested from Southwark and Knight to Canterbury and Parson "directly opposite in character to the 'circular' structure . . . we find in most poems of the period. . . . There is no reason to doubt that he would have finished the work in accordance with the proposals make by the Host. . . ." Donald R. Howard, *Pilgrims and Writers,* 97–98 and 120, notes that pilgrimage is, basically, a one-way activity. The account of this particular pilgrimage, however, reaches only as far as an unnamed "thropes ende" (10, 12), short of the shrine of Becket. Like other fictions that do not reach announced goals such as the stories of Alceste and Edward the Martyr, the unachieved fictional goal figures the pilgrims' and all man's unachievable goal of redemption. D. Knapp, "The Relyk of a Seint: A Gloss on Chaucer's Pilgrimage," *ELH* 39 (1972): 1–26, assumes on the basis of the account of Erasmus's and Colet's visit together to the shrine

that Canterbury was a tourist trap which, in Chaucer's day, was a "parody parading as a fact" (25). Perhaps, Knapp speculates, Chaucer doesn't want to get there.

17. Robert S. Knapp, "Penance, Irony and Chaucer's Retraction," *Assays* 2 (1983): 45–67, takes a semiotic approach to the leave-taking and concludes that restoring the text is tantamount to restoring the soul, and both are involved in the rhetorical trope of penance. I would add that penance, like irony, protects the author from judgment. The tales which "sownen unto synne" are those which attract man away from God, literally by their *sounds*. If confession must recall the sin to be absolved, and retraction the work to be retraced, how can we understand Chaucer's "cover confession" of those poems which are no longer in his remembrance?

18. Donald Howard, *The Idea of the Canterbury Tales,* 59, says à propos of the first sentence of the leave-taking, which he reads as the last line of the Parson's tale, "talk about the end of a work and your mind goes to the whole of it." For a radically different view, John Gardner, *The Life and Times of Chaucer* (New York: Vintage, 1977), 121, observes that "the retraction says plainly that Chaucer was aware of sex as a major theme in much of his life's work, both early and late."

19. Paul Ricoeur, *Time and Narrative,* vol. 2, 65, contrasts the "basic" time of fiction which locates a past event—"Bifil that in a seson on a day . . ."—and assertions about reality—"Whan that Aprille."

20. Curtius, *European Literature,* 92–94, reviews the topos of invocation to spring in the Latin tropological tradition, but notes no hierarchal order in them. Lydgate's imitation of Chaucer's opening in *The Siege of Thebes,* stuffed with meteorological and mythological allusions, extends the first sentence to sixty-five lines! Lydgate omits, however, the binding of vertical with horizontal designs. Malory's opening to "The Knight of the Cart" episode imitates and approaches Chaucer's conceptualization: "For lyke as trees . . . in lyke wyse every lusty hart . . . florryssyth in lusty dedis."

21. Aldo D. Scaglione, *Nature and Love in the Late Middle Ages* (Berkeley: University of California Press, 1963), 86–87, notes that Boccaccio credits *virtù*—Chaucer's *vertu*— with the principle of ordering things (*Il decamerone,* Second Day, Third Tale).

22. The form *inspire,* where Chaucer elsewhere uses *en*-for the proclitic particle, is an echo of the Vulgate *inspiravit*—God's breathing life into the form of Adam (Gen. 2, 7). God's breath is what Macrobius refers to in his Greek sources as the divine *logikon* which mediates between mortal *aesthetikon* and *phytikon* (*Commentary* 1, 14, 7). Russell A. Peck, "Number as Cosmic Language," *Essays in the Numerical Criticism of Medieval Literature* (Lewisburg, PA: Bucknell University Press, 1980), 27–29, recalls that *Universe* is *unus* and *versus,* a turning toward One, and that God's creative breath is, according to Photius, a *spermatitus logos,* akin to the Alexandrine School's *spermatologoi* and Dante's *seme operazione.* Aquinas explains that "our word is united to our speech by meaning of breathing [*spiritus*]. Therefore the Word of God is united to flesh by means of the Holy Spirit. And hence, by means of Grace which is attributed to the Holy Spirit according to 1 Cor. 12, 4" (*Summa,* 2, Q6, art. 6, obj. 3).

23. The most influential allegorical reading of the opening lines is Ralph Baldwin's *The Unity of the Canterbury Tales* (Copenhagen: Rosenkilde and Bagger, 1955), 54–57. Baldwin argues that the time and space of the passage render a perspective that reaches past Southwark toward the City of God. Thus, the pilgrimage is a static event.

24. Robert M. Jordan, "Reconstructing Chaucer," *SAC Proceedings* 1 (1984): 200, observes: "Chaucer is negotiating a delicate binary relationship between presentational voice and represented content."

25. For Platonic readings of the Milky Way as a reflection of a path containing the spirit of the gods, see Macrobius's *Commentary* 1, 12, 1–6.

26. The three major pilgrimage sites of Chaucer's day were Jerusalem (whose pilgrims

were palmers), Rome (whose pilgrims were roamers or Romeos, though the etymology is not certain), and Santiago de Compestello, the shrine of the first martyred apostle. The sign of an achieved pilgrimage to Santiago is the *coquille Saint Jacques,* more a gastronomic delight today than sign of spirit. Canterbury was a later fourth on the approved list because of the hardships of the Hundred Years War which made both land and sea voyages to Santiago perilous. Those who had gone to Santiago were earlier called "pilgrims," but by Chaucer's day, a voyager to any shrine could be called a pilgrim. For an informative scan of pilgrimage at that time, see Donald R. Howard, *Writers and Pilgrims* (Berekeley: University of California Press, 1980).

27. R. W. V. Elliott, *Chaucer's English* (London: André Deutsch, 1974), 368–69. Gabriel Josipivici, *The World and the Book* (London: Macmillan, 1971), 79–80, sees in this passage "a reporter dedicated to the 'truth' of what he says, even at the risk of offending those readers with sensitive tastes."

28. See P. B. Taylor, "Chaucer's *cosyn to the dede,*" *Speculum* 57 (1982): 315–27.

29. David H. Abraham, "*Cosyn* and *Cosynage:* Pun and Structure in the *Shipman's Tale,*" *ChauR* 11 (1977): 319–27, shows how the twin-senses of the word are present constantly in Chaucer's work. R. A. Shoaf, "The Play of Puns in Late Middle English Poetry: Concerning Juxtology," *On Puns,* ed. Jonathan Culler (Oxford: Basil Blackwood, 1988), 56–57, also comments on the play on *cosyn.*

30. The occasional homophony of *dede* [deed] and *deed* [dead] as in "Lak of Stedfastenesse," line 4) lends a remote sense: "Words can resemble the dead," if not dupe them.

# Epilogue: Memory and Design

1. Northrop Frye, "History and Myth in the Bible," *The Literature of Fact,* ed. Angus Fletcher (New York: Columbia University Press, 1976), 9–10, contrasts the bell-shaped curve of world history, with its rises and falls, with spiritual history, with its falls and rises. As the Parson's performance suggests, the curve does not close to a circle.

2. William W. Ryding, *Studies in Medieval Narrative* (The Hague: Mouton, 1971), 48, cites Aristotle's *Poetics* 17 (1455b) on amplification by addition, to characterize Chrétien's *Charrette* as a story whose "structure is like an accordion, flexible in the middle and steady at both ends." Jesse Gellrich, *The Idea of the Book,* 224–47, speaks of the indeterminacy of the book.

3. This is illustrated in ancient Greek thought by the powers of the river Lethe to remove memory. Dante's Hell, on the other hand, is a place of suffering an indelible memory.

4. Olive Sayce, "The Conclusion of the *Canterbury Tales* and its Place in Literary Traditions," *MAE* 40 (1971): 230–48, sees the retraction as conventional within the fiction of the pilgrimage, and that the lack of remembrance is ironic fiction. In his "Lenvoy" to "The Complaint of Venus," however, Chaucer regrets that age has reduced the *suffisaunce* of memory so that his poetic arts have been "bereft out of my remembraunce."

5. Ivan Illich and Barry Sanders, *The Alphabetization of the Popular Mind,* 92, remark: "If the existence of the world is contingent on the grace of the Word in 'divine authorship,' then Chaucer can only escape blasphemy by undercutting that singular, tremendous power that enables him to create—literacy."

6. Jean François Lyotard, *The Postmodern Condition,* trans. Geoff Bennington and Brian Massumi (Minneapolis: University of Minnesota Press, 1984), 22, expresses the postmodern view of the conjunction of memory and time in terms Chaucer could have appreciated:

By way of simplifying fiction, we can hypothesize that, against all expectations, a collectivity that takes narrative as it key form of competence has no need to remember its past. It finds the raw material for its social bond not only in the meaning of the narrative it recounts, but also in the act of reciting them. The narratives' reference may seem to belong to the past, but in reality it is always contemporaneous with the act of recitation. It is the present act that each of its occurrences marshals in the ephereal temporality inhabiting the space between the "I have heard" and the "you will hear."

7. Chaucer's art is not dedicated to purifying the dross of reality. There seems no reason to deny his possibility of "inventing" contradictions of fact in order to imitate life. Geographical references which seem contradictory might well be fictive faults of memory, a reportorial forgetting who said what when. On the other hand, "Loo, Rouchester stant heer faste by" (7, 3116) might be a topical joke or an idiom like "sending someone to Coventry." Glending Olsen, "Chaucer's Monk: The Rochester Connection," *ChauR* 21 (1986): 246, says that the artful purpose in mentioning Rochester and Sittingbourne is to avoid locating the pilgrims in time and space.

8. Aristotle, *De memoria et reminiscentia*, 1 (449b–451b), differentiates between memory which stores knowledge, and recollection which recalls facts. Recollection puts back into consciousness something that was once there, while memory holds conceptions and perceptions worked upon by the passage of time. Chaucer's sense of history has been examined at length recently by Lee Patterson in *Chaucer and the Subject of History*.

9. Michel Foucault, "Qu'est-ce qu'un auteur?" *Bulletin de la societé française de Philosophie* 63 (1969), 73–74. Caroline Dinshaw, *Chaucer and the Craft of Fiction: Two Views of the Author* (Ann Arbor, MI: University Microfilms, 1987), makes a dialectical distinction between the author as intrusive cause and as subsumed in the text's own integrity.

10. A. C. Baugh, *Chaucer's Major Poetry* (New York, 1965), notes that "Chaucer forgets that Justinus could not have heard the Wife of Bath's discourse." I read Justinus's reference (4, 1685) as an artful connecting of a tale with its performative context. Robert Worth Frank, Jr., "Inept Chaucer," *SAC* 11 (1989): 13–14, argues that Chaucer poses as inept to frustrate our attempts to perceive his real control of material.

11. R. W. Hanning, "Roasting a Friar, Mis-taking a Wife, and Other Acts of Textual Harassment in Chaucer's *Canterbury Tales*," *SAC* 7 (1985): 3–22, discusses the abuse of textual authority by tellers of tales.

12. Larry Sklute, *Virtue of Necessity: Inconclusiveness and Narrative Form in Chaucer's Poetry* (Columbus: Ohio State University Press, 1984), 120, argues that Chaucer composed by fragment and never intended to complete the narrative links between tales. Charles Owen, "The Alternative Reading of *The Canterbury Tales:* Chaucer's Text and the Early Manuscripts," *PMLA* 97 (1982): 237–50, argues that Chaucer's tales circulated unattached to one another and never had a fixed order in the author's mind. He says, 243, that good editing and glossing suggest a completeness "that the text by itself would not give." Ryding, *Medieval Narrative*, 44, calls frame stories such as the *Tales* "structurally unimaginative," and compares them to *roman à tiroirs*. John H. Fisher, "Animadversions on the Text of Chaucer, 1988," *Speculum* 63 (1988): 793, suggests that we deal with the book simply as a collection of tales, but he does not deny the possibility of finding patterns in their order.

13. Nicholas F. Blake, "The Debate on the Order of *The Canterbury Tales*," *RCEI* 10 (1985): 31–42; *The Textual Tradition of the Canterbury Tales* (London: Edward Arnold, 1985), especially, 187–202; and his review of the *Riverside Chaucer* in *SAC* 12 (1990): 258–59, argue against what he calls the arbitrary "tyranny" of the editorial preference for the Ellesmere order. The state of extant manuscripts, he says, is a result of scribal confusion. Fisher, "Animadversions," 789, considers the Ellesmere order as an editorial

tidying up of earlier copy texts which were in bundle form with marginal and interlinear emendations, whereas the Hengwrt is "Chaucerian." I know of no study of the consequences to criticism of different fragment orders.

14. *Paradiso* 31, 13. Patrick J. Gallacher, "The Conversion of Tragic Vision in Dante's *Comedy,*" *Romanic* 80 (1989): 609–10, explores the various manifestations of stupor which precede repentance and grace. Triadic designs are most obvious, perhaps, in religious literature. The "fair field full of folk" in *Piers Plowman* is bounded by the Dungeon of Falsehood and the Tower of Truth. The stage career of Everyman moves from his fear of the loss of his body to the free rendering of his soul to God. The stage of the morality plays displays man tugged by the contending attractions of God, the world, the flesh, and the devil. This pattern is figured throughout the *Tales* in various comic and groteque ways as well as in the religiously enlightened searches for desired goals. Absolon's blind thrust of his lips toward Alison's mouth, the miller's wife's grope in the dark for her bed, the greedy friar's grope for Thomas's gold, and the duped priest's reach for the Canon's false silver are all images of mediating movements between thought and deed, between expectation and reward.

15. The intricate relationship between visual image and spoken or written text in Chaucer's poetry has been suggested by a number of studies. Donald R. Howard, *The Idea of the Canterbury Tales,* and Robert M. Jordan, *Chaucer and the Shape of Creation,* point to mnemonic images of labyrinth and Gothic cathedral, respectively, as models for poetry. D. W. Robertson, Jr., *A Preface to Chaucer,* and V. A. Kolve, *Chaucer and the Imagery of Narrative,* demonstrate the tight mnemonic bond between medieval narrative and pictorial imagery. Frances A. Yates, *The Art of Memory* (London: Routledge & Kegan Paul, 1966), 82, cites Jacopo Ragone's explanation in the fifteenth century that memory consists of *loci et imagines* "memory places and images." Mary Carruthers, *The Book of Memory,* 5–6, discusses Bradwardine's visual systems of memory that Chaucer might well have known. Jean Seznec, *The Survival of the Pagan Gods,* 273, cites Giordano Bruno's *De Umbria Idearum* to the effect that "ideas can be conceived by the human mind only in the shape of images."

16. Gabriel Josipivici, *The World and the Book* (London: Macmillan, 1971), 73, says that while Dante and Langland move from a "failure to see" to a final "now I see how it is," Chaucer holds a poem up to us to say "the truth is not this."

17. Barry Windeatt, "Literary Structures in Chaucer," *The Cambridge Chaucer Companion,* 195–212, reviews several theories of organizational principles in the order of the tales. For recent examples, William Rogers, *Upon the Ways,* 25, 28, and 46, sees groups of tales following a thematic line until one asserts an issue "unsatisfactorily," at which point the next tale shifts to a new issue. C. David Benson, *Chaucer's Drama of Style,* 20, remarks on the ways in which each tale treats an issue in contrast with a preceding tale's treatment. Judson Boyce Allen and Theresa Ann Moritz, *A Distinction of Stories* (Columbus: Ohio State University Press, 1981), see the tales scanning ethical issues. Carl Lindahl, *Ernest Games: Folklore Patterns in the* "Canterbury Tales" (Bloomington and Indianapolis: University of Indiana Press, 1987), 87ff., adds new observations on insult strategies to revive the theory of dramatic interplay between pilgrims. Traugott Lawler, *The One and the Many,* reads the tales as successive reflections of Boethius's opposition between the One and the many, and Jerome Mandel, *Geoffrey Chaucer,* traces the reduplicative structural patterns in contiguous tales.

18. Robert M. Jordan, *Chaucer and the Shape of Creation,* 14ff. Martin Stevens, "Chaucer and Modernism: An Essay in Criticism," *Chaucer at Albany,* 203, notes that Chaucer "used his design when he needed it, but he was also entirely free to discard it when it did not serve his purpose." Helen Cooper *The Structure of the Canterbury Tales,*

69, takes the narrator's invitation to skip the Miller's tale and go on to another (1, 3176–77) as evidence that Chaucer did not care if the tales were read in any particular sequence.

19. Both Rogers in *Upon the Ways* and Benson in *Chaucer's Drama of Style* develop this idea profitably.

20. The story of Philomene in *The Legend of Good Women* draws primarily upon Chrétien's "Et de la hupe" in the *Ovide Moralisé.*

21. Since interdiction against prayer to the Virgin Mary and the saints was the eleventh point of accusation against the Lollards, it is unlikely that Chaucer was himself on the side of Lollard doctrine, as some have thought.

22. Robert B. Burlin, *Chaucerian Fiction,* 150, notes that the Knight's tale and *Troilus* "have the authenticity of philosophic poetry because Chaucer's adaptions of old authors are dramatic reenactments of the 'experience' of 'auctoritee.'"

# Abbreviations

The following abbreviations appear in the Notes and Bibliography:

| | |
|---|---|
| CN | *Chaucer Newsletter* |
| ChauR | *Chaucer Review* |
| DQR | *Dutch Quarterly Review* |
| EETS | *Early English Text Society* |
| ELH | *English Literary History* |
| ES | *English Studies* |
| ESA | *English Studies in Africa* |
| JEGP | *Journal of English and Germanic Philology* |
| JFH | *Journal of Family History* |
| JSA | *Journal of Structural Anthropology* |
| MAE | *Medium Aevum* |
| MH | *Medievalia et Humanistica* |
| MLQ | *Modern Language Quarterly* |
| MP | *Modern Philology* |
| NLH | *New Literary History* |
| NM | *Neuphilologische Mitteilungen* |
| N & Q | *Notes and Queries* |
| PL | Migne's *Patrilogia Latina* |
| PMLA | *Publications of the Modern Language Society* |
| PQ | *Philological Quarterly* |
| RCEI | *Revista Canaria de Estudios Ingleses* |
| SAC | *Studies in the Age of Chaucer* |
| SLI | *Studies in the Literary Imagination* |
| SN | *Studia Neophilologica* |
| SP | *Studies in Philology* |
| TSLL | *Texas Studies in Literature and Language* |

# Bibliography

## Primary Sources.

Alain de Lisle. *De Planctu Naturae.* Trans. James J. Sheridan. Toronto: PIMS, 1980.

*Alcuin, The Bishops, Kings and Saints of York.* Ed. Peter Godman. Oxford Medieval Texts. Oxford: Clarendon Press, 1982.

Aldhelm's *Riddles in the British Library MS Royal 12.C.xxiii, Through a Glass Darkly.* Ed. Nancy Porter Stork. Toronto: Pontifical Institute of Mediaeval Studies, 1990.

*Andreas Capellanus on Love.* Ed. and trans. P. G. Walsh. London: Duckworth, 1982.

Augustine. *Opera. Patrologia Latina.* Ed. J.-P. Migne, vols. 32–47.

———. *The Confessions, The City of God, On Christian Doctrine.* Vol. 18, Great Books of the Western World. Ed. William Benton. Chicago: Encyclopaedia Britannica, 1952.

Bede. *Ecclesiastical History of the English People.* Harmondsworth: Penguin Classics, 1955.

Bernard, Silvester. *Commentum super sex libros Eneidos Virgilii.* Ed. J. W. and E. F. Jones. Lincoln: University of Nebraska Press, 1972.

———. *Cosmographia.* Ed. Peter Dronke. Leiden: Brill, 1978.

Boccaccio, Giovanni. *Il decamerone.* Edizione critica secondo l'autografo hamiltoniano a cura di Vittore Branca. Florence: Presso l'accademia della Crusca, 1976.

*Boccaccio on Poetry.* Ed. Charles G. Osgood. Indianapolis: Bobbs-Merrill, 1956.

*Boethius, Philosophiae consolationis.* Ed. and trans. H. F. Stewart. London: William Heinemann, 1968.

"Boethius' *De consolatione* by Jean de Meun." Ed. V. L.Dedeck-Héry. *Mediaeval Studies* 14 (1952): 165–275.

Bruno, Giordano. *The Heroic Furies.* Trans. P. E. Memmo. Chapel Hill: University. of North Carolina Press, 1964.

———. *De Magia: De vinculis in genere.* Ed. Albano Biondi. Pordenone: Biblioteca dell'immagine, 1987.

Caxton, William. *Book of Courtesy.* Ed. F. J. Furnivall. London: EETS, 1868.

Chalcidius. *Platonis Timaeus, interprete Chalcidio.* Ed. Ioh. Wrobel. Frankfurt: Minerva, 1903.

*Claudii Claudiani Carmina.* Ed. J. Koch. Leipzig: Teubner, 1893.

Dante Alighieri. *Il convivio.* Ed. G. Busnelli and G. Vandelli. Florence: Felice Le Monnier, 1968.

———. *The Divine Comedy.* Ed. and trans. Charles S. Singleton. Princeton: Princeton University Press, Bollingen Series 80, 1970–75.

———. *La vita nuova.* Ed. Michele Berbi. Florence: B. Bemporad, 1932.

————. *De vulgari eloquentia.* Ed. Aristide Marigo. Florence: Felice Le Monnier, 1968.

*John Gower. The Complete Works.* Ed. G. Macaulay. Oxford: Clarendon Press, 1901.

*Hali Meiðhad.* Ed. Bella Millett. London: Oxford University Press, EETS OS 284, 1982.

Henryson, Robert. *The Works of Robert Henryson.* Ed. Denton Fox. Oxford: Clarendon Press, 1981.

Ibn Gabirol. *Avencebrolis Fons Vitae.* Ed. Clemens Bäumker. Münster, 1892–95.

*Innocent III: De miseria condicionis.* Ed. Robert E. Lewis. Athens: University of Georgia Press, 1978.

Isidore of Seville, *Etymologiae, PL* 57.

*John of Salisbury. Policraticus.* Ed. Murray F. Markland. New York: Frederick Ungar, 1979.

*Julian of Norwich's Revelations of Divine Love.* Ed. Frances Beer. Heidelberg: Carl Winter, 1978,

Kipling, Rudyard. *Limits and Renewals.* London: Macmillan, 1932.

Langland, William. *Piers Plowman, C Text.* Ed. Derek Pearsall. London: Edward Arnold, 1978.

————. *Piers Plowman: The B Version.* Ed. George Kane and E. Talbot Donaldson. London: Athlone, 1988.

*Latin Poetry and the Classical Tradition.* Ed. Peter Godman and Oswyn Murray. Oxford: Clarendon Press, 1990.

De Lorris, Guillaume, and Jean de Meun. *Roman de la rose.* Ed. Daniel Poirion. Paris: Garnier-Flammarion, 1974.

————. *The Romance of the Rose.* Trans. Charles Dahlberg. Princeton: Princeton University Press, 1971.

Lydgate, John, *The Troy Book.* Ed. Henry Bergen. London: EETS, 1906–35.

*Macrobius. Commentary on the Dream of Scipio.* Ed. and trans. William Harris Stahl. New York: Columbia University Press, 1952.

*Macrobius Opera.* Ed. F. Eyssenhardt. Leipzig: Teubner, 1893.

*Malory: Works.* Ed. Eugène Vinaver. London: Oxford University Press, 1971.

Marlowe, Christopher. *The Complete Plays of Christopher Marlowe.* Ed. Irving Ribner. New York: Odyssey, 1963.

Martianus Capella. *De Nuptiis.* Ed. Adolf Dick. Stuttgart, 1978.

*Mediaeval English Lapidaries.* Ed. Joan Evans and Mary S. Serjeantson. London: Oxford University Press, EETS series 190, 1960.

*Medieval Song.* Ed. James J. Wilhelm. New York: E. P. Dutton, 1971.

Milton, John. *Paradise Lost.* Ed. Merritt Y. Hughes. New York: Odyssey Press, 1933.

Momaday, N. Scott. *The Ancient Child.* New York: Harpers, 1989.

Norton, Thomas. *The Ordinal of Alchemy.* Ed. John Reidy. London: EETS, 1975.

*Ovid. Heroides.* Ed. and trans. Grant Showerman. London: Heinemann, 1963.

————. *Metamorphoses.* Ed. and trans. Frank Justus Miller. 2 vols. London: Heinemann, 1951.

*Ovide Moralisé.* Ed. C. de Boer. Vaduz: Hans R. Wohlend, 1984.

Plato. *Timaeus.* Ed. and trans. R. G. Bury. London: Heinemann, 1981.

Plato. *The Collected Dialogues.* Ed. and trans. Edith Hamilton and Huntington Cairns. New York: Pantheon Books, Bollingen Series 71, 1961.

*Sir Gawain and the Green Knight.* Ed. J. R. R. Tolkien and E. V. Gordon. 2d ed. rev. Norman Davis. Oxford: Clarendon Press, 1968.

Stevens, Wallace. *The Collected Poems.* London: Faber & Faber, 1959.

*The Travels of Sir John Mandeville.* Trans. C. W. R. D. Moseley. Harmondsworth: Penguin Classics, 1983.

*Lyrics of the Troubadours.* Ed. and trans. Frederick Goldin. New York: Anchor Books, 1973.

William of Malmesbury. *De gestis rerum anglorum.* Ed. Joseph Stevenson. Dyfed, 1989.

Williams, William Carlos, *Paterson.* New York: New Directions, 1958.

## Secondary Sources.

Abraham, David H. "*Cosyn and Cosynage:* Pun and Structure in the *Shipman's Tale.*" *ChauR* 11 (1977): 319–27.

Aers, David. *Chaucer.* Brighton: Harvester, 1986.

Allen, Judson Boyce. "The Old Way and the Parson's Way: An Ironic Reading of the Parson's Tale." *JMRS* 3 (1973): 255–71.

———. *The Ethical Poetics of the Later Middle Ages:* A Decorum of Convenient Distinction. Toronto: University of Toronto Press, 1982.

Allen, Judson Boyce, and Theresa Anne Moritz. *A Distinction of Tales.* Columbus: Ohio State University Press, 1981.

Allen, Michael J. B. *The Platonism of Marsilio Ficino: A Study of his "Phaedrus" Commentary, its Sources, and Genesis.* Berkeley: University of California Press, Publications of the UCLA Center for Medieval and Renaissance Studies 21, 1981.

———. *Marsilio Ficino and the Phaedran Charioteer.* Berkeley: University of California Press, 1981.

Anderson, J. K. "An Analysis of the Framework Structure of Chaucer's *Canterbury Tales. Orbis Litterarum* 27 (1972): 179–201.

apRoberts, Robert P., "The Central Episode in Chaucer's *Troilus,*" *PMLA* 77 (1962), 373–85.

Armstrong, A. Hilary. *Plotinian and Christian Studies.* London: Variorum Reprints, 1979.

———. "Negative Theology." *The Downside Review* 95 (1977): 176–89.

Arnheim, Rudolph. *Visual Thinking.* Berkeley: University of California Press, 1969.

Auden, W. H. *The Enchaféd Flood.* New York: Random House, 1967.

Bachman, W. Bryant, Jr. "'To Maken Illusioun': The Philosophy of Magic and the Magic of Philosophy in the *Franklin's Tale. ChauR* 12 (1977): 55–67.

Baldwin, Ralph. *The Unity of the Canterbury Tales.* Copenhagen: Rosenkilde and Bagger, 1955.

Bäuml, Franz H. "Varieties and Consequences of Medieval Literacy and Illiteracy." *Speculum* 55 (1980): 237–65.

Barney, Stephen A. "Troilus Bound." *Speculum* 47 (1972): 445–58.

Bayley, John, *The Characters of Love.* London: Constable, 1960.

Bembrose, Stephen, *Dante's Angelic Intelligences.* Rome: edizione di storia e letteratura, 1983.

Bennett, J. A. W. *Chaucer at Oxford and Cambridge.* Toronto: University of Toronto Press, 1974.

Bennett, J.A.W., and G. V. Smithers. *Early Middle English Verse and Prose.* Oxford: Clarendon Press, 1966.

Benson, C. David. *Chaucer's Drama of Style.* Chapel Hill: University of North Carolina Press, 1986.

———. "The *Knight's Tale* as History." *ChauR* 3 (1968): 107–23.

———. "Their Telling Difference: Chaucer the Pilgrim and His Two Contrasting Tales." *ChauR* 18 (1983): 61–76.

Benson, Larry D. *Morte Darthur.* Cambridge: Harvard University Press, 1976.

Benson, Larry D., and Siegrfried Wenzel, eds. *The Wisdom of Poetry.* Kalamazoo, MI: Medieval Institute Publications, 1982.

Bernstein, Alan E. "Esoteric Theology: William of Auvergne on the Fires of Hell and Purgatory." *Speculum* 57 (1982): 509–31.

Blake, Kathleen Ann. "Order and the Noble Life in Chaucer's *Knight's Tale.*" *MLQ* 34 (1973): 3-19.

Blake, N. F. "The Debate on the Order of the *Canterbury Tales. RCEI* 10 (1985): 31–32.

———. *The English Language in Medieval Literature.* London: J. M. Dent & Sons, 1979.

———. *The Textual Tradition of the Canterbury Tales.* London: Edward Arnold, 1985.

Bloch, R. Howard. "Chaucer's Maiden's Head: 'The Physician's Tale' and the Poetics of Virginity." *Representations* 28 (1989): 113–34.

Blodgett, E. D. "Chaucerian *Pryvetee* and the Opposition to Time." *Speculum* 51 (1976): 477–93.

Bloomfield, Morton W. "Chaucer's Sense of History." *JEGP* 51 (1952): 301–34.

———. "Fourteenth-Century England: Realism and Rationalism in Wyclif and Chaucer." *ESA* 16 (1973): 59–70.

———. "The *Franklin's Tale:* A Story of Unanswered Questions." Carruthers and Kirk, 189–98.

———. "The Miller's Tale—An UnBoethian Interpretation." *Medieval Literature and Folklore Studies: Essays in Honor of Francis Lee Utley.* Ed. Jerome Mandel and Bruce A. Rosenberg. New Brunswick, NJ: Rutgers University Press, 1970, 205–11.

———. *The Seven Deadly Sins.* East Lansing: Michigan State University Press, 1952.

Boitani, Piero. *Chaucer and the Imaginary World of Fame.* Cambridge: D. S. Brewer, 1984.

———. "Old books brought to life in dreams: the *Book of the Duchess,* the *House of Fame* and the *Parliament of Fowls.*" In Boitani and Mann, Cambridge Chaucer Companion, 39–57.

Boitani, Piero, and Jill Mann, eds. *Cambridge Chaucer Companion.* Cambridge: Cambridge University Press, 1986

Boitani, Piero, and Anna Torti, eds. *Poetics: Theory and Practice in Medieval English Literature.* Woodbridge: Boydell and Brewer, 1991.

Bolton W. F., ed. *The Middle Ages.* London: Sphere Books, 1970.

Brewer, Derek S. *Chaucer.* 3d ed. London: Longman, 1973.

———. *Chaucer: The Critical Heritage.* London: Routledge & Kegan Paul, 1978.

———. *Chaucer: The Poet as Storyteller.* Cambridge: D. S. Brewer, 1984.

———. "Class Distinction in Chaucer." *Speculum* 43 (1968): 290–305.

———. *Geoffrey Chaucer.* Woodbridge: D. S. Brewer, 1990.

———. "Trolius and Criseyde." In Bolton, *The Middle Ages,* 204–35.

Bridges, Margaret. "The Sense of an Ending: The Case of the Dream-Vision." *DQR* 14 (1984): 81-96.

Brody, Saul Nathaniel. "Truth and Fiction in the *Nun's Priest's Tale*. *ChauR* 14 (1979): 33–47.

Brooks, D., and Alastair Fowler. "The Meaning of Chaucer's *Knight's Tale*." *MAE* 39 (1970): 123-46.

Burnley, David. *A Guide to Chaucer's Language.* Norman: University of Oklahoma Press, 1983.

Burnley, J. D. *Chaucer's Language and the Philosopher's Tradition.* Cambridge: D. S. Brewer, 1979.

Burrow, J. A. *The Ages of Man.* London: Oxford University Press, 1986.

———. *Ricardian Poetry.* London: Routledge & Kegan Paul, 1971.

Bynum, Caroline Walker, "'And Woman His Humanity: Female Imagery in the Religious Writing of the Late Middle Ages," *Gender and Religion:* In Bynum, *On the Complexity of Symbols,* 257–88.

Bynum, Caroline Walker, Steven Harrell and Paula Richman, eds. *On the Complexity of Symbols.* Boston: Beacon Press, 1986.

Cannon, Christopher. "*Raptus* in the Chaumpaigne Release and a Newly Discovered Document Concerning the Life of Geoffrey Chaucer." *Speculum* 68 (1993): 74–94.

Carruthers, Mary J. *The Book of Memory.* Cambridge: Cambridge University Press, 1990.

Carruthers, Mary J., and Elizabeth Kirk, eds. *Acts of Interpretation: Essays in Honor of E. Talbot Donaldson.* Norman, OK: Pilgrim Books, 1982.

Carton, Evan. "Complicity and Responsibility in Pandarus' Bed and Chaucer's Art," *PMLA* 94 (1979): 47–61.

Cerquiglini, Jacqueline. "Le clerc et le louche: Sociology of an esthetic." *Poetics Today* 5 (1984): 479–91.

Cespedes, Frank V. "Chaucer's Pardoner and Preaching." *ELH* 44 (1977): 1–18.

Chamberlain, David. "The Music of the Spheres and the *Parlement of Foules*." *ChauR* 5 (1970): 32–56.

Cherniss, Michael D. "The Clerk's Tale and Envoy, the Wife of Bath's Purgatory, and the Merchant's Tale." *ChauR* 6 (1971): 235–54.

Clark, David W. "William of Ockham on Right Reason." *Speculum* 48 (1973): 13–16.

Cohen, Edward S. "The Sequence of the *Canterbury Tales*." *ChauR* 9 (1974): 190–95).

Colish, Marcia L. *The Mirror of Language.* Lincoln: University of Nebraska Press, 1983.

Cook, Robert G. "Chaucer's Pandarus and the Medieval Ideal of Friendship." *JEGP* 69 (1970): 407–24.

Cooper, Helen. *The Canterbury Tales.* Oxford Guides to Chaucer. Oxford: Clarendon Press, 1989.

———. *The Structure of the Canterbury Tales.* London: Duckworth, 1983.

Copeland, Rita. *Rhetoric, Hermeneutics, and Translation in the Middle Ages.* Cambridge: Cambridge University Press, 1991.

Cornford, Francis M. *Plato's Theory of Knowledge.* New York: Bobbs-Merrill, 1957.

Cosman, Madeleine Pelner, and Bruce Chandler, eds. *Machaut's World: Science and Art in the Fourteenth Century.* New York: The New York Academy of Sciences, 1978.

Coulter, James A. *The Literary Microcosm: Theories of Interpretation of the Later Neo-Platonists.* Leiden: Brill, 1976.

Courcelle, Pierre. *La Consolation de Philosophie dans la tradition litteraire*. Paris: Etudes augustiniennes, 1967.

Crampton, Georgia Ronan. *The Condition of Creatures: Suffering and Action in Chaucer and Spenser*. New Haven: Yale University Press, 1974.

Crane, Susan. "Alison's Incapacity and Poetic Instability in the Wife of Bath's Tale." *PMLA* 101 (1987): 20–28.

Culler, Jonathan, ed. *On Puns*. Oxford: Basil Blackwood, 1988.

Curry, Walter. *Chaucer and the Medieval Sciences*. 2d ed. New York: Barnes and Noble, 1960.

Curtius, Ernst Robert. *European Literature and the Latin Middle Ages*. New York: Pantheon, Bollingen Series 36, 1953.

Dahlberg, Charles. *The Literature of Unlikeness*. Hanover, NH: University Press of New England, 1988.

Dales, Richard C. "Discussions of the Eternity of the World during the First Half of the Twelfth Century." *Speculum* 57 (1982): 495–508.

———. "Robert Grosseteste's Place in the Medieval Discussions of the Eternity of the World." *Speculum* 61 (1986): 544–63.

Daniel, E. Randolph. "The Double Procession of the Holy Spirit in Joachim of Fiore's Understanding of History." *Speculum* 55 (1980): 409–83.

David, Alfred. "Literary Satire in the *House of Fame*." *PMLA* 75 (1960): 333–39.

Davis, R. Evan. "The Pendant in the Chaucer Portrait." *ChauR* 17 (1982): 193–95.

Dean, James. "The Ending of the *Canterbury Tales*." *TSLL* 21 (1979): 17–33.

Delany, Sheila. *Chaucer's House of Fame*. Chicago: University of Chicago Press, 1972.

———. *The Naked Text":The Legend of Good Women*. Berkeley: University of California Press, 1994.

Delasanta, Rodney. "Alisoun and the Cozening of our Expectations." *ChauR* 12 (1978): 218–35.

———. "Pilgrims in the Blean." *CN* 6 (1984): 1–2.

———. "The Theme of Judgment in *The Canterbury Tales*." *MLQ* 31 (1970): 298–307.

Diekstra, F. "Chaucer's Way with His Sources: Accidents into Substance and Substance into Accident." *ES* 62 (1981): 215–36.

Dinshaw, Caroline Louise. *Chaucer and the Text: Two Views of the Author*. Ann Arbor, MI: University Microfilms, 1987.

Donaldson, E. Talbot. "The Ordering of the Canterbury Tales." *Medieval Literature and Folklore Studies*. Ed. Jerome Mandel and Bruce A. Rosenberg. New Brunswick, NJ: Rutgers University Press, 1970, 193–204.

———. *Speaking of Chaucer*. New York: W. W. Norton, 1970.

Donoghue, Denis. *Ferocious Alphabets*. Boston: Little Brown, 1981.

Dove, Mary. *The Perfect Age of Man's Life*. Cambridge: Cambridge University Press, 1986.

Dronke, Peter. *Fabula: Explorations into the Uses of Myth in Medieval Platonism*. Leiden: Brill, 1974.

———, ed. *A History of Twelfth-Century Western Philosophy*. Cambridge: Cambridge University Press, 1988.

———. *Medieval Latin and the Rise of the European Love Lyric*. 2d ed., 2 vols. Oxford: Clarendon Press, 1968.

————. *The Medieval Poet and his World.* Rome: edizione de storia letteratura, 1984.

Dronke, Peter, and Jill Mann. "Chaucer and the Medieval Latin Poets." In Brewer, *Chaucer,* 1990, 154–183.

Drury, John. "Luke." In *The Literary Guide to the Bible.* Ed. Robert Alter and Frank Kermode. Cambridge: Belknap Press of Harvard University Press, 1987.

Duby, Georges. *The Knight, The Lady, and the Priest: The Making of Modern Marriage in Medieval France.* New York: Pantheon, 1983.

Dwyer, Richard A. *Boethian Fictions.* Cambridge: Medieval Academy of America, 1976.

Eade, J. C. *The Forgotten Sky.* Oxford: Clarendon Press, 1984.

Eckhardt, Caroline D. *Essays in the Numerical Criticism of Medieval Literature.* Lewisburg, PA: Bucknell University Press, 1980.

Edwards, Robert R. "Narration and Doctrine in the Merchant's Tale." *Speculum* 66 (1991): 342-67.

Elbow, Peter. *Oppositions in Chaucer.* Middletown, CT: Wesleyan University Press, 1975.

Eliade, Mircea. *The Sacred and the Profane.* New York: Harcourt Brace and World, 1959.

————. "The Yearning for Paradise in Primitive Tradition." In Ohmann, *The Making of Myth,* 84–98.

Eliason, Norman. *The Language of Chaucer's Poetry.* Anglistica 17. Copenhagen: Rosenkilde and Bagger, 1972.

Elliott, Ralph W. V. *Chaucer's English.* London: André Deutsch, 1974.

Ellis, Roger. *Patterns of Religious Narrative in the Canterbury Tales.* London: Croom Helm, 1986.

Erler, Mary, and Maryanne Kowalski. *Women and Power in the Middle Ages.* Athens: University of Georgia Press, 1988.

Ferrante, Joan M. *Woman as Image in Medieval Literature from the Twelfth Century to Dante.* New York: Columbia University Press, 1975.

Ferster, Judith. *Chaucer on Interpretation.* Cambridge: Cambridge University Press, 1985.

Fichte, Jörg O. *Chaucer's Art Poetical.* Tübingen: Gunter Narr, 1980.

————. "Man's Free Will and the Poet's Choice: The Creation of Artistic Order in Chaucer's *Knight's Tale.*" *Anglia* 93 (1975): 335–60.

Fisher, John Hurt. "Animadversions on the Text of Chaucer, 1988." *Speculum* 63 (1988): 779–93.

————. *John Gower.* London: Methuen, 1965.

Fleming, John. *The Roman de la Rose:* A Study in Allegory and Iconography. Princeton: Princeton University Press, 1969.

Fletcher, Angus, ed. *The Literature of Fact.* New York: Columbia University Press, 1976.

Foucault, Michel. "Qu'est-ce qu'un auteur?" *Bulletin de la société française de Philosophie* 63 (1969): 73–104.

Fowler, Alastair. *Silent Poetry: Essays in Numerological Analysis.* London: Routledge & Kegan Paul, 1970.

Frakes, Jerold C. *The Fate of Fortune in the Early Middle Ages: The Boethian Tradition.* Leiden: Brill, 1988.

Frank, Robert Worth, Jr. *Chaucer and the "Legend of Good Women."* Cambridge: Harvard University Press, 1972.

————. "Inept Chaucer." *SAC* 11 (1989): 5–14.

Frye, Northrop. "History and Myth in the Bible." In Fletcher, *Literature of Fact,* 1–19.

———. *Secular Scripture*. Cambridge: Harvard University Press, 1976.

Fyler, John M. *Chaucer and Ovid*. New Haven: Yale University Press, 1979.

Gallacher, Patrick J. "The Conversion of Tragic Vision in Dante's *Comedy*. *Romanic* 80 (1989): 607–25.

———. "Dame Alice and the Nobility of Pleasure." *Viator* 13 (1982): 275–93.

———. "Food, Laxatives, and Catharsis in Chaucer's Nun's Priest's Tale." *Speculum* 51 (1976): 49-68.

———. *Love, the Word and Mercury:* A Reading of John Gower's *Confessio Amantis*. Albuquerque: University of New Mexico Press, 1975.

Gallagher, Joseph E. "Theology and Intention in Chaucer's *Troilus*." *ChauR* 7 (1972): 44–66.

Gardner, John. *The Life and Times of Chaucer*. New York: Vintage Books, 1977.

———. *The Poetry of Chaucer*. Carbondale: Southern Illinois University Press, 1977.

Gass, William H. "The Ontology of the Sentence, or How to Make a World of Words." *The World Within the World*. New York: Alfred A. Knopf, 1979.

Gaylord, Alan T. "The Moment of *Sir Thopas:* Towards A New Look at Chaucer's Language." *ChauR* 16 (1982): 311–29.

Gellrich, Jesse. "Parody of Medieval Music in the *Miller's Tale*." *JEGP* 73 (1974): 176–88.

———. *The Idea of the Book in the Middle Ages*. Ithaca: Cornell University Press, 1985.

Georgianna, Linda. "Love So Dearly Bought: The Terms of Redemption in *The Canterbury Tales*." *SAC* 12 (1990): 85–116.

Gilson, Etienne. *History of Christian Philosophy in the Middle Ages*. London: Sheed and Ward, 1955.

Godman, Peter. "Literary Classicism and Latin Erotic Poetry of the Twelfth Century and the Renaissance." In Godman and Murray, *Latin Poetry,* 149–82.

Godman, Peter, and Oswyn Murray, eds. *Latin Poetry and the Classical Tradition*. Oxford: Clarendon Press, 1990.

Grant, Edward. *Planets, Stars, and Orbs: The Medieval Cosmos, 1200–1687*. Cambridge: Cambridge University Press, 1944.

Gray, Douglas. "The Five Wounds of Our Lord." *N & Q,* 208 (1963): 82–89.

Green, Richard Firth. "Chaucer's Victimized Women." *SAC* 10 (1988): 3–21.

Halvorsen, John. "Aspects of Order in the *Knight's Tale*. *SP* 57 (1960): 606–21.

Hamilton, Marie. "Chaucer's 'Marcia Catoun.'" *MP* 30 (1933): 361–64.

Hanning, R. W. "Roasting a Friar, Mis-taking a Wife, and Other Acts of Textual Harassment in Chaucer's *Canterbury Tales*." *SAC* 7 (1985): 3–22.

Hansen, Elaine Tuttle. "Irony and the Antifeminist Narrator in Chaucer's *Legend of Good Women*. *JEGP* 82 (1983): 11–31.

———. "The Powers of Silence: The Case of the Clerk's Griselda." In Erler and Kowalski, *Women and Power,* 230–49.

Harding, Alan. *The Law Courts of Medieval England*. London: George Allen & Unwin, 1973.

Harper-Bill, Christopher, and Ruth Harvey, eds. *The Ideals of Medieval Knighthood*. Woodbridge: Boydell and Brewer, 1986.

Harwood, Britton J. "Language and the Real: Chaucer's Manciple." *ChauR* 6 (1972): 268–79.

Hawking, Steven W. *A Brief History of Time*. New York: Bantam Books, 1988.

Heiatt, A. Kent. *Chaucer, Spenser, Milton: Mythopoeic Continuities and Transformations.* Montreal: McGill-Queens University Press, 1975.

Herlihy, David. "The Making of the Medieval Family." *JFH* 8 (1983): 116–130.

Herman, John P, and John J. Burke, Jr., eds. *Signs and Symbols in Chaucer's Poetry.* University: University of Alabama Press, 1981.

Heyworth, P. L., ed. *Medieval Studies for J. A. W. Bennett.* Oxford: Clarendon Press, 1981.

Hill, John M. *Chaucerian Belief: The Poetics of Reverence and Delight.* New Haven: Yale University Press, 1991.

Hornsby, Joseph Allen. *Chaucer and the Law.* Norman, OK: Pilgrim Books, 1988.

Howard, Donald R. *The Idea of the Canterbury Tales.* Berkeley: University of California Press, 1976.

———. "The Philosophies in Chaucer's *Troilus.*" In Benson and Wenzel, *Wisdom of Poetry,* 151–75.

———. *Writers and Pilgrims.* Berkeley: University of California Press, 1980.

Howell, Wilbur Samuel. *The Rhetoric of Alcuin and Charlemagne.* Princeton: Princeton University Press, 1941.

Illich, Ivan, and Barry Sanders. *The Alphabetization of the Popular Mind.* San Francisco: North Point Press, 1988.

Jameson, Fredric. *The Political Unconscious: Narrative as a Socially Symbolic Act.* London: Methuen, 1981.

Jones, Terry. *Chaucer's Knight.* London: Weidenfield and Nicolson, 1980.

Jordan, Robert M. *Chaucer's Poetics and the Modern Reader.* Berkeley: University of California Press, 1987.

———. *Chaucer and the Shape of Creation: The Aesthetic Possibilities of Inorganic Structure.* Cambridge: Harvard University Press, 1967.

———. "Reconstructing Chaucer." *SAC Proceedings* 1 (1984): 195–200.

Josopivici, Gabriel. *The World and the Book.* London: Macmillan, 1971.

Kermode, Frank. *The Sense of an Ending.* London: Oxford University Press, 1967.

Kiser, Lisa J. *Telling Classical Tales. Chaucer and the "Legend of Good Women."* Ithaca: Cornell University Press, 1983.

———. "*The Legend of Good Women:* Chaucer's Purgatories." *ELH* 54 (1987): 741–60.

Klipansky, Raymond. *The Continuity of the Platonic Tradition.* London: Warburg Institute, 1951.

Knapp, D. "The Relyk of a Seint: A Gloss on Chaucer's Pilgrimage." *ELH* 39 (1972): 1–26.

Knapp, Peggy A. "Deconstructing *The Canterbury Tales:* Pro." *SAC Proceedings* 2 (1987): 73–81.

———. "The Nature of Nature: Criseyde's 'Slydyng Corage.'" *ChauR* 13 (1978): 133–40.

Knapp, Robert S. "Penance, Irony, and Chaucer's Retraction." *Assays: Critical Approaches to Medieval and Renaissance Texts* 2. 1983, 45–67.

Koff, Leonard Michael. *Chaucer and the Art of Storytelling.* Berkeley: University of California Press, 1988.

Kökeritz, Helge. *A Guide to Chaucer's Pronunciation.* Toronto: University of Toronto Press, 1978.

Kolve, V. A. *Chaucer and the Imagery of Narrative.* London: Edward Arnold, 1984.

———. "From Cleopatra to Alceste: An Iconographic Study of *The Legend of Good Women.*" In Herman and Burke, *Signs and Symbols,* 130–78.

————. "'Man in the Middle': Art and Religion in Chaucer's *Friar's Tale.*" *SAC* 12 (1990): 5–46.

————. *The Play Called Corpus Christi.* Stanford, CA: Stanford University Press, 1966.

Kooper, E. S. "Inverted Images in Chaucer's *Tale of Sir Thopas.*" *SN* 56 (1984): 147–54.

LaBarge, Margaret Wade. *Women in Medieval Life.* London: Hamish Hamilton, 1986.

Lacan, Jacques. *Ecrits.* Paris: Seuil, 1966.

Langlois, C. V. *La Connaissance de la nature et du monde.* Paris: Hachette, 1911.

Laplanche, J., and J. B. Pontalis. *The Language of Psycho-Analysis.* London: Hogarth Press, 1983.

Lawler, Traugott. *The One and the Many in the Canterbury Tales.* Hamden, CT: Archon Books, 1980.

LeGoff, Jacques. *The Medieval Imagination.* Chicago: University of Chicago Press, 1988.

————. *La Naissance de purgatoire.* Paris: Gallimard, 1981.

Leff, Gordon. *The Dissolution of the Medieval Outlook.* New York: New York University Press, 1976.

————. "Wycliff and the Augustinian Tradition, with Special Reference to his *De Trinitate.*" *MH* 7 (1976): 29–39.

Lepley, Douglas, L. "The Monk's Boethian Tale." *ChauR* 12 (1978): 162–70.

Lévi-Strauss, Claude. *Structural Anthropology.* New York: Basic Books, 1963.

Lewis, C. S. *The Discarded Image.* Cambridge: Cambridge University Press, 1964.

Lewry, Osmund. *On Time and Imagination.* London: Oxford University Press, 1987.

Lindahl, Carl. *Ernest Games: Folklore Patterns in the Canterbury Tales.* Bloomington: University of Indiana Press, 1987.

Lock, Richard. *Aspects of Time in Medieval Literature.* New York: Garland Press, 1985.

Lovejoy, Arthur O. *The Great Chain of Being.* Cambridge: Harvard University Press, 1966.

Luria, Maxwell. *A Reader's Guide to the Roman de la Rose.* Hamden, CT: Archon Books, 1982.

Lynch, Kathryn L. "Despoiling Griselda; Chaucer's Walter and the Problem of Knowledge in the *Clerk's Tale.*" *SAC* 10 (1988): 41–70.

Lyotard, Jean François. *The Postmodern Condition.* Trans. Geoff Bennington and Brian Massumi. Minneapolis: University of Minnesota Press, 1984.

McAlpine, Monica. *The Genre of "Troilus and Criseyde."* Ithaca: Cornell University Press, 1978.

McCall, John P. *Chaucer among the Gods.* University Park: Pennsylvania State University Press, 1979.

McKeon, R. "Poetry and Philosophy in the Twelfth Century." *MP* 43 (1946): 217–34.

Mandel, Jerome. "Courtly Love in the *Canterbury Tales.*" *ChauR* 19 (1985): 277–89.

————. *Geoffrey Chaucer: Building the Fragments of the Canterbury Tales.* Rutherford, NJ: Fairleigh Dickinson University Press, 1992.

Mann, Jill. *Chaucer and Medieval Estates Satire.* Cambridge: Cambridge University Press, 1973.

————. "Chance and Destiny in *Troilus and Criseyde* and the *Knight's Tale.* In Boitani and Mann, *Cambridge Chaucer Companion,* 75–92.

————. "Satisfaction and Payment in Middle English Literature." *SAC* 5 (1983): 17–48.

Meech, Sanford B. *Design in Chaucer's Troilus.* New York: Greenwood Press, 1969.

Meletinskij, E. "Scandinavian Mythology as a System." *JSA* 2 (1973): 43–57.

Mencken, H. L. *A New Dictionary of Quotations*. New York: Alfred A. Knopf, 1942.

Middleton, Anne. "The Idea of Public Poetry in the Reign of Richard II." *Speculum* 53 (1978): 94–114.

Miller, J. Hillis. "Ariachne's Broken Woof." *Georgia Review* 31 (1977): 36–48.

Miller, Nancy K. "Arachnologies: The Woman, the Text, and the Critic." In Miller *Poetics of Gender,* 270–95.

———. ed. *The Poetics of Gender*. New York: Columbia University Press, 1988.

Minnis, A. J. *Chaucer and Pagan Antiquity*. Cambridge: Derek Brewer, 1982.

———. *The Medieval Boethius. Studies in the Vernacular Translations of* "De consolatione philosophiae." Cambridge: D. S. Brewer, 1987.

———, and A. B. Scott, *Medieval Literary Theory and Criticism, c. 1100–c. 1375.* The Commentary Tradition. Oxford: Clarendon Press, 1988.

Mitchell, W. J. T., ed. *On Narrative*. Chicago: University of Chicago Press, 1981.

Mudrick, Marvin, "Tall Stories and Short Hairs." *The Hudson Review* 38 (1985): 133–39.

Murdoch, John E. "The Analytic Character of Late Medieval Learning: Natural Philosophy without Nature." In Roberts, *Approaches to Nature,* 171–213.

———. "*Subtilitatis Anglicaenae* in Fourteenth-Century Paris: John of Mirecourt and Peter Coffins." In Cosman and Chandler, *Machaut's World,* 51–86.

Musa, Mark. *Dante's Vita Nuova*. Bloomington: Indiana University Press, 1973.

Muscatine, Charles. *Chaucer and the French Tradition*. Berkeley: University of California Press, 1957.

Nabokov, Vladimir. *Lectures on Literature*. Ed. Fredson Bowers. New York: Harcourt Brace, 1988.

Newman, Francis X., ed. *The Meaning of Courtly Love*. Binghampton: CMRS, 1967.

North, John D. *Chaucer's Universe*. London: Oxford University Press, 1988.

———. "Kinematics—More Etheral than Elementary." In Cosman and Chandler, *Machaut's World,* 89–102.

North, Sally. "The Ideal Knight as Presented in Some French Narrative Poems c. 1090–c.1240: An Outline Sketch." In Harper-Bill, *The Ideals and Practice,* 111–32.

Norton-Smith, John. *Geoffrey Chaucer*. London: Routledge & Kegan Paul, 1974.

Ohmann, Richard M., ed. *The Making of Myth*. New York: G. P. Putnam, 1962.

Olsen, Alexandra Hennessey. "In Defense of Diomede: 'Moral Gower' and *Troilus and Criseyde.*" *In Geardagum* 8 (1987): 1–12.

Olsen, Claire C. "Chaucer and the Music of the Fourteenth Century." *Speculum* 16 (1941): 64–92.

Olsen, Glending. "Chaucer's Monk: The Rochester Connection." *ChauR* 21 (1986): 246–56.

Olsen, Paul. *The Canterbury Tales and the Good Society*. Princeton: Princeton University Press, 1987.

Olsson, Knut. "*Securitas* and Chaucer's Knight." *SAC* 9 (1987): 123–53.

Owen, Charles A., Jr. "Undergraduate and Graduate Courses: New Patterns." *CN* 2 (1980): 7–10.

———. "The Alternative Reading of *The Canterbury Tales:* Chaucer's Text and the Early Manuscripts." *PMLA* 97 (1982): 237–50.

———. "The Design of the Canterbury Tales." In Rowland, *Companion,* 192–207.

Panofsky, Erwin. *Studies in Iconology*. London: Oxford University Press, 1939.

Patterson, Lee W. *Chaucer and the Subject of History*. Madison: University of Wisconsin Press, 1991.

———. "The 'Parson's Tale' and the Quitting of the *Canterbury Tales*." *Traditio* 34 (1978): 331–80.

Payer, Pierre. "Prudence and the Principle of Natural Law: A Medieval Development." *Speculum* 54 (1979): 55–70.

Payne, F. Anne. *Chaucer and Menippean Satire*. Madison: University of Wisconsin Press, 1981.

Payne, Robert O. *The Key of Remembrance: A Study of Chaucerian Poetics*. New Haven: Yale University Press, 1963.

Pearsall, Derek. *The Canterbury Tales*. London: George Unwin, 1985.

Peck, Russell A. "Chaucer and the Nominalist Questions." *Speculum* 53 (1978): 745–60.

———. "Number as Cosmic Language." In Eckhardt, *Essays in the Numerical Criticism*, 15–64.

———. "Sovereignty and the Two Worlds of the Franklin's Tale." *ChauR* 1 (1967): 253–71.

Pelen, Marc. *Latin Poetic Irony in the Roman de la Rose*. Liverpool: F. Cairns, 1987.

Pratt, John H. "Was Chaucer's Knight Really a Mercenary?" *ChauR* 22 (1987): 8–27.

Pratt, Robert A. "Chaucer's Title: The Tales of Canterbury." *PQ* 54 (1975): 19–25.

Randall, John Herman, Jr. *Aristotle*. New York: Columbia University Press, 1960.

Ricoeur, Paul. "Narrative Time." In Mitchell, *On Narrative*, 165–86.

———. *Time and Narrative*. Trans. Kathleen McLaughlin and David Pellauer. 3 vols. Chicago: University of Chicago Press, 1984–88.

Robbins, Rossell Hope, ed. *Chaucer at Albany*. New York: Burt Franklin, 1975.

Roberts, Lawrence D., ed. *Approaches to Nature in the Middle Ages*. Binghampton, NY: Center for Medieval and Renaissance Studies, 1982.

Robertson, D. W., Jr. "The Concept of Courtly Love." In Newman, *Meaning of Courtly Love*, 1–18.

———. *The Literature of Medieval England*. New York: McGraw-Hill, 1970.

———. *A Preface to Chaucer*. Princeton: Princeton University Press, 1963.

———. "Some Medieval Literary Terminology." *SP* 68 (1951): 669–92.

Rogers, William. *Upon the Ways: The Structure of The Canterbury Tales*. Victoria, B.C.: University of Victoria Press, ELS Series 36, 1986.

Rose, Donald M., ed. *New Perspectives in Chaucer Criticism*. Norman, OK: Pilgrim Books, 1981.

Rowe, Donald W. *O Love, O Charite! Contraries Harmonized in Chaucer's* Troilus. Edwardsville: Illinois University Press, 1976.

———. *Through Nature to Eternity:* Chaucer's "Legend of Good Women." Lincoln: University of Nebraska Press, 1988.

Rowland, Beryl, ed. *Companion to Chaucer Studies*. London: Oxford University Press, 1968.

Ruggiers, Paul G. *The Art of the Canterbury Tales*. Madison: University of Wisconsin Press, 1965.

———. "Platonic Forms in Chaucer." *ChauR* 17 (1983): 366–81.

Rutledge, Sheryl P. "Chaucer's Zodiac of Tales." *Costerus* 9 (1973): 117–43.

Ryding, William W. *Studies in Medieval Narrative.* The Hague: Mouton, 1971.

Sayce, Olive. "The Conclusion of the *Canterbury Tales* and its Place in Literary Tradition." *Medium Aevum* 40 (1971): 230–48.

Scaglione, Aldo D. *Nature and Love in the Late Middle Ages.* Westport, CT: Greenwood, 1986.

Scarry, Elaine. "The Well-Rounded Sphere: The Metaphysical Structure of the *Consolation* of Boethius." In Eckhardt, *Essays in the Numerical Criticism,* 91–140.

Seznec, Jean. *The Survival of the Pagan Gods.* New York: Harper, 1961.

Shoaf, R. A. *Dante, Chaucer, and the Currency of the Word.* Norman, OK: Pilgrim Books, 1983.

———. "Dante's *Commedia* and Chaucer's Theory of Mediation: A Preliminary Sketch." In Rose, *New Perspectives,* 83–103.

———. "The Play of Puns in Late Middle English Poetry: Concerning Juxtology." In Culler, *On Puns,* 44-61.

Singleton, Charles S. *An Essay on the Vita Nuova.* Baltimore: Johns Hopkins Press, 1949.

Sklute, Larry. *Virtue of Necessity: Inconclusiveness and Narrative Form in Chaucer's Poetry.* Columbus: Ohio State University Press. 1984.

Smyser, Hamilton M. "A View of Chaucer's Astronomy." *Speculum* 45 (1970): 359–73.

Sorabji, Richard. *Matter, Space, and Motion.* Ithaca: Cornell University Press, 1988.

———. *Time, Creation, and the Continuum.* London: Duckworth, 1983.

Southern, R. W. *Robert Grosseteste.* Oxford: Clarendon Press, 1986.

Spearing, A. C. "Al This Mene I Be Love." *SAC Proceedings* 2 (1986): 169–77.

Spitzer, Leo. *Classical and Christian Ideas of World Harmony.* Baltimore: Johns Hopkins Press, 1963.

Steiner, George. *After Babel.* London: Oxford University Press, 1975.

Stevens, John. *"Angelus ad virginem:* The History of a Medieval Song." In Heyworth, Medieval Studies, 297–328.

Stevens, Martin. "Chaucer and Modernism: An Essay in Criticism." In Robbins, *Chaucer at Albany,* 193–216.

———. "The Royal Stanza in Early English Literature." *PMLA* 94 (1979): 62–76.

Stevens, Martin, and Kathleen Falvey. "Substance, Accident, and Transformation: A Reading of the *Pardoner's Tale," ChauR* 17 (1983): 142–58.

Stock, Brian. *The Implications of Literacy.* Princeton: Princeton University Press, 1983.

———. *Listening for the Text.* Baltimore: Johns Hopkins Press, 1990.

———. *Myth and Science in the Twelfth Century: A Study of Bernard Silvester.* Princeton: Princeton University Press, 1972.

Szittya, Penn R. *The Antifraternal Tradition in Medieval Literature.* Princeton: Princeton University Press, 1986.

Taylor, Davis. "The Terms of Love: A Study of Troilus's Style." *Speculum* 51 (1976): 69–90.

Taylor, P. B. "The Alchemy of Spring in Chaucer's *General Prologue," ChauR* 17 (1982): 1–4.

———. "Chaucer's *Cosyn to the Dede." Speculum* 57 (1982): 315–27.

———. "Chaucer's Names." *NM* 95 (1994): 243–48.

———. "The Parson's *Amyable Tongue." ES* 64 (1983): 401–9.

Thundy, Zacharias. "Chaucer's Quest for Wisdom in the *Canterbury Tales. NM* 77 (1976): 582–96.

Thurston, Paul T. *Artistic Ambivalence in Chaucer's Knight's Tale.* Gainesville: University of Florida Press, 1968.

Todorov, Tzvetan. *Introduction to Poetics.* Trans. Richard Howard. Minneapolis: University of Minnesota Press, 1981.

Traversi, Derek. *The Canterbury Tales.* London: Bodley Head, 1983.

Underwood, Dale. "The First of the *Canterbury Tales.*" *ELH* 26 (1959): 455–69.

Van, Thomas A. "Theseus and the 'Right Way' of the *Knight's Tale.*" *SLI* 4 (1971): 83–100.

Vance, Eugene. "Mervelous Signals: Poetics, Sign, Theory, and Politics in Chaucer's *Troilus.*" *NLH* 10 (1979): 293–337.

———. "*Pearl:* Love and the Poetics of Participation." In Boitani and Torti, *Poetics,* 131–47.

Wallace, William A. *Causality and Scientific Explanation.* Ann Arbor: University of Michigan Press, 1972.

Walsh, P. G. *Love Lyrics from the Carmina Burana.* Chapel Hill: University of North Carolina Press, 1993.

Waswo, Richard, "*The Narrator of Troilus and Criseyde.*" *ELH* 50 (1983): 1–25.

Weisheipl, James A., O. P. *Nature and Motion in the Middle Ages.* Ed. William E. Carroll. Washington, D.C.: Catholic University of America Press, 1985.

Wenzel, Siegfried. *The Sin of Sloth.* Chapel Hill: University of North Carolina Press, 1967.

West, Michael D. "Dramatic Time, Setting, and Motivation in Chaucer." *ChauR* 2 (1968): 172–87.

Westlund, Joseph. "The Knight's Tale as an Impetus for Pilgrimage." *PQ* 43 (1964): 526–37.

Wetherbee, Winthrop. *Chaucer and the Poets.* Ithaca: Cornell University Press, 1984.

———. "Philosophy, Cosmology, and the Twelfth-Century Renaissance." In Dronke, *Fabula,* 21–53.

———. *Platonism and Poetry in the Twelfth Century.* Princeton: Princeton University Press, 1972.

White, Gertrude M. "The Franklin's Tale: Chaucer or the Critics." *PMLA* 89 (1974): 454–62.

Windeatt, Barry. "Literary Structures in Chaucer." In Boitani and Mann, *Cambridge Chaucer Companion,* 195–212.

Wolff, Emil. *Die goldene Kette: Die Aurea Catena Homeri in der englischen Literatur von Chaucer bis Wordsworth.* Hamburg: Hanischer Gildenverlag, 1947.

Wood, Chauncey. "Chaucer's Portrait of the Prioress." In Herman and Burke, *Signs and Symbols,* 81–101.

Yates, Frances A. *The Art of Memory.* London: Routledge & Kegan Paul, 1966.

Ziolkowski, Jan. *Alan of Lille's Grammar of Sex.* Cambridge: Medieval Academy of America, 1985.

# Index

Abraham, David H., 192

Aers, David, 176

Alain de Lisle: *De Panctu Naturae*, 25, 33, 100, 172n. 42; *Anticlaudianus, 26, 36*

Albertus Magnus, 28, 187n. 33

Alcuin, 90

Aldhelm: *De Creatura, 23*

Alfred, King: *Consolatione,* 109

Allen, Judson Boyce, 164, 190, 194

apRoberts, Robert P., 174, 175

Apuleis: *Metamorphosis,* 169n. 19

Aquinas, Thomas, Saint: *Summa,* 30, 164n. 64, 180n. 29, 182n. 15, 191n. 22

Arendt, Hannah, 50

Aristotle, 24–25, 60; *De Anima,* 25, 37; *De memoria,* 193n. 8; *De sensu,* 173n. 3; *Ethics,* 172n. 49; *Metrologica,* 184n. 49; *Physics,* 77

Auden, W. H., 26, 167n. 20

Auerbach, Eric, 165n. 1

Augustine of Hippo, Saint: *Confessions,* 43; *Contra mendacium,* 149; *De bono conjugali,* 105. *De civitate Dei,* 27, 143–44, 149, 162n. 43, 168n. 5, 179n. 11, 185n. 17, 187n. 32; *De doctrina,* 170n. 26, 177n. 52, 187n. 32; *De magistro,* 172n. 49; *De mendacio,* 188n. 21; *De musica,* 31; *Soliloquum,* 175n. 34,

Bachman W. Bryant, Jr., 178

Baldwin, Ralph, 190, 191

Barney, Stephen A., 179

Baswell, Christopher C. 164

Baugh, A. C., 193

Bayley, John, 173, 175

Bede: *Ecclesiastical History,* 158n. 7

Benson, C. David, 170, 177, 187, 194 195

Benson, Larry B., 116, 188

Berkeley, George, *Siris,* 160n. 1

Bernard Silvester: *Commentary* on *The Marriage of Mercury and Philology,* 22–23; *Cosmographia,* 23, 61

Bible: Gen. 1:22–28, 73, 2:7, 191n. 22, 2:9, 35, 2:20, 174n. 19; Job 10:20–22, 183n. 27, 26:7, 160n. 3; Ps. 33:9, 30; Prov. 15:4, 190n. 14; Eccles. 2:14, 182n. 14; Song of Sol. 4:12, 101; Isa. 45:3, 182n. 14, 49:19, 183n. 26; Jer. 6:17–19, 190n. 11; Matt.12:37, 90, 16:19 and 18:18, 20, 24:43, 182n. 14, 27:46, 188n. 35; Mark 15:34, 188n. 35; Luke 1:19, 167n. 25, 23:46, 188n. 35; 24:25–28, 189n. 46; John 5:30, 112, 14:6, 46, 19:30, 188n. 35, 177n. 48; Rom. 5:13–14, 173n. 13, 13:12, 187n. 31; 1 Cor. 12:4, 191n. 22, 15:42–44, 139, 15:53–54, 185n. 16; 2 Cor. 6:7, 187n. 31, 6:8, 188n. 37; Eph. 5:32, 114, 6:11, 187n. 31; Col. 1:15, 42, 4:5, 167n. 28; 1 Tim. 2:5–7, 127, 6:16, 42, 14:16, 186n. 25; Apoc. 10:6, 168n. 32, 21:18, 158n. 1

Blake, Kathleen Ann, 176

Blake, Nicholas F., 193

Blake, William, 163n. 48, 182n. 6

Bloch, R. Howard, 163, 171

Blodgett, E. D., 166, 183

Bloomfield, Morton W., 178, 182

Boccaccio, Giovanni: *De genealogia deorum,* 30: *Il decamerone,* 69, 123, 149, 181n. 35, 184n. 4, 191n. 21

Boethius: *Consolatione Philosophiae,* 20–24, 31, 33, 35, 38–39, 42–46, 48, 50, 59, 72–73, 81, 86, 93, 100, 102, 130, 147–48, 158n. 3, 170n. 22, 173–74n. 15, 188n. 42; *De Trinitate,* 60

Boitani, Piero, 17, 170

Bonaventura, Saint, 37

Brewer, Derek, 159, 165, 175, 177

Brinton, Thomas, 112

Brody, Saul Nathaniel, 189

Brooks, D., 177

Bruno, Giordano: *De magia,* 160n. 2

Burlin, Robert, 159, 195

Burnley, J. D., 187

211